Faithful Passages

STUDIES IN AMERICAN THOUGHT AND CULTURE

Faithful Passages

American Catholicism in Literary Culture, 1844–1931

James Emmett Ryan

THE UNIVERSITY OF WISCONSIN PRESS

Publication of this volume has been made possible,
in part, through support from
the Anonymous Fund of
the College of Letters and Science
at the University of Wisconsin–Madison.

The University of Wisconsin Press
1930 Monroe Street, 3rd Floor
Madison, Wisconsin 53711-2059
uwpress.wisc.edu

3 Henrietta Street
London WC2E 8LU, England
eurospanbookstore.com

Printed in the United States of America

Library of Congress Cataloging-in-Publication Data

Ryan, James Emmett.
Faithful passages : American Catholicism in literary culture, 1844–1931 / James Emmett Ryan.
p. cm. — (Studies in American thought and culture)
Includes bibliographical references and index.
ISBN 978-0-299-29064-1 (pbk. : alk. paper) — ISBN 978-0-299-29063-4 (e-book)
1. American literature—Catholic authors—History and criticism. 2. Christian literature, American—History and criticism. 3. Catholics—United States—Intellectual life. 4. Catholic Church—In literature. 5. Catholics in literature. I. Title. II. Series: Studies in American thought and culture.
PS153.C3R93 2013
810.9'921282—dc23
2012013606

Revised versions of the following articles have been included with permission from the original publishers: "Orestes Brownson in Young America: Popular Books and the Fate of Catholic Criticism," *American Literary History* 15, no. 3 (2003): 443–70; "Sentimental Catechism: Archbishop James Gibbons, Mass-Print Culture, and American Literary History," *Religion and American Culture* 7, no. 1 (Winter 1997): 81–119.

Contents

Acknowledgments vii

Introduction 3

1 Orestes Brownson in Young America: Popular Books and Catholic Criticism 21

2 Print Evangelism: Father Hecker's American Mission 45

3 Entering the Mainstream: The Fiction of Jedediah Huntington and Anna Hanson Dorsey 77

4 Sentimental Catechism: James Gibbons and Literary Devotionalism 117

5 Trading Religion for Feminism: Kate O'Flaherty Chopin's Bayou Catholics 145

6 "A Kind Woman in Heaven": Willa Cather's Religious Aesthetic 164

Conclusion 182

Notes 189
Works Cited 225
Index 241

Acknowledgments

Warm friendships and generous assistance have helped me during the research for this project. The English Department at Auburn University has been a congenial scholarly home, and I am grateful to colleagues and students there for their support. My research assistant, Sydnee Doolittle, did important work in tracking down obscure but necessary historical details. The professional staff of Ralph Brown Draughon Library at Auburn University was tireless in obtaining interlibrary loan materials for use in the research, and I thank them for their consistent efforts on my behalf.

The University of North Carolina at Chapel Hill supplied an ideal setting for the early phases of study and writing that eventually grew into a larger endeavor. In the Department of English, Philip F. Gura was instrumental in many ways, but especially by supplying his unique blend of collegiality and inspiring scholarly example. I will always be thankful for his confidence in me and for his unwavering support. The UNC–Chapel Hill Department of Religious Studies was an important intellectual resource; Laurie F. Maffly-Kipp and Thomas A. Tweed were generous with their time, and they taught me much about the complexities of American religious historiography. At Duke University, Thomas J. Ferraro provided encouragement, memorable teaching, and insights into the aesthetic dimensions of Catholic religious life.

As a 2012 US Fulbright Lecturer at Nanjing Normal University (NNU) in Nanjing, China, I have enjoyed additional support and friendship from numerous colleagues and graduate students. Professor Yan Zhijun of the School of Foreign Languages and Cultures at NNU welcomed me as a visitor on his faculty and ensured that my research and writing could proceed without interruption. Professor Wu Yidong and Ms. Cai Neng of the NNU Office of International Affairs facilitated every aspect of my teaching and writing while in China.

At the University of Wisconsin Press, Gwen Walker was an ideal editor, once again guiding my work with warmth, skill, and professionalism. The anonymous reviewers made incisive suggestions that improved many aspects of the manuscript. I regret that the late Paul S. Boyer did not live to see publication of this book. As series editor for the University of Wisconsin Press, Paul worked with me over the past few years through all phases of writing and revision. Paul was unfailingly generous in supporting my research into American religion, and he consistently found ways to move my project in the most fruitful directions.

Along the way, a number of people made the journey richer and more satisfying. For their friendship and support, I thank Phillip Beard, Craig Bertolet, Jonathan Bolton, Michael Everton, Leslie Frost, Lou Freitas-Caton, Laura Gribben, Christopher Keirstead, A. J. Meir, Christine Meir, Laura Mielke, Carol Robicheaux, Francis Robicheaux, Susan M. Ryan, Mark Simpson-Vos, David Syracuse, James Truman, Karen Weyler, Claire Wilson, and Hilary Wyss. Among my family members, Cecilia Hughes, David Hughes, Mary Onstead, Jim Onstead, Kevin Ryan, Cindy Connelly Ryan, Theresa Ryan, Tom Kumpf, Maureen Hay, Allan Hay, and Karen Ryan have been an enduring resource. Many years ago, Krista Wilbanks, Richard Wilbanks, the late Michael Twombly, Kathy Zens, Gerry Twombly, Faith McCormack, Mark Twombly, Susie Twombly, Steve Twombly, and Patti Twombly adopted me as one of their own and have sustained me with their family's energy, talent, and affection. My father, William C. Ryan, and my mother, the late Alice L. Ryan, supplied the rich conversations, unfailing encouragement, and solid grounding that have sustained my work.

Renee Twombly and Thea Ryan are my perennial touchstones and soundest allies. I am fortunate to enjoy their affection, brilliance, wisdom, and good humor.

Faithful Passages

Introduction

This study aims to bring attention and analysis to a neglected dimension of American religious discourse and literary history: episodes in Roman Catholic literary life as it was conducted during a century of the nation's rapid development into an industrialized print culture, beginning with the first significant wave of professional authorship that emerged in the 1840s. Not surprisingly, literary and religious activities during this period were profoundly shaped by rapidly changing political, economic, scientific, and social contexts in the United States. During this tumultuous phase of national development, religion and literature functioned powerfully as mutually reinforcing discourses. As the historian Daniel Walker Howe has recently observed about the antebellum American scene, "Religious awakening, expansion of education, interest in science, and technological progress all went hand in hand. Evangelists welcomed technological advances along with mass education as helping them spread the good news of Christ. Literature, like education and science, was saturated with religious meanings and motivations."[1] Bringing before the American people literary works with evangelical ambitions was increasingly possible for religionists of all kinds, and such works flooded the antebellum literary marketplace. The quality of this writing varied tremendously, and many of the religious books, pamphlets, and tracts circulated among antebellum readers have limited appeal today as literature. Nevertheless, although much of the evangelical or religiously themed literature of the antebellum period has now been forgotten, a great many of the major American writers of the antebellum period—among them Nathaniel Hawthorne, Frederick Douglass, Herman Melville, Harriet Beecher Stowe, Emily Dickinson, and Walt Whitman—were closely attuned to the issues and themes from contemporary religious discourse, and used these religious ideas extensively in their works.

Immigration and annexation—demographic vectors seldom considered sufficiently in American literary history—were also significant factors in the reshaping of American religious life after the colonial and early national era. During the nineteenth and early twentieth century, the United States experienced dramatic and influential population increases, in large part by absorbing a significant influx of European immigrants. Many of these immigrants traveled to America from countries known for their Roman Catholic traditions, most notably Ireland, but significant immigrant populations arrived from Italy and Germany as well. Substantial numbers of Catholic immigrants also arrived in the United States during this period from Austria-Hungary, the Russian Empire, and Canada. This tide of Roman Catholic immigration changed the religious landscape of the United States, tripling the number of American Roman Catholics within a very short time. The changing political landscape of the United States was an additional factor in the religious transformations of this period, as the country's settlement and population continued their westward passage. Shifting American political boundaries contributed to the increasingly Catholic religious flavor of the United States, as a host of other newly colonized American Catholics, many of them from French, Mexican, and Spanish backgrounds, were absorbed into the United States following the acquisition of large territories in present-day Louisiana (1803), Florida (1820), and Texas/New Mexico/California (1848).

During these nineteenth-century demographic and political upheavals, Roman Catholicism, which had been the religion of only a rather small American minority since the early seventeenth century, became the largest single religious denomination in the United States. Given this very significant result, even considered abstractly as census data, it would be reasonable to predict that certain aspects of American culture would have been transformed, proportionally refashioned in response to the influence of Roman Catholic styles of worship, social arrangements, and moral habits. Historians have yet to assess completely the role of Roman Catholicism in the development of United States culture, although it is well known that Catholicism since the mid-nineteenth century has been the religion by birth or choice for a substantial number of Americans. Demographic changes and expanding territories tell a story of unmistakable growth in the number of American Catholics, but it remains to determine with greater specificity what the growth of Roman Catholicism in America has meant for the nation's textures of life: its patterns of morality, its modes of socialization, and—crucial for the literary historian—its habits of reading and writing. One might reasonably ask, then, given the enlarged presence of Catholics in nineteenth- and early twentieth-century America: what are the specific adjustments in the cultural sphere that can be traced to the increased presence of Roman Catholicism in the United States?

The essential and more immediate questions for the historian of American literature, though, are somewhat narrower: how, by whom, and with what consequences have Roman Catholic values and ideas been written into the literary discourse of this crucial period of national growth and consolidation? Scholarship has long made clear that American literary culture was dramatically transformed during the long nineteenth century, as it grew to industrial scale with the assistance of improved transportation infrastructure and the development of a national publishing industry, but the role of Roman Catholic religion in shaping and responding to print-media growth during this period has not been sufficiently investigated. These questions are complicated by the various objectives that diverse American writers had in mind when they engaged with Catholicism in their writing and publishing activities, objectives that ranged quite widely depending on the particulars of each writer's socioeconomic background, intellectual aims, and religious identity. These objectives are important because perspective matters immensely when evaluating how religious discourse works in literary culture, particularly in light of the sociological turn that has been so central to religious studies since the early twentieth century. For instance, the social theorist Emile Durkheim observed in *The Elementary Forms of Religious Life* (1912), "Religion is . . . above all a system of ideas by which men imagine the society of which they are members and the obscure yet intimate relations they have with it." Using analogous terms, the religious historian Thomas A. Tweed has recently noted that "Religions are cultural processes whereby individuals and groups map, construct, and inhabit worlds of meaning."[2] As these comments suggest, the idea that certain dimensions of human religious understanding are socially constructed is pivotal to the contemporary study of religion, and thus the development and evolution of print culture—the vehicle for so much of the conversation about modern religious experience—figures powerfully as a discursive mechanism for the social processes that function to make religious meanings.

The discourse circulating through the Roman Catholic map of meaning in the United States can look radically different according not only to the kind, quantity, and circulation of writing produced but also according to how the writer is positioned and aimed. Consider a few of the many possibilities included in this study: Irish American publishers selling Bible commentaries and devotional books for Catholics in the late eighteenth and early nineteenth century; a Catholic priest writing theological tracts directed at fellow clergymen; an anti-Catholic Protestant author of salacious convent exposés; male and female Catholic authors of historical romances featuring Catholic protagonists; former transcendentalists who become Catholic converts and devote long careers to writing for Catholic intellectuals; a prominent Catholic bishop who writes a best-selling catechism, which remains popular for decades; and women writers with no obvious religious commitment who nevertheless craft proto-feminist fiction that relies heavily on Catholic characters and culture. Some of these writers were able to reach large audiences of American readers, while others (in spite of their evangelical ambitions) were mostly unsuccessful in circulating their work. But each of these experiences in commercial print culture helps illuminate the evolving relationship between Roman Catholicism and American literary culture during the nineteenth and early twentieth century.

Religious publications were not without difficulty placed into the hands of ordinary American Catholics; immigrants had much to cope with in addition to absorbing religious ideas through print, and the still-maturing print marketplace lacked the efficiencies of national distribution that would be in place during the twentieth century. Even well into the later nineteenth century, many immigrant Catholics had little formal education in either secular or religious matters and were, understandably, focusing their attentions on the kinds of concerns that all immigrants confront: access to prosperity and respectability. In addition, the infrastructural improvements in transportation and print technologies necessary for the development of industrial print culture, and thus essential for the efficient circulation of religious publications, were still being developed in the antebellum period as Roman Catholic immigrants streamed into the United States. As a very young nation-state with underdeveloped systems of communication and print distribution, the United States until the mid-nineteenth century was an example of what the historian Trish Loughran has described as "the virtual nation—a term [that describes] the extended but nonintegrated republic in the years between the Revolution and the Civil War."[3] Still, vastly increased numbers of Roman Catholics in America had put that religion into the spotlight by the 1850s, and writers on different sides of the Catholic question began, with varying degrees of success, to use the increasingly powerful and important industrial print marketplace to disseminate their views. Even the noted Harvard College professor of foreign languages, Henry Wadsworth Longfellow, then the most popular and influential of American poets and a man closely linked to the Harvard Unitarian tradition, tried his hand at Roman Catholic imaginings. Although he did not devote much of his career to Catholic religious writings, Longfellow's widely circulated epic poem *Evangeline: A Tale of Acadie* (1847), perhaps his most famous work, is notable for its sympathetic depiction of exiled Acadian Catholics.

Print culture is, of course, only one dimension of Roman Catholic life in United States, and consequently this study must admit the practical limits of its scope. The episodes in literary culture presented here do not investigate the lived experience of religion for ordinary people (most helpfully charted by social historians) or the intricacies of theology (better understood using methodologies familiar to intellectual historians). Those topics are vitally important for understanding the way religious ideas are transmitted and undergo change. By contrast, this study aims to be mindful of lived religion and theology but also to chart some of the ways that Catholicism came to be produced in rhetorical terms by a diverse array of American writers at work in an evolving commercial print culture. Religious practice and theology are by no means irrelevant to a study grounded in rhetorical analysis and print culture, because religious practice and theology structure inform the intellectual and moral worlds of the writers considered in this book. However, a good deal of the story that unfolds here, especially in the opening chapters, has to do with the transformation of print media and the opportunities and obstacles that commercial publication offered to American men and women who wanted to read or write about Roman Catholicism.

In recognition of its significant growth, development, and complexity, nineteenth-century American Catholicism has been assessed to some extent by demographers and historians of social and material practices, and some excellent histories have provided a good framework for understanding the development of Roman Catholic hierarchy and parish development. However, the literary practices and texts devoted to, and preoccupied with, Catholicism for this period have not yet been given their due. Roman Catholic literary culture in the United States did not attract much scholarly attention until the latter half of the twentieth century. In her pioneering 1954 study of Catholic publishers of the period 1784–1850, Sister Mary Stephana Cavanaugh highlighted this lack of attention to American Catholic literary history: "The existing histories of American printing ignore, almost completely, Catholic publishing activities. A careful checking of Isaiah Thomas's *History of Printing in America* [1810] yields not one Catholic publisher." While acknowledging the significant influence of Isaiah Thomas—the early professional bookman and founder of the American Antiquarian Society—in the historiography of American print culture, Cavanaugh called into question Thomas's intellectual honesty "because he fails to include the Catholic Mathew Carey, his greatest rival in the publishing field, who had been in business a quarter of a century when Thomas's history was published, and of whose existence Thomas could scarcely been ignorant."[4] In neglecting the contributions of Roman Catholic writers, Thomas was hardly exceptional and in fact typifies a long-standing tendency among American literary historians of the nineteenth century who, unlike their counterparts in social history, have only recently have begun to investigate the relationship between Roman Catholicism and the broader literary culture.[5]

Attending to the presence of Roman Catholic discourses is necessary in order to provide a more complete American literary history, but at the same time it is important not to oversimplify the complexities of religious affiliation and practice. This study assesses a series of Catholic writers and texts in nineteenth- and early twentieth-century America with particular reference to their attempts to promote and to imagine a diverse range of Catholicisms for America. The plural form "Catholicisms" is intentional here. Never a monolithic enterprise (in spite of anti-Catholic accusations about systematic papal plots against the American people[6]), the rhetoric of American Catholicism during the nineteenth century was intellectually fragmented, regionally variant, often produced without official church sanction, and subject to a wide range of interpretations, which draw on the specificity of American social, economic, and political conditions. Social historians have only rather recently come to grips with the complexities of lived religion generally, and the social history of nineteenth-century American Catholicism especially has much work to accomplish before that period can be understood with real particularity and nuance. The texts discussed in the following chapters, drawn from a number of genres—sermons, theological tracts, novels, essays, autobiography, and catechisms—demonstrate both the range of imaginative proposals for American Catholicism and the cultural negotiations that were required for writers whose rhetoric engaged with the idea of Catholic religious practices. In all of the works examined, within "fictional" and "nonfictional" genres alike, the desire for American Catholicism finds its expression in rhetoric infused with a host of vital concerns: political debates, personal morality and virtue, the business of publishing, Catholic immigration and its discontents, gender identity, and of course the time-honored evangelical tradition of promoting Catholicism over Protestantism. The conclusions reached about these matters were, however, far from unanimous.

Although Roman Catholicism did not provide unanimity among those who incorporated it into their literary work, Roman Catholicism became a vital and complex part of the nation's literary culture during the nineteenth and early twentieth century. Catholic ideas and Catholic culture provided rich materials for American writers of various stripes: professional novelists, literate evangelists, publishing priests, and intellectuals. Moreover, their many published works and literary entrepreneurship, as well as their diverse modes of engagement with the broader literary culture of the United States, demonstrate that significant intellectual and artistic work was performed by Catholic writers and others who found Roman Catholic traditions and aesthetics to be morally and artistically energizing. The following chapters also point toward the limitations encountered by this cohort of writers working within the sphere of Roman Catholic influence. While admitting their modest successes in the literary marketplace, it is necessary to concede that no Catholic writer of the nineteenth century achieved anything like the popular success of Harriet Beecher Stowe, the intellectual prominence of Ralph Waldo Emerson, or the autobiographical charisma of Frederick Douglass. To a certain extent, the rather limited popular success achieved by most nineteenth-century Roman Catholic writers, especially those with an overtly didactic or moralistic style, can be explained by admitting their lesser talents when compared with the canonical writers just mentioned. It is just as likely that as American Roman Catholic writers and readers began to emerge as a major constituency in literary culture during the middle and later years of the nineteenth century, the evangelical force of print media had declined substantially, even as some Catholic activists like Isaac Hecker and James Gibbons were working tirelessly to promote the specifics of orthodox Catholic theology through their publications.

Evangelical publishing was a major component of American literary culture during the antebellum period, and this book builds on previous scholarship, which has established that Roman Catholic writers were a presence on the nineteenth-century commercial publishing scene. In fact, the work of demonstrating that Roman Catholic writers were quite active in the marketplace of religious fiction has been conducted thoroughly by the literary historian David S. Reynolds, in *Faith in Fiction* (1981), whose research lays much of the groundwork for this project, especially for the period before 1850. The work of Reynolds and other book historians has shown that Roman Catholic writers joined Protestant writers in doing their best to take advantage of the revolution in commercial publishing by seeing to it that American readers were provided with relatively inexpensive religious books, periodicals, and tracts. Like their Protestant counterparts, Catholic publishing entrepreneurs throughout this time frame were enthusiastic about mass print's potential to shape religious sensibilities and shrewdly adopted inexpensive printed materials as a way of promulgating Christian faith.[7]

To take an early example of this phenomenon, consider the Irish American printer Mathew Carey, whose Bible edition was one of the first Catholic books printed in America. Carey, who carved out a successful business in part by selling Catholic pamphlets, devotional books, catechisms, and Bibles, was one of the most prescient in seeing the moral need (and commercial advantages) of producing books aimed at Catholic readers. In 1791, a half-century before the potato famine of the 1840s brought a great tide of Irish immigration to the United States, Carey wrote a circular to the clergy attending the first synod of the American Catholic Church, held in Baltimore. In his message, Carey focused on the importance of the Catholic press in the United States, the practical challenges of marketing books, and the relationship between reading habits and the development of religious commitment: "Without religious books, it is impossible to awaken or preserve a religious spirit among the people, especially in this country, where pastors are so few, and the flock scattered at such vast distances from each other." Carey admitted the scarcity of suitable books and also the sometimes weak commitment of individuals to a religion about whose precepts they lacked sufficient knowledge: "For want of proper books numbers of Roman Catholics are utterly unacquainted with the most essential and fundamental principles of their religion—some of whom have become wholly regardless of religion—and many embraced other religious persuasions, whose books they had opportunity of perusing." Recommending that the Church take it upon itself to fund the publication and distribution of Catholic books (because "the languor of the Roman Catholics, with respect to religious books," meant that "no printer will . . . venture to print them at his own risk"), Carey forcefully concluded his appeal to the Catholic clergy by observing the critical link between reading, religion, and social order. Lacking significant support from the Church, "the scarcity of books will continue, and be productive of consequences not only disgraceful and injurious to the Roman Catholics (who, in this respect, stand on much worse ground than any other body of people in America, all the others being abundantly supplied with books of religion) but hurtful to the community at large; as want of religion is almost always the parent of immoral and disorderly conduct."[8]

Carey's remarks to the 1791 Baltimore synod illustrate both a keen perception of religious books as a vital technology of evangelism and a shrewd business sense, which led him to survey his market of potential readers while considering with care how best to monetize their piety through targeted book sales. For Carey, a pious Catholic and a serious businessman, the crucial outcomes for American literary culture are the elevation of morals, the advancement of Catholic reading, and the successful commercial enterprise of selling large numbers of religious books. In light of his latter aim, which Carey shared with the following generation of Catholic writer-activists, another theme emerges of a constantly changing literary marketplace. This modernizing print marketplace both produced and reflected a steady transformation in American habits of reading. Certain dimensions of this transformation have been well charted by historians of the book, who have shown how major developments in print technology and distribution allowed for the proliferation of all kinds of relatively inexpensive printed materials. In addition, the book historian Ronald J. Zboray has argued that "the social distribution of literature followed closely the march of American economic development," meaning that much of the way that transformation in reading habits occurs is by means of an increasingly wealthy nation but also—and most crucially—a nation whose improved transportation and shipping networks by the middle and later nineteenth century began to make it a profoundly interconnected nation.[9]

Even before the communication and transportation revolutions of the nineteenth century, Roman Catholic thought had gradually begun to seep into in the American public sphere. For example, the early history of American Catholic writing surely cannot be understood without reference to the literary production of Catholic priests, for prior to the early decades of the nineteenth century, missionary priests—many of them European born—were the primary intellectual force working on behalf of Catholicism in the United States.[10] An exemplary figure in this regard, Anthony Kohlmann, S.J. (1771–1836), was a superbly educated theologian and cosmopolitan missionary who became president of Georgetown College in 1819 and also founded Old St. Patrick's Cathedral in New York City. Born in Alsace and well traveled in the European Catholic missions, Kohlmann devoted his writings to the production of highly erudite sermons and controversial works, and eventually became the general superior of the Jesuits in the United States. But Kohlmann, along with many other missionary priests of the colonial and early national period, remains a marginal figure in American religious history, largely because during his career as a theologian the population of Catholics was still so small. Moreover, Kohlmann's scholarly works were destined to remain the province of a tiny intellectual elite: the classically educated few who could fully grasp his recondite theological positions. Lacking the population base of religious adherents that might have provided him greater status, and writing well above the intellectual limits of the average literate person, Kohlmann was fated to obscurity as an American author.[11] Kohlmann's very modest profile in American literary culture exemplifies the marginality of most Catholic priests as writers in the United States before the mid-twentieth century, when the novelist Andrew Greeley began his long career as a chronicler in fiction of the American Catholic experience (with a particular focus on the religious world of Irish Americans). My focus in this book is divided between writers with official ties to the Catholic Church (the ordained priests Isaac Hecker and James Gibbons); writers like Anna Dorsey, Jedediah Huntington, and Orestes Brownson, who were ardent Catholics at work as popular authors; and the modernist writers Kate Chopin and Willa Cather, for whom Catholicism would function not as an evangelical goal but as a dimension of their literary aesthetic.

Because he was in many ways far more significant and influential than the early missionary American priests, the essayist and editor Orestes A. Brownson serves as the subject of my first chapter, in which I introduce some of the concerns that infused the antebellum rhetoric of American Catholicism. Much of Brownson's importance to Catholicism in the United States was a matter of timing. Converting from Protestantism to Catholicism in 1844, the mercurial and prolific Brownson—who had been one of the leading Unitarian thinkers during the 1830s—provides a critical early link between long-neglected Roman Catholic writings and the better-known intellectual and religious sphere of Brownson's friend Ralph Waldo Emerson and his transcendentalist circle. Brownson's several decades of greatest literary activity—during which he edited and served as primary contributor to the *Boston Quarterly Review* and *Brownson's Quarterly Review*—also coincide with the peak midcentury years of Irish immigration to the United States, thus making his works a useful resource for gauging the effect of demographic change on attitudes about American religious identity. At the same time, Brownson—who was born in Vermont—is a significant figure because his view of Catholicism was not primarily formed out of the Irish experience. The historian Thomas J. Meehan has observed that while Catholic controversy was a vital concern for early Catholic writers in the United States, "the progress of the movements for Catholic Emancipation and the repeal of the Union in Ireland" took up most of the space in Catholic newspapers of the first half of the nineteenth century. Brownson's self-appointed role as Catholic public intellectual was thus self-consciously American; it de-emphasized Irish politics by comparison with other Catholic journalists of the day, many of whom were recent immigrants from Ireland.[12]

A number of themes resonate throughout subsequent chapters. First, Brownson notes the importance of knitting politics and religion together in his arguments for religious change in America. The ideology of "Young America," an antebellum publishing slogan, which had become linked in the United States to notions of postcolonial pride, manifest destiny, and literary ambition, in Brownson's hands becomes a critical lens for examining the moral and religious failures of the nation. Equal parts intellectual contrarian and stubborn advocate for Catholic traditionalism, Brownson used "Young America" as an epithet denouncing what he saw as an irreligious, immature, and salacious popular culture. Second, Brownson appears as an early advocate of popular writing and widely distributed books as a means for promoting religion. Although his own attempts at fiction and popular writing had only limited success in the marketplace, he was an astute observer of the changes in print distribution and professional authorship in America. Finally, Brownson's attitudes about American femininity and the representation of women in literature initiate a theme that persists in subsequent chapters, in which tensions are revealed about women's place in Roman Catholic reading and writing. Dismayed at the increasing power of women in the print marketplace, and convinced that the failure (as he saw it) of American popular writing was a function of its pandering to women's interests and feminine weaknesses, Brownson advocated a larger role for a more masculine and conservative brand of Roman Catholicism in American literary culture.

The discourse about women in this period formed a natural terrain for exploration by writers concerned with Roman Catholic faith and practice. A large segment of the broader American literary culture was doing its part to critique, redefine, and improve woman's sphere, and so it was inevitable that this rhetoric would find its way into literary efforts that explored Catholicism. For all of its strongly patriarchal theology and ecclesiastical practice, Roman Catholic culture had always been concerned with the concept of idealized types of womanhood, as evidenced by its female saints, nuns and other women religious, and above all popular devotions to the Virgin Mary. American writers under the sway of Roman Catholic faith expressed a variety of opinions about how women should participate in religious and secular culture, and many—notably Orestes Brownson and James Gibbons—had grave reservations about expanding women's rights. But, somewhat ironically, the prominence of women as important figures in the history of the Church, along with the centuries-old cult of the Virgin, allowed American writers who worked with Catholic themes a decidedly gendered array of intellectual resources. These resources would prove crucial to representations of Roman Catholicism within a national literary culture whose growth owed so much to the emergence of women's professional authorship, burgeoning numbers of female readers, and representations of feminine sentiment in popular books.

For nineteenth-century immigrant Catholics, the appeal of sentimental structures of feeling, notably those advanced through popular books, would have been quite compelling. The cultural historian Karen Halttunen has argued that "the sentimental demand for sincerity was a defensive strategy against the perceived dangers of placelessness in the open society and of anonymity in the urban world of strangers." Consequently, women were important mediators and interpreters of socioeconomic status and were thus the reason that "sentimentalism emerged as an offensive strategy for defining what it was to be middle-class in America."[13] In some cases, writers and readers committed to (or oriented toward) Roman Catholic principles were then presented with the challenge of not only navigating the broader cultural changes associated with women's sphere in American culture but also reconciling these changes with attitudes about gender specific to their religious tradition. Brownson wrote learnedly about many subjects, and his turbulent literary career resists easy summary, but with his highly articulate and prolific opposition to women's expanding cultural influence, the American Catholic literary tradition had produced one of its most profoundly conservative voices.

Chapter 2 examines the career of Father Isaac Hecker, who, after some years as a Romantic transcendentalist and resident at the Brook Farm commune in Massachusetts, converted to Roman Catholicism with his friend Orestes Brownson. After his brief affiliation with the transcendental movement, Hecker founded the first order of American priests, the Congregation of Missionary Priests of Saint Paul the Apostle, commonly known as the Paulist Fathers, dedicated to the mission of evangelizing the American continent. In his role as leader of the Paulists, Hecker became a public missionary figure in the nineteenth century, a prominent lecturer evangelizing for a Catholic America, and a key spokesperson for the organized Church. Hecker's contributions to Catholic literature during the period begin with his diary, written before his conversion in 1844, continue with his two popular Catholic apologetical tracts that appeared in the 1850s, and continue with his editorial work with the *Catholic World*, an "eclectic magazine of general literature and science" that he founded after the Civil War.

Hecker's literary work, produced as a record of his conversion and as a vehicle for his missionary work, reveals a set of idiosyncratic and evolving attitudes about the possibilities for Catholicism in America. His writings, generated from positions both inside and outside of the organized Church, also provide shifting perspectives on Roman Catholic thought while suggesting some key scenes for this Catholic intellectual in the nineteenth century: self-examination before his conversion, the frustrations of his seminary years in Europe, and the extended career as a liberal Catholic leader and editor during which he came into serious conflict with Roman Church authorities over his desire for a moderate form of American Catholicism. Like Brownson, Hecker was becoming increasingly alert to the potential influence of widely distributed books in the literary marketplace. The *Catholic World* under his editorship thus became a clearinghouse for reviews and reprints of literary texts, and was aimed directly at the growing and increasingly literate class of American Catholics. Although his early writings show him to be mainly self-directed and preoccupied with the intricacies of his personal spiritual condition, his mature editorial work and his two most important books clearly demonstrate his belief that American Catholicism required a significant leadership in the field of letters. The shape of Hecker's career during the transformative decades of the middle and later nineteenth century demonstrates his conviction that the expanding print marketplace held unsurpassed opportunities for cementing the bonds between religious commitment and national identity.

Because of the centrality of fiction to nineteenth-century literary culture, chapter 3 examines several overtly pro-Catholic novels written during the antebellum period by Anna Hanson Dorsey and Jedediah Vincent Huntington. These writers were selected as transitional figures in American Catholic authorship; compared with the writings of Brownson and Hecker in the previous chapter, their work more successfully negotiated a balance between literary entertainment and religious instruction, and thus reached out to a more mainstream audience of readers. Literary fiction was not the predominant element in early nineteenth-century Roman Catholic writing, but by the late antebellum period the works of Dorsey and Huntington began to stake out a real claim on the attentions of American Catholic readers of fiction. In his excellent study of antebellum American Catholic fiction, Willard Thorp observed that Dorsey and Huntington (as well as Charles James Cannon, George Henry Miles, and Mary Anne Sadlier) were part of a new cohort of lay novelists that emerged before the Civil War. According to Thorp, "In the 1840s the writing of Catholic novels began to pass from the priests into the hands of professional authors." As the print marketplace matured and its commercial potential was recognized and exploited during the mid-nineteenth century, these novelists joined their non-Catholic contemporaries as participants in the national literary conversation about Christian religion. As novels became increasingly profitable products, Thorp continues, American Catholic publishers expanded their offerings from cheap devotional books to highlighting fiction as well: "In the early years the chief sources of revenue for the Catholic publishers were cheaply printed devotional works, sold at missions, over the counter in Catholic supply stores, or through religious book societies. By 1850 Catholic novels were advertised prominently in the publishers' lists alongside devotional works." At midcentury, then, Roman Catholic writers had joined the ranks of American novelists for whom industrial-scale publication and wide distribution offered not only the promise of national evangelism but also the possibility of lucrative work.[14]

The expansion and diversification of commercial publishing in the nineteenth century provided the means to promote and distribute various narratives and propositions for American Catholicism, and these developments were witnessed not just by professional writers and evangelists but also by writers whose primary work lay in other fields of endeavor. Bearing in mind the importance of talented literary amateurs, chapter 4 discusses the priest and writer James Gibbons, a Catholic archbishop best known previously for his leadership of the Baltimore archdiocese, for his political influence in the early twentieth century, and for his status as the second American Catholic appointed as cardinal. My discussion of Gibbons acknowledges his career as an important Catholic bishop but also positions him as one of the most successful, influential, and enterprising popular catechists of his day. Conceived during his years as an itinerant priest in North Carolina, his catechism *Faith of Our Fathers* (1876) stands as a deft and successful adaptation of Catholic faith in response to prevailing literary themes and the exigencies of the print marketplace.

Gibbons presented a simple version of Catholic principles and dogma, such as the veneration of the Virgin Mary and the seeming paradox of papal infallibility, and so *Faith of Our Fathers* in some ways resembles other catechisms in its didacticism and appeal to a broad readership. And yet what distinguishes the book from other examples of the genre is Gibbons's extensive use of literary devices drawn from the nineteenth-century sentimental tradition. Specifically, *Faith of Our Fathers* figures the Catholic Church as a beautiful and yet suffering young woman, oppressed by Protestantism and in need of rescue by the faithful. This adaptation of traditional representations of the Church as a nourishing mother links his catechism to the more familiar (to literary historians) discourses of ideal womanhood, sentiment, domesticity, and benevolence. Ambitious to create a popular book to use in the service of Catholic evangelism, Gibbons framed his work as a catechism but inflected it with literary themes and gender politics that would have been familiar to any American reader of nineteenth-century popular fiction.

In chapter 5, short fiction and the novel take center stage once again, in my consideration of writings by Willa Cather and Kate Chopin. These important figures, who might fairly be described as participants in both the local-color school as well as the early modernist literary movement, have rarely if ever been described as "Catholic" writers, and I make no claim that they evangelize on behalf of the Catholic Church in anything like the same fashion as nineteenth-century pro-Catholic novelists like Jedediah Vincent Huntingdon, Anna Hanson Dorsey, and others. Instead, Cather and Chopin deploy the symbols and textures of Roman Catholicism for purposes that cannot be described as or reduced to apologetics on behalf of organized religion. Nor does their fiction serve as a marker on a path to secularization, with religious motifs merely emptied of devotional and spiritual content. Instead, their work points to a new way of using religious rhetoric, a mode that harmonizes with the philosopher Marcel Gauchet's assertion that "modern society is not a society without religion but one whose major articulations were formed by metabolizing the religious function."[15]

The legacy of nearly a century of religious activism in the culture of print has some of its most vital elements in American popular fiction, but the religiosity of missionary zeal—far more evident in an earlier Victorian era dominated by such Protestant evangelical publishers as the American Tract Society—had by the era of Chopin and Cather given way to a religiosity deployed in "metabolized" form. While the deeper religious commitments of Chopin and Cather are somewhat obscure by comparison with the previous generations of American Catholic writers, they are just as much engaged with issues of gender, and they use religious representations and themes in order to explore women's lives and the politics of gender in the early twentieth century. As with their antecedent, the American local-color pioneer Henry Wadsworth Longfellow, whose evocative and popular poetry featured references to Roman Catholicism in North America, Catholicism provides a deep well for the literary picturesque in the work of Chopin and Cather. Resolutely averting their authorial gaze from the actual scenes of contemporary Catholicism (the great majority of which were located in urban areas), these writers produced a scenic Catholicism set on the American geographic margins, notably Chopin's Louisiana coasts and Cather's desert Southwest, from which to explore complex ideas about religion and gender.

These new tendencies exemplified by Chopin and Cather suggest a number of important shifts in American religious and literary culture during the late nineteenth and early twentieth century. The enculturation and assimilation of Irish Catholic immigrants had eventuated in the successful establishment of churches, schools, and parish organizations to the point that Catholic identity in America had become something more complex than merely being associated with a servant class. For instance, the 1891 joint conversion to Roman Catholicism by Nathaniel Hawthorne's daughter Rose Hawthorne Lathrop and her husband, George Parsons Lathrop, created a nationwide sensation in the newspapers, but it also demonstrated that Catholic identity had become a viable religious option even for America's intellectual elites.[16] Perhaps as a result, American writers who valued Roman Catholic faith and traditions found new and less dogmatic ways of using religious themes in their work. Ironically, during a period when James Gibbons's popular catechisms—brimming with Catholic dogma and evangelical zeal—continued to roll off the presses, innovative writers like Cather and Chopin eschewed both evangelism and Catholic Church membership, and yet they were able to locate in the fabric of both traditional and contemporary Catholic culture many powerful resources for charting modernist sensibilities and evolving American identities.

Across many decades of American intellectual history, the explanatory power promised—and in many ways delivered—by such influential studies as Vernon Louis Parrington's *Main Currents in American Thought* (1927), Perry Miller's *The New England Mind* (1939), Sidney Ahlstrom's *The Religious History of the American People* (1972), and Sacvan Bercovitch's *The Puritan Origins of the American Self* (1975) has also served to situate Protestantism as the nation's literary master discourse: America's religion by default. Moreover, subsequent generations of literary scholars have not yet done enough to alter the conclusion that ours is a literary history whose religious contours have been shaped almost exclusively by evangelical Protestant Christianity. By contrast, the perspectives offered here that traverse literary genres and range across writers with various types and degrees of religious commitment suggest an American literary history in which Roman Catholicism in fact played a very significant role. The mere presence of Roman Catholic discourse in our literary history is only part of the story that deserves telling. That some of these writers discussed were adult converts to Catholicism and that others were not members but used aspects of Roman Catholicism to advance their literary purposes obliges us to acknowledge as well the complexity of religious discourse in American literary history. Each of the writers under consideration here participated in a collective and yet de-centered process of literary invention applied to questions of faith and morality. While their aims were as various as their temperaments, beliefs, and literary talents, their involvement in this process of invention allowed them to play a role in fashioning the religious dimensions of our literary culture through encounters with the realities, the possibilities, and the limits of Roman Catholicism in a rapidly changing nation.

1

Orestes Brownson in Young America

Popular Books and Catholic Criticism

> Nor is it true that the general tendency of art, or aesthetic culture, is to liberate the mind. The panders to vice know very well that art is one of the most effectual means of enchaining their victims, and do not fail to enlist architecture, poetry, music, painting, sculpture, in their service . . . and we may lay it down as an invariable rule, that art uniformly tends to corrupt, when not preceded and accompanied by high spiritual, or moral and religious culture.
>
> Brownson, "Schiller's Aesthetic Theory" (1846)

More than any other American writer, Orestes A. Brownson (1803–76) worked at the intellectual confluence of nineteenth-century Protestant and Catholic literary cultures. In a career that spanned numerous religious conversions and produced a daunting body of publications, Brownson during his most productive years (1844–70) also became the preeminent American Catholic intellectual of his generation. Because of his rigorous program of self-education and his close contacts with the leading New England thinkers of his day, Brownson's intellectual interests were diverse and wide-ranging; he not only wrote extensively about religious topics but also tried his hand at composing fiction, published substantial essays on political theory and philosophy, lectured widely about religion on the lyceum circuit, and fashioned himself into a book reviewer with considerable influence among Catholic intellectuals. And like many of the leading thinkers and writers of his day, Brownson was acutely conscious of the emerging power and influence of the United States in the nineteenth century and sought to shape its literary culture in ways commensurate with both his own religious commitments and his belief in American political ascendancy. Herman Melville, one of Brownson's contemporaries, provides a useful way of illustrating the high stakes that Brownson and other American Catholic activists—enamored with the idea of a "Young America" with limitless creative potential—believed to be in play in the rapidly expanding literary marketplace of the middle nineteenth century.

The intensity with which the brash concept of American "manifest destiny" was joined by a correspondingly fervent drive for the development of "Young American Literature" may be registered at numerous junctures in antebellum writing, but nowhere more bitterly than in Melville's scathing chapters on the subject in *Pierre; or, the Ambiguities* (1852). Late in that novel, upon his arrival in New York City, the ingenuous and ill-fated protagonist Pierre Glendinning discovers the ruthless market forces and shallow literary talents at work in harnessing a powerful—and lucrative—American desire for books and reading. Melville's *Pierre* constitutes an important fictional example of how the opportunities of commercial publishing, conditioned by political and cultural forces, were confronted by a new professional class of American writers.

Disowned by his wealthy mother and faced with an impoverished life in New York City with his half-sister/lover Isabel, Pierre Glendinning sets out to make his name as a "Young American" professional author, only to encounter grave difficulties in reconciling his own lofty ideas with the crassness of a profit-driven and politically shallow literary marketplace. Pierre's failure to align his views with the practical demands of this prevailing theme in antebellum literary circles—the idea of an immensely gifted and youthful nation on the cusp of a cultural power so profound as to require new modes of literary representation—figures as a part of his tragic decline in Melville's novel. It is also a reminder of the imaginative energy that Young America embodied for a generation of media-savvy antebellum writers and reformers of all kinds.[1]

The concept of Young America inevitably found its way into antebellum religious debates, particularly those advanced by Brownson, a former leading transcendentalist, a sometime colleague of Emerson and Thoreau, and later a self-appointed cultural critic on all subjects related to Roman Catholicism.[2] In Brownson's essays during the middle decades of the nineteenth century (most of them published in the *Boston Quarterly Review* and *Brownson's Quarterly Review*), Young America is adapted from its originally nationalistic politico-literary stance into a flexible weapon of religious cultural critique. Young America, rather than signifying political idealism and literary innovation (however misguided that innovation might have appeared to skeptics like Melville), in Brownson's hands was crafted as an epithet suggesting the naiveté and shallowness of American social mores and cultural production that obstruct the development of American Catholic religion. In particular, Brownson's polemic against Young America comes to indicate corrosive forces preventing the broad implementation of orthodox Catholicism: family disruption, resistance to authority of all kinds, salaciousness in popular fiction, and so on. Above all, however, Brownson's project of dismissing Young America as a misguided and immoral set of social trends lays the blame for cultural problems in the nineteenth century squarely upon the shoulders of women, and especially what he perceived as their tendency to "feminize" (and thus to weaken and debase) American literary practices and social habits, which he saw as requiring the necessarily "masculine" intervention of Roman Catholic principles.

Unsurprisingly, the urgency felt by those who promoted the idea of addressing moral issues through uniquely American literary practices—an idea that drew on the recognition that the widely distributed modern book or essay could now do tremendously effective cultural work—eventually made itself known in a variety of religious circles. Didactic religious operations like the Protestant evangelical American Tract Society, with its ubiquitous leafleting during the antebellum years, figure as only the most prominent examples of religious interest in an increasingly powerful and inexpensive form of modern media.[3] Nor did the utility of Young America as a descriptor of nineteenth-century social, political, aesthetic, and religious imperatives escape the notice of the mercurial Brownson. He, along with his friend and fellow-convert Father Isaac Hecker, had become formidable advocates for American Catholicism during the pivotal decades before and after the Civil War. Given his iconoclastic and disputatious temperament, though, Brownson's views on the cultural work of literature often diverged sharply from other advocates of a new national literature, even as he echoed their voices in chanting for American cultural ascendancy. One of Brownson's biographers has pointed out that even from his earliest years as a literary reviewer—when he was known mainly as a prominent intellectual associated with the transcendentalist movement in New England—Brownson typically took it upon himself to "[measure] the worth of literary authors according to the degree they promoted social reform, or advanced the cause of democracy."[4] Or, as Brownson himself remarked dourly in his ambivalent review of Nathaniel Hawthorne's *The Scarlet Letter*, "Mere literature for its own sake we do not prize. . . . [Men] are moral and accountable beings, and we look only to the moral and religious effect of their works. Genius perverted, or employed in perverting others, has no charms for us."[5] Apart from what he saw as the relatively minor interest they held as works of art, for Brownson the utility of literary texts lay primarily in their ability to motivate society in the right directions, morally and religiously.

In spite of austere views like these, Brownson nevertheless took on the burden of reviewing as many literary works as possible that dealt with subjects and issues of potential value for his Catholic readership. While his own early reputation as a critic, before his conversion to Catholicism, had been built largely on his published reviews of complex philosophical and political tracts—as with his prodigious explications of Kant's philosophy in the early numbers of the *Boston Quarterly Review*—he became increasingly convinced that the royal road to moral development for literate Americans lay with widely distributed popular literature. And so, to the extent that using the literary slogan "Young America" served as a tactic for representing to readers his own more particular blend of Catholicism and cautious republicanism, Brownson at first was willing to use that slogan to his advantage.

By the waning years of his long reviewing career, however, and especially after the Civil War, Brownson concluded that his early optimism about popular American books had been misguided. Having once embraced the idea that the United States might fulfill what he saw as the crowning religious achievements of Western civilization by embracing Roman Catholicism, he became convinced that it was unrealistic to expect popular literature to have the kind of wholesome effect he had once envisioned for it. Moreover—and here is the point at which his theology and criticism betray a strain of misogyny—Brownson's early polemics against irreligious and immoral literary works, writings he deemed to be corrosive of true religion and likely to foster lust and sentimentality among their readers, gradually solidified into a direct critique of American women's influence as writers and readers of these books.[6]

"Sentiment," as he described the troublingly emotional reader-responses of women—and men sympathetic with women—"is almost sure, if indulged, to become lust, and to pave the way for wide-spread licentiousness and impurity."[7] Indulgence in irreligious sentiment or prurient topics, as Brownson understood them, was the surest way to earn a disapproving notice in *Brownson's Quarterly Review*. Eventually, his views about the matter hardened so that even the term "Young America," which once had signified for him an auspicious national destiny tied to refined aesthetic sensibilities and the formation of a new democratic literature, became a pejorative term that he linked to moral decay—a cultural rot exacerbated not simply by a hegemonic Protestantism but by women's activities within nineteenth-century American culture.

For a time during the middle part of his career (1844–55), he had held out hope for an incipient Young American spirit that would represent in literature the religious morality, authoritarian principles, and social dictates of Catholicism. However, in later essays like those on "The Woman Question" (1869 and 1873), the Young America of Brownson's lexicon had become an ironic synonym for a religiously bankrupt younger generation that had lost its moral bearings. Older generations writing critically about the young is of course a time-honored practice, but this generational tension is complicated in Brownson's reviews because women and women's sensibilities are blamed directly for the diseased state of American literary and religious culture. For example, the campaign for woman suffrage was, for Brownson, merely another indication of deteriorating family life and a sure path toward failed religious values among the young: "There is nothing which more grieves the wise and good, or makes them tremble for the future of their country, than the growing neglect or laxity of family discipline; than the insubordination, the lawlessness, and precocious depravity of Young America. . . . And whose fault is it? It is chiefly the fault of the mothers, who fail to govern their households, and to bring up their children in a Christian manner."[8] This theme is extended in his 1873 essay on woman suffrage, where Brownson again ties the fate of Young America to troubled gender roles in society: "The children catch the spirit of disobedience from the reluctance of the wife to obey, or her actual disobedience to her husband. Children early become disobedient to their parents, and the distinctive qualities of 'Young America' are inherited or learned from the mother."[9] One of Brownson's final essays, on "Women's Novels" (1875), implicates women and mothers directly as key actors in the failure of Young America to realize its potential in literature and religion, claiming that "the faults of what we call Young America are in great measure due to maternal weakness on the one hand, and the absence of paternal authority on the other."[10] In effect, then, Brownson's once-sweeping program for American Catholicism had foundered, according to his view, not merely because of Protestant resistance to the truths of Catholicism but also because necessary patriarchal structures (in government, literature, and religion) had been undermined by women's failure to submit to authority in all its forms. No longer content to frame popular culture alone as the foe of religiosity and morality, Brownson once again goes to considerable lengths to assert that the new American literature—and its promise as a useful voice for Catholicism—met with failure precisely because of women's strengthening influence over the nation's cultural life.

For all of his strident criticism of mass-print culture, Brownson continued to acknowledge that the best popular writing could be deployed in the service of high literary achievement and the religious improvement of society, and he was perennially attentive to popular writers in his book reviews. As Brownson admitted in a lengthy 1850 essay-review praising his favorite American literary artist, Henry Wadsworth Longfellow, certain contemporary writers did indeed have "a perception, if not of the truth of the Catholic Church, at least of her beauty."[11] Part of Brownson's aim in reviewing popular Longfellow poems like *Evangeline* was "to show the Catholic reader how easy it is for genius to mould the simplest elements of Catholic life into a story full of instruction and beauty, without cramming it full of inconsequent controversy and questionable theology. . . . If our religious novelists could get Protestants to *feel* the beauty of Catholic customs and Catholic life, they would accomplish much in thus removing a load of prejudice that impairs the proper exercise of reason."[12] Longfellow's great virtue, according to Brownson, lay in his ability to exert a wide "influence [in] the world of letters," while gaining "the consideration of that very exclusive, but passive and obedient creature, the reading community." Although he was a Unitarian, Longfellow's artistic and aesthetic interest in Catholic-themed poetry combined with his popularity among American readers to position him as one of the more important American writers with sympathetic views about Roman Catholic culture.[13]

Brownson's reviews praised James Fenimore Cooper's fiction as well, finding him to be "an earnest-minded man, and, though a novelist, he is no trifler." Overlooking the inconvenient detail that Cooper (like Longfellow) was not a Catholic and did not deal with Roman Catholic themes in many of his writings, Brownson's admiration for his moral and religious sensibility convinced him that Cooper should be given "an honorable place in what we call 'secular Catholic literature.'"[14] By contrast, in a later essay concerned with "Beecherism and Its Tendencies" (1871), Brownson sharply criticized what he perceived as the corrupting power of Henry Ward Beecher's Protestant evangelism. And Brownson reserved some of his harshest disapproval for the literary applications of Beecherism that the novelist Harriet Beecher Stowe had disseminated to enormous effect in her own books. "Beecherism," complained Brownson, "without explicitly affirming universal salvation, decidedly doubts that the sufferings of the damned, if any damned there are, will be everlasting, as we may see in *The Minister's Wooing*, and in the *Defence of Lady Byron*, by Mrs. Beecher Stowe" (478).[15] The point to be emphasized here is that a significant part of what Brownson gleaned from the Young America debates may be found in his conviction that changing practices of reading and writing were shaping antebellum morality and religiosity in disturbing ways. Or, as Brownson put it in his essay "The Literary Policy of the Church of Rome," "books are companions, and bad books are as dangerous as any other species of companions. Evil communications corrupt good manners, and we may be corrupted by reading bad books as well as by frequenting bad company." So it was that one of his self-appointed tasks as a reviewer was to alert his readers about how best to furnish literature suitable for the American Catholic reader.[16]

As his own efforts as a self-described "Catholic publicist" and champion of Young *Catholic* America continued and became a vital part of a deeply conservative interpretation of antebellum Catholicism, Brownson became convinced that—Longfellow and Cooper notwithstanding—few if any works of modern literature could fulfill his demand that books be socially appropriate and theologically correct from the perspective of Catholicism. While pointing out such difficulties as theological error and the pernicious influence of competing Protestant religious ideas, his assessments of Catholic literature also consistently point to the grave failure of Catholic writing to discipline itself against problems even more intractable than doctrinal controversy: the influence of women's writing and the intrusion of "feminized" emotions and religiosity into popular books.[17]

Long before his conversion to Catholicism, in essays that ponder the role of public scholarship and the relation between mind and materialism in the young republic, Brownson had argued that the desire for a national literature would not be realized until the educated classes committed their intellectual energies to great moral projects, without which American writing would never reach the highest excellence. However, energy alone, according to Brownson in an 1849 review of James Russell Lowell's poetry, would not suffice for the task of generating a suitable American literature unless that energy were joined within the culture by a more somber mode of scholarship: "Everybody knows that the great poets, the great artists, have never flourished, save in epochs and countries marked by severe discipline, and ennobled by serious and solid studies. The flourishing period of true art is always immediately preceded or accompanied by a flourishing period of philosophy, of moral science, and of religious truth." Although he had at one time been an advocate of Lowell's poetry, Brownson's concern is that while his Arthurian poem about a knightly quest for the Holy Grail, *The Vision of Sir Launfal*, amply demonstrated Lowell's technical gifts as a poet, it nevertheless failed miserably in moral terms. The moral objection here, in Brownson's view, is related to Lowell's depiction of a knight who performs benevolently, not for reasons of chastity and authentic religious devotion but for the warm glow of pleasure that benevolent acts bring to the knight. Seeing Lowell as emblematic of a "superficial and frivolous age," Brownson awaited the arrival of an American literary culture worthy of the name, while suggesting to his Catholic readers that "the first American poet is probably not yet born."[18]

By 1844, when he converted to Catholicism, Brownson had located the great moral and religious project—the "serious and solid studies"—that would occupy him for the remainder of his career. Catholicism, embraced by Brownson as the religious manifest destiny for an American nation and a tradition worthy of his own talents, had appeared to him as a true and ideal faith. He saw in Roman Catholicism a religion that would greatly benefit a country with high political ideals and ambitions for moral improvement. And yet Catholicism also became Brownson's critical theory: a fulcrum for raising a long line of objections, first, against the traditions of American "Protestant" literature, and second, against the various and often misconceived efforts at creating an indigenous American "Catholic" literature. As the Civil War years approached, Brownson, always attuned to the interpenetrations of religion and politics, became more explicit about the connections he wished to forge between a nation with growing power and geopolitical potentiality, and the fates of a religious cohort of Americans, which grew radically in size and importance at precisely the same historical juncture:

> There is more than meets the eye in the popular expression, "Manifest Destiny." We have a manifest destiny, and the world sees and confesses it, some with fear and some with hope; but it is not precisely that supposed by our journalists, or pretended by our filibusterers,—although these filibusters may be unconsciously and unintentionally preparing for its fulfillment. It may be our manifest destiny to extend our government over the whole American continent, but that is in itself alone a small affair, and no worthy object of true American ambition. . . . The manifest destiny of this country is something far higher, nobler, and more spiritual,—the realization, we should say, of the Christian ideal of society for both the Old World and the New.[19]

It is with Catholic literature that Brownson rather grudgingly places the responsibility for resisting the morally corrosive themes extant in Protestant writing, which he calls "essentially heathen—a reproduction, under varied forms, of the literature of pagan antiquity."[20] So contaminated with paganism has so-called Protestant literature become, he wrote in his essay "Modern Idolatry" (1845), that "there is and must be the same hostility between Catholic and Protestant literatures as between the Catholic and Protestant religions."[21]

What separates Brownson so dramatically from other midcentury critics engaged in working toward their own versions of an authentically American literature, however, are his unwillingness to adopt a straightforward literary-nationalism attitude and his marked ambivalence about literary work not aimed at developing religious values. Working partly against the grain and spirit of Young Americanism, Brownson promoted instead a literature of weighty morality, but one operating in the service of Catholicism rather than merely in the service of nationalism: "No doubt, each nation has its peculiar wants, and its peculiar modes or habits of thought and feeling, which to some extent are to be consulted and addressed; but that which is addressed to them should be peculiar to no particular time or place, but universally true and applicable in its principle."[22] For this reason, he advocated "subject[ing] literature to the empire of religion" through a controlled and steady critical gaze and by doing everything possible so as to ensure the ascent of a generation of writers willing to acknowledge that "only a Christian literature . . . is desirable or allowable."[23]

Along with his reluctance to climb aboard the literary-nationalist bandwagon in the antebellum period, Brownson also had much to say about the rise of that distinctive new Young American character on the nineteenth-century cultural stage—the professional author—remarking acerbically: "We have no respect for mere professional authors, whether American or not." Because they do not work in service for the higher vocation of religious work,

> an author class, whose vocation is simple authorship, has no normal functions, in either the religious or the social hierarchy. Our Lord, in organizing his church made no provision for professional authors. . . . They constitute one of the greatest pests of modern society. Nothing can be conceived more ruinous to the state, more destructive of faith and manners, of all that constitutes the work or glory of society or individuals, than a class of men of which your Bulwers, Byrons, Shelleys, Dickenses, Victor Hugos, Balzacs, Eugene Sues, Paul de Kocks, and, pardoning the bull, George Sands, not to mention a whole host of Germans and some Americans, are distinguished specimens.[24]

The irony of this statement in light of his own career as professional author notwithstanding, it is clear that Brownson is persuaded of print media's increasing power to shape morality, and by extension to shape the religious beliefs of Americans. Simply put, the grave danger that motivates Brownson to warn against professional authorship turns out to be secularism, but especially—and here Brownson concurs with others in the Young America literary movement—the temptation of writing primarily to earn money rather than to advance morals and religion. In the decades after his Catholic conversion, he concluded that the rise of a professional class of writers with no obligation other than profit must necessarily lead to a plenitude of texts that are widely distributed and yet morally dubious and nonreligious. As a younger writer, Brownson had witnessed the advance of Jacksonian ideologies in the popular press, which he saw as perilous invitations to mob rule and anarchy, concluding that "—when the people became indocile, disloyal, restless,—when literature became the rage,—when all the passions were stimulated into fearful activity, and all questions, sacred and profane, were wrested from the schools and brought before the multitude, . . . new modes of meeting the enemies of religion [became] indispensable."[25] Brownson's book reviews, for all their sophistication, were thus intended to move beyond mere aesthetic judgment in order to function as conservative mechanisms of social control and cultural stability calibrated with Catholic religious premises.

Brownson was attuned to political developments in the United States, and he was equally alert to representations of Roman Catholicism in popular American books. Among the manifestations of mob consciousness and the rule of popular writing that Brownson had in mind in his harsh critiques of contemporary print culture would have been the enormous wellspring of interest generated by Maria Monk's infamous convent exposé, *Awful Disclosures of Maria Monk, or, the Hidden Secrets of a Nun's Life in a Convent Exposed!* (1836), an oft-reprinted potboiler that capitalized on the enthusiasm for anti-Catholicism and promoted violent acts such as convent-burning.[26] But Brownson was occasionally forced to admit that "little can be done in a direct way in relation to literature, either in checking the growth of a corrupt and licentious literature, or in the production of a pure and wholesome literature." Adopting a fatalistic attitude in this comment, he positioned the practices of literature-for-its-own-sake (whether aimed at aesthetic or pecuniary ends) outside of the realm of American Catholicism rightly understood: "As literature in general, and American literature in particular, is no primary want of individuals or of society, we may leave it to take care of itself, and trouble ourselves no further about it than to guard, as far as possible, against its corruptions."[27] For the diligent critic, however, the work of filtering culture so as to eliminate the various toxins of non-Catholic, anti-Catholic, or insufficiently Catholic religious themes and motives of its literature proved to be no simple matter:

> We speak of literature proper, of works intended for popular reading. These are the works which need the most to be looked after. The most influential writers, whether for good or evil, are those who are taken from the ranks of the people, and who write for the people. They may exert an influence wholly repugnant to our holy religion, and do immense harm, without departing in a single instance from the strict letter of the faith. . . . It is the unconscious life of the author diffused through the work, and which he could not avoid diffusing through it, if he would,

> that determines its influence for good or evil. . . . [The Church] knows that a literary work of any worth, in a literary point of view, must be, to a considerable extent, the expression of the life of the author, and therefore, if the author be a heretic, it must contain a secret poison which will prove at least hurtful to the purity and strength of Catholic life.[28]

As for the writers and publishers of popular books, religious purpose must assert itself, and although Brownson insists that American Catholics need not "wield the tomahawk and battle-axe of controversy," he lobbied for a distinctively Catholic mode of writing whereby "whoever takes up one of our works . . . shall feel that its author could have been none other than a Catholic."[29]

Although his own efforts at popular fiction were neither well-wrought nor popular, Brownson always recognized the importance of participating in the struggle for Catholic ideas and the contest for popular religiosity within the marketplace of popular print.[30] Much of the evidence for this may be found in his interest in literary criticism and his book reviews that emphasize the possibility and promise of various kinds of Catholic publications. Especially notable, in Brownson's view, was the tremendous expansion of journalism and the periodical press, whose reach and influence were vastly increasing during the antebellum years:

> The ablest, the most energetic and living writers of the day, instead of writing folios, or pamphlets as formerly, write leaders in the journals, or contribute articles to reviews and magazines. Journalism has become the most approved and the most efficient means through which modern thought is expressed, and the public mind is formed and directed. . . . It becomes necessary therefore for Catholics to have their journals, and to use them as a means of neutralizing the effects of the non-Catholic press, and of promoting what may be called the external interests of religion. It seems but right that they should do what they can to turn the weapon invented for their destruction against their enemies.[31]

With the use of such tools as intellectual journalism and measured commentary on popular culture in the form of widely disseminated reviews and criticism, then, the American people, in whom Brownson harbored no deep religious confidence or illusions about predisposition for Catholicism, would eventually be drawn inexorably to the truths of the Catholic faith, and "the progress of the American mind . . . will force them before long to choose between Catholicity and no religion . . . and will prefer Catholic religion. Having finally undergone the necessary conversion, these newly Catholic Americans will "carry into their Catholic life those natural virtues of boldness, energy, enterprise, and perseverance for which they are now so remarkable, because our religion does not destroy the natural, but elevates, purifies, and directs it."[32] Success in converting Protestants to Roman Catholicism, a difficult task given the traditions of American religion, as Brownson so clearly recognized, would prove even more elusive if Catholicism failed to make itself legible, accurate, and compelling as a national literature.

The traditional genealogy of national literary emergence during the American Renaissance years—a narrative of literary history tied closely to the ideological imperatives of Young America—has relied upon a sequence of events that begins with postcolonial literary anxiety during the early republic, followed by early Americanizing efforts in fiction by writers such as Charles Brockden Brown, Washington Irving, and James Fenimore Cooper. Familiar and canonical American Protestant authors such as Hawthorne, Melville, Whitman, Dickinson, Thoreau, and others thus emerge within a reshaped nationalist cultural milieu, which included technological transformations in the sphere of publishing, along with the philosophical transformations wrought by Unitarianism and transcendentalism, and voiced preeminently in the antebellum period by Ralph Waldo Emerson. This familiar—although lately contested—narrative of American literary values, aesthetics, and praxis works usefully to chart voices of increasingly secular and liberalizing disposition during the nineteenth century, but it is a story whose dimensions are less than adequate for explaining the links between American literary nationalism and pro-Catholic discourse voiced by Orestes Brownson. In particular, the traditional emphasis on a national literature featuring themes of self-reliance and self-consciousness does not account for a variant ideology developing within Brownson's works and the writings of his American Catholic contemporaries. In his post-conversion essays, the pressing need from at least some Catholic perspectives was not so much for a nationalizing literature per se but for a cadre of writers and critics who could better express Roman Catholic traditionalism in the context of antebellum social and political turmoil. These elite Catholics, Brownson and his supporters believed, would in turn foster the kinds of popular reading materials that were necessary to bolster the Catholic piety of ordinary Americans.

Though only slightly less mandarin in intellectual temperament than Ralph Waldo Emerson and William Ellery Channing (both of whom were New England contemporaries who shared his enthusiasm for a new American literature), Brownson held the opinion that good literature must be provided for ordinary people as well as the elite few. In his January 1839 essay "American Literature" (part 1), his response to Emerson's 1838 lecture on "Literary Ethics," he remarked that "the whole people must constitute" the audience for any national literature worthy of the name. Using the lexicon of Emerson's "American Scholar" essay, Brownson had already recognized the implications of popular reading practices for the mass of citizens, noting: "He who would be an American scholar must address himself to the whole American people; and his own attainments cannot far outrun the capacity of the masses to comprehend and relish his speech. It follows from this . . . to make the whole nation a nation of readers, and to secure to the great mass of the people the leisure necessary to attend to the [scholar's subjects]."[33] Reading, an ever more vital American cultural practice, had been empowered to a large extent, according to Brownson, by the remarkably high level of national literacy. However, broad participation in the enlivening world of popular reading—especially as it related to the fiery rhetoric of antebellum newspapers—also ushered in a host of cultural problems. And it is these problems that Brownson traced, soon after his conversion, to the failure of moral and religious authority to hold sway over these modes of popular nineteenth-century expression: "The press makes readers, but does little to make virtuous and intelligent readers. The newspaper press is, for the most part, under the control of men of very ordinary abilities, lax principles, and limited acquirements. It echoes and exaggerates popular errors, and does little or nothing to create a sound public opinion. Your popular literature caters to popular taste, passions, prejudices, ignorance, and errors. . . . On what then, are we to rely?"[34] Despite these reservations, Brownson complains and moralizes far less than some others about the putative lack of an effective and vibrant national literature—one that could merit comparison with the great European literary traditions—because he sees the development of a national spirit of reading in the welter of periodicals and newspapers that the country produced and consumed, day by day. For Brownson, a careful sifting of these periodicals brought to light "more fine writing, more true poetry, genuine eloquence, vigorous thought, original and comprehensive views, than can be found in the classics of either France or England."[35]

Given such remarks, it seems evident that Brownson's urgings for a vibrant American literary culture have roots in some of the very same intellectual sources that fueled Ralph Waldo Emerson's "The American Scholar" (1837), his manifesto for a budding American literary exceptionalism. Another key text that can be linked to Brownson's religiously based reviews and criticism is William Ellery Channing's early essay "Remarks on National Literature" (1830), which was first delivered before the American Philosophical Society in 1823. Channing, whose Unitarian theology would prove so important for the development of transcendental thought in subsequent decades, also finds common ground with the urge—central to Roman Catholicism—toward religious structure and authority. Like Emerson, Channing voiced the need for a generation of great scholars at work for the young nation. For him, intellect must work in service to social change: "We regard . . . gifted men, whether devoted to the exact sciences, to mental and ethical philosophy, to history and legislation, or to fiction and poetry, as forming a noble intellectual brotherhood, and it is for the purpose of quickening all to join their labors for the public good, that we offer the present plea in behalf of a national literature."[36] Since the highest calling for the developed intellect is to work toward the perfection of social structures, so must national literature—understood as an intervention within print media—serve instrumentally to reshape the collective national morality. "Books," according to Channing the literary nationalist, "penetrate everywhere. . . . Writing is now the mightiest instrument on earth. Through this, the mind has acquired a kind of omnipresence."[37]

With Brownson, Channing shared the certainty that religion, rather than eros, mere sentimentality, or populist Jacksonian politics, must serve as motivation for the anticipated generation of nationally significant writers. Likewise, the Unitarianism of Channing and the Catholicism of Brownson, however differently motivated, set forth similar critical principles that serve the conservative cause of order and authority. An optimistic Channing could thus proclaim that "the patriotism of antiquity and the sexual love of chivalrous ages, which inspired so much of the old literature, are now seen to be feverish and vicious excesses of natural principles, and have gone, we trust, never to return."[38] Frivolity and romanticism alike are the forbidden ground of literature for Channing and Brownson, as may be seen in Brownson's assessment of James Russell Lowell's poetry in 1849: "We love art, and . . . we love poetry best. But we have too high an appreciation of its character and office, to receive with favor the light and frivolous productions of our modern race of poetasters and versifiers, however beautiful their print and paper, or rich and tasteful their binding."[39]

Sharing a distrust with regard to the morals of antiquity that Brownson had disavowed in his essay "Modern Idolatry," Channing joined Brownson in mapping the moral propriety of an incipient American literature. Writing essays that would eventually fuel the religious and intellectual iconoclasm of the transcendental movement, Channing's early thoughts on elite intellectual groups and the pragmatic function of writing thus correspond in a surprising number of particulars with Brownson's growing cultural conservatism. The roots of social control through the development of a carefully monitored and precisely instituted national literary movement, which Channing and Brownson alike describe during the Jacksonian era, may in fact serve as a way of understanding what a number of Brownson scholars have pointed to as a dichotomy between the early political critic and the later, post-conversion "conservative" commentator. Rather than being elements of what Brownson scholar Charles C. Hollis has called the "separate periods of his life" as a critic,[40] the pre- and post-conversion literary criticism produced by Brownson might also be understood as a rather consistent drive toward shaping—through critical interventions—a body of popular literature that in his view seemed to increase in cultural power with each passing decade, and thus compelled his efforts to harness that power for the benefit and improvement of Roman Catholics.

Soon after the publication of Emerson's "The American Scholar," Brownson made one of his more urgent appeals for a new literary tradition, this time delivering a lecture titled "American Literature" (part 2) before a literary society at Brown University in September 1839. As in an earlier essay by the same title, Brownson reminded his audience of his disagreement with Emerson over the developmental pattern for an emerging national literature during an era marked by what Emerson had called "the new importance given to the single person."[41] Denying that true literature can be formed by the force of will or training of the self along aesthetic or moral lines—an approach that Emerson, following Channing and a standard line of Unitarian thought, had been proposing—the argument of even Brownson's early critical writings links great literature to periods of social change: "Literature is no arbitrary creation. It is dependent on higher laws than human enactment. It comes only when it is needed, and comes always in a shape and of a quality, in commercial phrase, to suit the market."[42] An activist analysis of literary history is consistently present here, as elsewhere in Brownson's early pre-conversion writings about the genesis and utility of national letters. Because "literature comes not when it is bidden, but at those epochs when there is work to be done for the human race," the appearance of great writers and great works figures as a sign of social change; to await the arrival of a formidable literary tradition is likewise to await "a work for humanity to perform which demand[s] at literature" so that "if [America is] to have a literature we must have some great work to do which will need it."[43] Or, as he exhorted an audience of students at Dartmouth College in 1843, "a great national literature . . . [is possible] if it comes at all, only on condition that brave and true-hearted men engage in some great and good work for their country or their race, to the performance of which literature is indispensable; and it will be true and noble, rich and varied, living and profound, just in proportion to the nobleness of the work."[44] Viewing all non-Catholic literatures as fundamentally flawed and transient texts, Brownson, especially in the years just after his conversion, was convinced that "there need be no question . . . as to the fact that Catholic America will be the author of our national literature," even as he acknowledged that the conditions for Catholic literary preeminence had not yet arrived.[45]

In the course of his career as a public intellectual, Brownson adopted several characteristic postures toward religious debates as they were carried out in widely distributed books. Above all, he defended Catholicism against what he called spurious charges of wrong-headed medievalism and idolatry, that is, the accusation that Catholicism's failure to adopt fully the premises of modernity led it to rely on antiquated devotional practices. Equally forceful in his literary reviews, however, are his tireless arguments against what he perceived as the excessive emotionalism, the "sentimentality" of popular fiction.[46] In this way, his defense of the Catholic church against the error of idolatry coexisted in his essays with a deep suspicion about the emotional and rhetorical excesses that Nathaniel Hawthorne had famously attributed to the successful women writers of the mid-nineteenth century. Even Hawthorne himself, though, for all of his own criticism of popular women authors, cannot avoid censure by Brownson, who lamented Hawthorne's *The Blithedale Romance* (1852) as representing the worst tendencies of women's sensibility: "All the pretty things said of women's love in novels and romances are mere moonshine. . . . [Woman] craves not so much love as strong emotion of some sort, it matters little to her of what sort, and hence she is most captivated by the man who gives her the most excitement, produces in her the strongest emotions, though nine tenths of the time they are anger or grief."[47] These twin aversions to idolatry and sentimentality exemplify Brownson's broader project to create and implement a mode of *masculine* Catholicism that could claim ancient theological authority while sloughing off any investment in the iconographic modes of Catholic tradition. Brownson thus eschewed ethnic and folk traditions of Catholic piety and iconography, which he associated with overly feminine modes of religion, and he was equally suspicious of the focus on feminine sentiment and sensation in the midcentury print marketplace.

Much of Brownson's sensitivity to charges of what his own critics identified rather broadly as Catholic "idolatry" appears to have flowed from his awareness of the American nativist movement and its incendiary anti-Catholic rhetoric. Indeed, one of the factors that must have contributed to the astonishment of Brownson's intellectual colleagues upon hearing of his conversion to Catholicism in 1844 was the enormous surge in the power of that most famous of anti-Catholic political parties, the Know-Nothings. By 1844, as the historian Ray Allen Billington has shown, the linked attack by politicians and Protestant church leaders against Catholicism, an attack driven in large part by the new presence of a vast wave of new immigrants, had placed anti-Catholic nativism in a new position of respectability and self-righteous activism. The year before Brownson's conversion, one virulently anti-Catholic periodical of the day, the *Spirit of the XIX Century*, editorialized about the newly pious forms that anti-Catholic activism had taken: "Truly a great revolution in public sentiment is already accomplished, when in the same city, the same cause which in 1832 endangered a man's life, in 1835 jeopardized his character, and as late as 1840 exposed him to indictment, fine and imprisonment—in 1843 looms gloriously up on the top of a general movement of the piety of the community, and becomes the very center of Christian unity."[48]

Extending only reluctant support to the literary nationalism of the Young America movement, Brownson's reactions to the ubiquitous nativist rhetoric of midcentury are remarkably muted, as he typically does not engage directly in debates or polemic with Know-Nothing writers themselves. Apart from a few essays refuting the Know-Nothing political agenda, Brownson does not mention the nativist party at all, except for the occasional publicist's acknowledgment that "the Know-nothing movement has done more in two years to bring our religion before the

American people and to force them to examine it, than all our journals could have done in twenty."[49] Instead, his responses to the question of nativism usually took the form of discussions of various kinds of Catholic or American unity, which he saw to be possible and desirable. In a sense, Brownson's method of sidestepping Know-Nothing rhetoric and the racist idiom of anti-immigrationism shows him attempting to rise above the fray of popular debate in order to carry on a more sophisticated intellectual argument about the practical ramifications of ethnic proliferation in antebellum America. But his avoidance of ethnic concerns in his writing—even as ethnicity came increasingly to be one of the unavoidable facts in American cities of the nineteenth century—betrays an anxiety about certain iterations of Catholicism that failed to align themselves with his own preferences for political unity and religious homogeneity.

When Mary Anne Sadlier's Irish-centric and pro-Catholic novel *The Blakes and the Flanagans: A Tale Illustrative of Life in the United States* (1855) appeared for his review, Brownson took her to task for her ethnic allegiances, specifically her careful distinction between the Irish and Saxon races. In so doing, Brownson encouraged immigrant Catholics to shed their multicultural sympathies in favor of a more profound unity based on Catholicism and American citizenship: "We think the time has come when we should cease to speak of ourselves as Irish, German, English, French, or even as American Catholics, and accustom ourselves to think and speak of ourselves in religion simply as Catholics, and in all else as men and Americans. . . . The foreign national distinctions are, for the most part, obliterated with the first generation, and all attempts to perpetuate them, especially where English is the mother tongue, are and must be fruitless. Catholics in this country, of whatever national origin, are in general heartily tired of them." Rather than aiding the cause of Catholicism, the religio-cultural inventions of Mary Anne Sadlier's widely popular fictions take on the cast of nativist political debate, in Brownson's judgment, since she "writes as if Irish and Catholic, and American and non-Catholic, were synonymous, and thus unintentionally adopts the views of the Know-nothings, and plays into their hands by representing Catholics as an alien body or a foreign colony in the bosom of the commonwealth."[50]

What is perhaps most compelling in reviewing Brownson's controversy with Protestantism during the nineteenth century are some of the recurring elements within his many anti-Protestant polemics. In particular, he found a number of problematic layers within the structures of Protestant theory and practice. What begins as a broad-based theoretical refutation of Protestant religion (see, for example, the early break with William Ellery Channing in Brownson's *The Mediatorial Life of Jesus*) leads eventually to investigations of the *causes* of Protestant failure. Underlying the ruins of contemporary Protestantism, Brownson found an unseemly preoccupation with humanism or philanthropy (both of which are pejorative terms within his lexicon). Subsequently, at the deepest level of humanism, he found idolatrous impulses to erect false gods. Furthermore, motivating and conditioning the impulse toward the false gods of humanism, he finds culpable the drenchingly femininized sentimentality of nineteenth-century religious and literary culture.[51] Finally, he concludes that the problem of feminine sentimentality grows directly out of what he complains is a sexually provocative and culturally dangerous female nature. In this way, the problems of misguided idolatry (an error in Catholic piety) and feminized religion resolve into roughly congruent problems, with both attributable to the presence and influence of women in the religious sphere. Sentimentality, as Brownson understood it, fostered a reshaped version of the provocative feminine in religious and secular culture, to the extent that certain forms of idolatry may be read within the proprieties and decorum of the cult of true womanhood and its attendant moral structures.

This twinned critique—of inappropriately emotive women and their adoption of incorrectly "idolatrous" forms of piety—had long been familiar ground for Brownson. In his review of Margaret Fuller's visionary feminist manifesto, *Woman in the Nineteenth Century* (1845), Brownson savaged Fuller for her literary and feminist embrace of the classical age and of the "ancient heathens." In so doing, he rendered in sharp focus his notion of the literal and rhetorical proximity of pagan idolatry and female sexuality. At the crux of his attack on Fuller's feminist appropriation of the classical period, he argued that the history of religious idolatry and the history of women's sexuality are coterminous with an anarchy of sexual corruption and licentiousness: "[Fuller] is greatly taken with Isis, Sita, Egyptian Sphynx, Ceres, Proserpine. Would she recall these ancient heathen deities, their ancient worship, filled with obscene rites and frightful orgies?"[52] After providing a description of these "obscene rites" from the classical period, which range from forced prostitution to assorted Bacchanalian revels, Brownson proceeds to allege the complicity of women in these pagan practices. He implies even more directly that pagan corruptions and idolatry stemmed naturally from undisciplined female sexuality: "Has it never occurred to our learned and philosophic lady to ask, if there was not some relation of cause and effect between the part women took in these ancient religions, and these filthy rites and shameful practices?"[53] This sort of aversion to the influence of women on culture led to a corresponding anxiety about the evolving modes of political participation for women in the United States. As Barbara Welter has pointed out in commenting on his contributions to the debates between nineteenth-century Catholics and their nativist adversaries, Brownson "used the presumed model of the Blessed Virgin to speak against the women's movement . . . [and] identified the demand for the vote with 'hostility to the marriage law, and the cares and drudgery of maternity and human life.'"[54] So it was that the most important American Catholic intellectual of the nineteenth century, a man who understood the relationship between religion and mass-print media as well as anyone else during that period, concluded that the problem with contemporary women had to do with their inability to sufficiently model their behavior after the Virgin Mary: the preeminent female person in the Roman Catholic tradition.

To the extent that it tended to express the feminine dimension of religion and other human experiences, Brownson came to believe that American literature was destined to fail as a suitably religious force: "The curse of the age is its femininity, its lack, not of barbarism, but of virility. It is the age of woman-worship. Women are angels; men are demons. . . . Though moderately well-read in feminine literature, we cannot call to mind a single heroine, drawn by a female hand, that is really frank and truthful."[55] It is here that Brownson's cultural critique becomes most ardent, disclosing on the one hand his concern about attenuated American masculinity and on the other hand his adversarial engagement with a popular literary culture infused with representations of women's piety and emotional life.[56] Registering his opposition to women's sentimentality at both the individual and mass-market levels, Brownson complained that because "it depends more on physical than rational causes," sentimental attachments (as, for example, in courtship or marriage) lead inevitably to social interactions, which are debased by individualistic desires. All of which leads him to conclude that "nothing is more uncertain, variable, and fickle, than sentiment."[57] As this survey of his career has demonstrated, Brownson recognized that what he sometimes called "light literature," the mainstay of mass-print culture, could have tremendous powers of popular influence, as could thematically violent (and often gory) religious art and venerated relics. But Brownson also notes despairingly that "under pretence of *realism*" (emphasis in original) a flood of immorality accompanied many popular texts of the day, debasing readers to such an extent that they "can see no merit and find no relish in works not highly spiced with vice, crime, or disorderly passion."[58] Even Jonathan Swift, whom Brownson claimed to admire, given that Swift's "genius was great, his patriotism praiseworthy, and he [was] one of the most elegant writers in the language," is deemed to have been a purveyor of "smut" for authoring works such as *Tale of a Tub*. To make judgments like this, according to Brownson, indicates not that he has no sense of humor but that serious and mature critical responses are required when confronting literature's increasing power in commercial print media. Thus, he could claim about his own tastes that, far from being overly prim or humorless, "We love amusement, and can enjoy mirth, whether in old or young . . . but only on condition that neither is purchased at the expense of faith or morals, or suffered to interfere with the grave duties of our state in life."[59]

Vexing moral dangers lurked in the aisles of the American bookseller and even on the parlor bookshelves of literate Catholics. Because of the difficulties in persuading the young to read serious theological tracts and the systematic theology of which Brownson was so enamored, the impressionable American reading public had become susceptible to the debasements and idolatries of enervating sentimentality: "The staple literature of our times, the staple reading of our youth of both sexes, is sentimental novels and love-tales, and the effect is manifest in the diseased state of the public mind, and in the growing effeminacy of character and depravation of morals."[60] Brownson was far from alone in expressing his reservations about contemporary American reading. Similar concerns would be voiced by other Catholic observers of literary culture during the later nineteenth century, who lamented the influence that reading had begun to exert among the young and impressionable working classes: "If we go into the large workshops of the principal cities, or the factories of New England, where so many young persons are engaged, at the hour of dinner we will see every second boy and girl devouring with more eagerness than their food the contents of some flashy journal or specimen of what is generally known as 'yellow-covered literature,' in which vice is hidden under a thin veil of romance only to make it the more seductive."[61] Here, a familiar nineteenth-century complaint about the dangers of novel reading is reinforced by a shrewd observation about readership that is too seldom made by literary historians: in the era before electronic entertainments, popular fiction figures as an extremely important element in youth culture. When concerns about the salacious quality of American and European novels are voiced by commentators like Brownson and others writing for the major Catholic publications, the dangers that freely disseminated "sentimental" writing poses are directed most forcefully at the impressionable youth of the nation. For the nineteenth-century urban adolescent, farm youth, or teenaged factory worker, the pleasures of consuming literary fantasies of romance, intrigue, sensation, and sentiment are easy to imagine.

The effect of this theology-resistant, Euro-American culture of literary sentiment Brownson diagnoses in gendered medical terms: sensational literature, which opposes the moral righteousness of what he called "a robust faith, and strong and masculine virtues," also releases unwholesome masculine desires. Consequently, the market for virtuous Catholic works steadily erodes, because "the literary stomach has been so weakened by vile stimulants that it cannot bear a sound or a wholesome literature."[62] If the religious trouble with light literature is its sentimentality, then the largely feminine market for these texts absorbs the debasement through reading; by definition, sentimental literature fails in religious terms, and its failure Brownson links to its diseased femininity. The prototypical reader of such irreligious popular works therefore embodies and enacts the largest threat to Brownsonian Catholicity: "Her heart is *blase* before she is out of her teens. Her whole being, body and soul, heart and mind, inside and out, from top to bottom, is diseased, full of wounds and putrefying sores."[63] Even as he registered the failure of Young American literature to fulfill its moral promise, Brownson knew that the ability to direct the popular press led directly to control and influence among the widest range of readers and potential converts. His book reviews and essays thus aspire to undermine the female ethos of idolatry that he saw at the heart of both anti-Catholicism and popular literature.

Brownson's hopes for a morally unassailable American Catholic literature are constantly under threat from popular works that trafficked in sentimental or sensational representations of women's experience (however circumscribed by Victorian morality and the cult of true womanhood), as well as by the more explicit and graphic representations found in such works as convent exposés. For Brownson, the ceaselessly proliferating representations of women in popular books would lead inevitably to moral decay among ordinary readers: "The deification of woman in the natural order, or the institution of woman-worship characteristic of America, if not all modern society, and to which every modern novelist brings an offering, is only the worship of lust . . . the god of the modern world."[64] Concerns like these show the extent to which Brownson's religious essays, conversion memoirs, and book reviews, for all their intellectual range and power, are haunted by more than just an abstracted theology of Protestantism. Brownson's obsessive polemical style in his literary criticism does indeed register his devotion to the nuances of Catholic theology, but it also shows a deeply apprehensive relation to women as a presence at the crossroads of American religious and literary culture. It was this feminine strain in commercial print that he saw as conspiring to deprive the nation of a virile "Young American" literature that might have recuperated an immoral and irreligious popular culture for modern Catholicism.

2

Print Evangelism

Father Hecker's American Mission

No people are more susceptible of religious impressions, no people more in earnest in all that regards religion, than the American people.

Isaac Hecker (1857)

I desire you to look forward, as I do, to a new and glorious era in the Church's history, an era of the triumph of faith and holiness, in which I trust [the United States] is destined to become the theatre of a brilliant development of the Catholic religion.

Isaac Hecker (1869)

[I] saw Father Hecker for the first time on the lecture platform. He was then in the full tide of success, conscious of his opportunity and of his power to profit by it. We never can forget how distinctly American was the impression of his personality. We had heard the nation's greatest men then living, and their type was too familiar to be successfully counterfeited. Father Hecker was so plainly a man of that type, so evidently an outgrowth of our institutions, that he stamped American on every argument he proposed.

Walter Elliott, *Life of Father Hecker* (1891)

Like his close friend Orestes Brownson, Isaac Hecker (1819–88) was a convert to Roman Catholicism. Hecker had been influenced early by experiences and exchanges with the close circle of key players in the antebellum New England intellectual, philosophical, and religious ferment that came to be known as "transcendentalism." In part for that reason but also because of a unique personality that combined a mystical temperament with substantial measures of evangelical ambition and intellectual elitism, Hecker arrived at his own distinctive American Catholic views and promoted those views during a long career as a Catholic writer, editor, and evangelist. After converting to Catholicism, Hecker tried to promote his newly adopted religious ideas in a variety of ways, most notably through his ordination as a Redemptorist priest and the leadership of the Congregation of Missionary Priests of St. Paul the Apostle (the Paulists), the first order of American Catholic priests, which he founded in 1858. Hecker later attempted to bring his message of Roman Catholicism to larger audiences by means of several books of advanced theological writings as well as through his work as a professional man of letters.

Given his program of self-education as a young man, the development of Hecker's philosophical tendencies and bourgeois intellectual preferences—which would be reflected in his post-conversion publishing activities—come as little surprise. He, like Brownson, had shocked his friends by taking the unexpected course of fleeing the secular world of New England transcendentalism and exchanging it for the life of a missionary Catholic priest.[1] By the early 1840s, Hecker, the son of an immigrant German metalworker and brother to two enterprising men who would grow wealthy as commercial bakers in New York City, had made his way to the epicenter of New England transcendentalism: the Fourierist utopian community near Boston at Brook Farm, Massachusetts. While at Brook Farm, Hecker became intimately acquainted with most of the transcendentalist thinkers of the day, such as Bronson Alcott, Henry Thoreau, Ralph Waldo Emerson, and Orestes Brownson. Restless still, Hecker decamped from Brook Farm to take up a six-month residency at Bronson Alcott and Charles Lane's small, short-lived, and wildly unsuccessful Fruitlands experimental community in Harvard, Massachusetts. But these remarkable communal adventures among the postreligious New England intelligentsia were unsatisfying for Hecker, who had ingratiated himself for a time among that group of brilliant eccentrics but later became disaffected with the unconventional freedoms that they proposed. Instead, influenced strongly by the charismatic Brownson, whose false starts in a variety of Protestant religious denominations eventually led him to an unswerving commitment to the authority and tradition of Roman Catholicism, Hecker himself became a Catholic convert soon after emerging from his sojourns at the Brook Farm and Fruitlands communities. Having resolved to take up a life devoted to Roman Catholicism, however, Hecker was not content to lead a life of private faith and solitary contemplation. He built an evangelical career while operating with a strong awareness, which he shared with Brownson himself, that mass-print media held enormous potential for the advancement of a Catholic agenda suitable for American circumstances. Whereas the Brook Farm and Fruitlands utopian experiments had been markedly unsuccessful in practical terms and limited to only a tiny group of like-minded New England intellectuals, Hecker saw the project of evangelizing the United States for the Catholic Church as a mission worthy of his newfound religious zeal and his transatlantic evangelical ambitions.

After joining the Roman Catholic Church in 1844, just a few months after his close friend Orestes Brownson, Isaac Hecker almost immediately expressed his desire to be ordained as priest to his bishop in New York, John Hughes. Before he was well acquainted with Catholic religious doctrines but eager to join a missionary order, Hecker next journeyed to Belgium, where several Redemptorist houses had been established in the early nineteenth century. Following a novitiate in St. Trond, Belgium, and a studentiate year in Wittem, Holland, Hecker turned to a course of personal study that eventually led to his ordination at the Redemptorist house in Clapham, England, on October 15, 1849. He returned to the United States with a group of convert priests in 1851. Having completed his education in seminary, though, Hecker found himself confronting a tension between his desire to be active as a religionist in the public sphere and his more private mystical tendencies. He later expounded upon these mystical impulses in his theological writings, which were well received among the American Catholic intelligentsia who found his religious ideas to be suitably pious but also refreshing in their avoidance of strict dogma. His biographer John Farina observed of Hecker, "In theology, as in the arts, Isaac was largely a self-educated man. He never was taught the rigors of Scholastic logic, never was made to memorize formulas and pat answers to the criticisms leveled against Catholic doctrine."[2] A decade later, the unconventionally educated and mystically inclined young German American priest published his first serious writings in *Questions of the Soul* (1855), a book that would be accepted as a fresh and timely theological contribution by the tight-knit community of American Catholic priests and intellectuals who seem to have been its primary audience and who approved of Hecker's call to renew their spiritual and ascetic religious practice. Hecker's intellectual reputation among American Catholic elites grew steadily during the two decades following his ordination, and his program of self-education in theology was sufficiently impressive to gain appointment as theologian to Martin John Spalding, archbishop of Baltimore, and to serve as a delegate to Rome in that capacity for the Vatican Council of 1869–70.[3]

Although for years Hecker had been attracted to Ralph Waldo Emerson's brand of intellectual optimism, he had finally and decisively repudiated the humanistic New England philosophy of transcendentalism in favor of Roman Catholicism. In so doing, Hecker was not alone among American elites of the mid-nineteenth century. In an astute retrospective essay on nineteenth-century Catholicism, the literary critic George N. Shuster wrote in 1922 that although neither Hecker nor Brownson demonstrated first-rate talents during their literary careers, they were in important ways representative of intellectual converts of their generation: "Together with Brownson [Hecker] typifies the response which a great many intellectual New Englanders made to Catholicism: the recognition of dogma as an escape from unbridled idealism and materialistic despair."[4] With no regrets at his abandonment of Emerson and his circle, and having firmly accepted the Roman Catholic tradition as his own moral and intellectual harbor, Hecker lost no time in setting about an evangelical mission of bringing the Catholic message before his fellow Americans, using every means at his disposal.

After his return from European seminary training in 1851, Hecker spent some of his first years as a Redemptorist priest doing the work of a missionary preacher at Catholic revivals in the Northeast. The historian Ruth M. Kelly describes these events as resembling contemporary Protestant revivals: "These missions used the modified model of the Protestant revival meetings popularized earlier by Charles G. Finney. Hecker and his group of American Redemptorists traveled from Watertown, New York, to New Orleans, preaching to thousands of Catholics."[5] This preaching had influence among a wide audience, some of whom would have considerable influence on religious matters in subsequent years. For example, James Gibbons, a future bishop and cardinal of Baltimore and a young man who lived in New Orleans at the time of Hecker's mission visit, credited Hecker's preaching as having influenced him to join the priesthood.

During these years of missionary preaching, Hecker continued to monitor developments in the burgeoning American print marketplace, which came to commercial maturity and national reach at about mid-century. Hecker's most notable early talents, however, were expressed in the pulpit and on the lecture stage, which was one of the few ways that Catholic intellectuals of his generation were able to earn a substantial income (a problem pointed out earlier by the Catholic convert and popular novelist Jedediah Vincent Huntington).[6] Their modest success as professional lecturers—both of these charismatic men were well received by nineteenth-century Catholic lyceum audiences—was not matched by a corresponding literary popularity. In an era when many professional writers had begun to earn substantial incomes, and a fortunate few had even become wealthy from the book business, neither Hecker nor Huntington earned a living wage from his publications. Their paltry book sales would not have been sufficient to yield substantial earnings; indeed, the very publication of those books was made possible mainly by the support of the Church and its benefactors.[7] Having honed his religious oratory during those years, lecturing and public preaching would remain the most effective staple of Hecker's evangelism.[8] By most accounts, he also became an impressive figure on the lyceum circuit; he preached in many locations to substantial audiences during the decades following the large-scale Irish Catholic migration to the United States that occurred as a result of the Irish potato famine, but it is not clear that those immigrants were well represented in his audiences.

The challenge of bringing immigrants into the Church and into the mainstream of American culture was obvious to most nineteenth-century Catholic religionists; they recognized that Irish Catholic arrivals in the United States meant that significant religious changes were in store for the nation. Those same observers understood that the enormous potential for enlisting the new immigrants as orthodox American Catholics was at odds with the reality that many of these immigrants were only nominally Catholic. For example, the noted Swiss American religious historian Philip Schaff would write in 1855 that because of the "perfectly massive emigration from Catholic Ireland" and the increasing political importance of the United States, "the ultimate fate of the Reformation will be decided in America." Anticipating the ongoing collision of

Protestant and Catholic religious energies on American soil, especially in large American cities, Schaff expressed serious reservations about the immigrant Irish and their version of Catholic faith: "The emigrants from the southern parts of Ireland have, indeed, many good traits, among which are prominent, generosity, chastity, and a love for the religion of their fathers undestroyed by years of oppression and misery; but they are in general terribly neglected, ignorant, addicted to drunkenness and profanity, quarrelling and fighting, not seldom in the open street; and they form on the whole the roughest class of the American population [and] they do not seem to be morally improved by any number of masses and confessions, which they scrupulously attend."[9] The barely Americanized Irish singled out with alarm by Schaff joined a substantial population of European American Catholics as well as a host of other newly colonized American Catholics, many of them from French, Mexican, and Spanish backgrounds, who were absorbed into the United States following the acquisition of large territories in Louisiana (1803), Florida (1820), and Texas (1844). Technologies of travel such as the railroad, which was instrumental for allowing itinerant missionaries like Hecker's Redemptorists to preach on the antebellum revival circuit, also figured significantly in the rapid expansion of Catholic America. As the sociologists of religion Roger Finke and Rodney Stark have observed, a number of midwestern bishops, such as John Ireland of St. Paul, Minnesota, worked with the railroads to encourage Catholic homesteaders to create settlements in Iowa, Minnesota, Nebraska, and the Dakotas.[10] All of these circumstances combined in a way that located Hecker's work of evangelism squarely in the middle of tectonic changes in the religious character of the United States, whose demographics and geography were being altered substantially thanks to forces of immigration and national expansion.

In less than a generation, the United States had acquired a Catholic population to be reckoned with, and the newly ordained Father Isaac Hecker appeared on the scene at precisely the right moment to attempt harnessing and guiding American Catholic culture through his work as theologian, lecturer, and literary man. Along with Orestes Brownson, he would remain for many years a prominent figure, well known for his work promoting American Catholic intellectual positions. His ability to reach the masses of American Catholics, though, never matched his ambitions, for he failed to become the kind of writer or publisher who could substantially influence ordinary readers and thus stem the tide of anti-Catholic discourse that flowed unabated through the commercial presses during those years. Positive representations of Catholicism in popular books were relatively hard to find, even though by midcentury a small cohort of American Catholic novelists had begun to publish their works. The anti-Catholic press of the antebellum period held sway especially during the first half of the century, so that if American readers happened upon representations of Roman Catholic culture, it would more than likely come to them in salacious books like the best-selling pseudo-exposé by Maria Monk, *Awful Disclosures of Maria Monk, or, the Hidden Secrets of a Nun's Life in a Convent Exposed!* (1836) or one of the many anti-Catholic novels that appeared during the peak years of Irish immigration, such as Isaac Kelso's virulent attack on Jesuit priests in his novel *Danger in the Dark: A Tale of Intrigue and Priestcraft* (1855).

A large immigrant population ripe for conversion and catechism, a growing national transportation infrastructure that made possible a nationally circulated print media, and deep-seated resistance to the rising Roman Catholic presence in the United States were some of the cultural circumstances faced by both Brownson and Hecker, who nevertheless emerged during the nineteenth century as redoubtable activists for Catholic literary values and a Catholic national identity. Furthermore, and even more than Brownson and others—many of whom were devoting their energies to building parishes and schools for immigrant Catholics—Hecker remained convinced of the importance of nurturing a cohort of intellectual leaders while converting large numbers of Americans to Catholicism. This conviction eventually led him to part ways with the Redemptorist order of priests, who expelled Hecker from their ranks because of his reluctance to limit his evangelism to the German American Catholics that had been the main focus of the Redemptorists. Undeterred, in 1858, with permission granted by the Vatican, Hecker set about founding and leading the first order of American priests, the Paulists.

To further his Catholic evangelism during his years with the Paulists, Hecker founded and wrote frequently for the *Catholic World: A Monthly Eclectic Magazine of General Literature and Science*, an important Catholic intellectual journal since its inception in 1865. He also published an illustrated monthly magazine for children, the *Young Catholic*, first issued in 1870; founded the Catholic Publication Society in 1866 in order to circulate free or inexpensive pamphlets for a broad readership, including schools and prisons;[11] and spent much of the period from 1863 to 1873 on the American lyceum circuit as a Catholic evangelist, bringing his religious message to many thousands of non-Catholics and Catholics alike.[12] Toward the end of Hecker's lifetime, the Paulists established the Columbus Press, a New York City publishing house that began selling religious books in 1881 and in 1913 was renamed the Paulist Press. By the 1960s, the Paulist Press was reputed to be the largest Catholic publisher in North America, claiming to distribute about 20 million religious books, pamphlets, and magazines every year. When commercial radio became viable in the 1920s, the Paulists started a radio station in New York City; by the 1950s, Paulist Productions was airing made-for-television films, documentaries, and feature films. As Ruth M. Kelly explains, "The Paulists perpetuate the mission of Isaac Hecker by evangelizing through print, radio, television, video, and the Internet."[13]

Despite these accomplishments, though, Hecker's largest influence on the American Catholic tradition, ironically enough, occurred some years after his death, when his ideas became central to the so-called Americanism controversy of the late nineteenth century, which arrayed his relatively progressive Catholic views in opposition to ultramontane papal Catholic authority. His published views of the United States as a venue for a relatively enlightened mode of Roman Catholicism, which would encourage individual initiative and a more collaborative relationship between priests and lay Catholics, resulted in a strong reaffirmation of Roman authority over the American Catholic hierarchy.[14]

For all of his various efforts at evangelizing the American people—taking to the revival pulpit as a touring preacher, lecturing to Catholics and non-Catholics on the lyceum circuit, serving as spiritual adviser to prominent intellectuals, and working to enlist larger audiences by writing books and trying his hand as a magazine and tract publisher—Hecker's missionary accomplishments fell short of his grand ambitions. As an adult convert to Catholicism, he shared Orestes Brownson's zest for evangelizing Americans and saw his own missionary goals clearly, but as a young man who had been exposed to some of the leading New England thinkers of his generation, he had become accustomed to the larger ambitions of intellectual life and also to a strong sense of literary propriety. Consequently, he was committed to a form of Roman Catholic practice that included his participation not just in the ordinary activities of priesthood but also an engagement with literary issues, commercial publishing, and the possibility of shaping the larger culture through media. At the same time, he expressed a strong preference for refined company, bourgeois values, and a markedly recondite strain of literary and theological discourse. Perhaps as a consequence of his intellectual elitism, while he was undeniably zealous to convert Americans to the Catholic faith, a survey of Hecker's writings and an assessment of his publishing efforts show that he lacked the commercial and populist instincts that would have made his evangelism more successful and his preaching more relevant to immigrant Catholics—the ordinary Americans who made up the largest segment of the Church during the nineteenth century.

Hecker joined Brownson as a public intellectual working on behalf of their newly adopted religion by appealing to American cultural elites and to the Catholic hierarchy in Rome, whose relationship to American Catholicism remained extremely important well into the twentieth century. When the international debates over the "Roman Question" were spawned in the wake of the 1848 attack on the papal states that led eventually to the creation of the kingdom of Italy, American Catholic support of the temporal power of the pope and their opposition to Italian nationalism were crucial issues that divided American Catholic intellectuals from mainstream opinion.[15] This appeal to elites came at the expense of a wider readership, as Hecker's preferred engagement with theological and philosophical issues kept him at a wary and highly critical distance from the more turbulent avenues of commercial publishing and the many readers whose views of religion were shaped in part by inexpensive books and periodicals.

Brownson, an influential role model for Hecker and the Paulists (for many years Brownson made regular monthly visits from his home in Elizabeth, New Jersey, to the Paulist house in New York City), appears in certain respects to have set the tone for Hecker's career as a Catholic man of letters. In 1875, near the end of his long career as a public intellectual, Brownson had expressed some of his own frustrations about the shortcomings of American Catholic authors and readers: "We are obliged to confess that our authors lack both depth and freshness, as well as vigor of thought, and our Catholic public cares little about literature except newspapers and sensational novels. We are wofully [*sic*] behind-hand in literature. . . . Here is a reproach to us which it is time for us to wipe out. It is time for us to show that we are neither imbecile nor indolent; and the Catholic public should feel their responsibility as a missionary people."[16] The Irish American physician and historian John O'Kane Murray—a great admirer of Brownson's critical writings and a contributor to Hecker's flagship journal, the *Catholic World*—echoed

Brownson's opinion about the power and importance of industrial print media, proclaiming in 1876 that "an immoral, unprincipled [periodical] is capable of doing a vast amount of evil. A good one does the work of a score of missionaries. We can almost tell the moral tone and character of a family by knowing what journal of journals its members patronize. A newspaper is an intellectual bill of fare. . . . Woe to the Catholic parents who allow questionable newspapers to enter their doors—to corrupt the purity of their children's minds."[17] Like his literary colleagues, Hecker took to the higher ground of theological writing and periodical publications aimed squarely at more well-educated Catholic readers and potential converts rather than setting his sights on the larger cohort of recent immigrants who made up such a large proportion of the growing American Catholic population. Like so many of his Protestant contemporaries who understood the power and reach of industrial print culture, Hecker remained sensitive to the ways that publishing could shape moral and religious values. But by contrast to the most successful of evangelical Protestant writers—Harriet Beecher Stowe being the most obvious and influential example, and she was joined by a host of other popular writers who used the print marketplace for religious advantage—Hecker pursued his literary goals with only a small and select audience for most of his own writings and edited publications.[18]

Perhaps even more tellingly for a country in which immigrants made up a large share of potential Catholics, Hecker's literary evangelism would never match the influence of the successful Catholic revival missions that his own Paulist order had helped to promote earlier in the nineteenth century.[19] Although he had himself done the hard work of missionary preaching, when it came time to write his books, he had more lofty intellectual goals in mind for his evangelism.[20] Writing to a friend in 1853, he boldly proclaimed his oft-repeated ambition in imperial terms, insisting that "we must make Yankeedom the Rome of the modern world—or at least work hard to make it Catholic," but in a letter to Brownson the same year he made an appeal for a more refined Catholic sensibility, complaining that "until we have a higher tone of Catholic life in our country we shall do nothing."[21] Several years later, after Hecker had successfully founded the Paulist Fathers, Hecker wrote in similar terms to his fellow traveler and friend, Father Adrienne-Emmanuel Rouquette, a Romantic poet, novelist, and Louisiana missionary to the Choctaw tribes: "The conversion of the American people to the Catholic faith has ripened into a conviction with me that lies beyond the reign of doubt. My life, my labours, and my death is [*sic*] consecrated to it. No other aim as an end outside of my own salvation and perfection can occupy my attention a moment. . . . In the union of Catholic faith and American civilization a new birth awaits them all, and a future for the Church brighter than any past."[22] Joining Rouquette in his enthusiasm for missionary work and never lacking for sheer optimism or boundless conviction, Hecker's fatal shortcoming as an evangelist was his inability to apply significant force to the lever of popular publishing in ways that could bring to fruition his dream of a Catholic America.[23]

Hecker easily recognized the evangelical significance of best-selling books in the antebellum period, but he echoed Brownson in questioning the morality of certain publications that did not meet his standards of propriety and right religion. For instance, in his own first book, *Questions of the Soul* (1855), which was aimed primarily at well-educated Catholics and potential converts, he expressed his censorious opposition to the dangers of popular books marketed to the masses of ordinary people who seemed immune to persuasion by Roman Catholic evangelism:

> You need no confession! Why, then, do you make the wide world the witness and confidant of your crimes, your misdeeds, and your shameful weaknesses? For what else is the great mass of our modern popular literature but an examen of conscience, publicly made by the author, before his readers, and the whole wide world? And so deeply are his vices rooted in his heart, that not satisfied with presenting them under the attractive disguise of imagery, they must be spread out to cater to the tastes of his readers, in all their filthy and disgusting details. Why, no one whose conscience is not blinded by sin, can take up a volume of the popular literature of our times, and read a page of it, without detecting some inordinate passion, or deadly sin, rankling in the heart of the author.[24]

The attack on contemporary literature that Hecker mounts in his chapter on the sacrament of confession in *Questions of the Soul* is fervent and squares with views expressed by his culturally conservative literary friends, among them Orestes Brownson and the Catholic writer and editor John Hassard. For Hecker, modern literature too often hinges on the human impulse to confess and disclose misdeeds, which in Catholic tradition is placed into sacramental terms but in literary discourse could range from the high-minded confessionalism of Romanticism or religious conversion to the more tawdry confessionalism of salacious fiction. It is crucial for his analysis that Americans recognize the need for penitence and confession, while at the same time coming to understand that the confessional impulse must be structured not by salacious curiosity but by sacramental penitence. Here we can see Hecker merging two distinct but overlapping concerns about the transatlantic literary culture in which he had been immersed: the frank confessionalism of Romantic writers and the pandering licentiousness that certain styles of popular fiction seemed to promote.

It is clear that, for all his stated ambitions about literary evangelism, Hecker lacked both the will and the narrative talent to reach out to make inroads with popular audiences using his own religious writings. In subsequent decades, even writers for the *Catholic World* began to complain about the tension between commercial popularity and strident religious writing. In an essay for the *Catholic World* in 1909, Agnes Repplier made this point bluntly: "If a book be solely designed for Catholic readers, if it be controversial in its tone, or treat of matters which concern only Catholics and Catholics only, we can hardly expect the secular press and the secular public to welcome it unless it be a great literary masterpiece."[25] Repplier's comments were both astute and prescient. Hecker's books reached only small audiences among the Catholic clergy and laity, and his attempt at publishing a popular magazine failed to turn a profit and at its peak had only a few thousand subscribers.[26]

Even Hecker's greatest successes in the publishing would not have been possible without funding from his wealthy family. Catholic historians have frequently referred to the *Catholic World* as a highly significant voice for the American Catholic Church during the later nineteenth and early twentieth century, but in fact its financial support and its readership were in no way indicative that it had the support of ordinary American Catholics. For example, the Catholic Publication Society, which Hecker had helped to found and which his wealthy brother George Hecker funded lavishly, claimed better results and successfully managed to distribute hundreds of thousands of books and inexpensive four-page tracts in the years after the Civil War. Nonetheless, like other religious tract societies of the nineteenth century, the CPS was never a viable business and required substantial funding from benefactors. The society was finally sold by Hecker in December 1883 to a group of investors, a move that postponed its bankruptcy until 1894, when the business was placed into receivership. According to the Catholic publisher Lawrence Kehoe, by 1882 Father Hecker's brother George had spent in excess of $200,000 in a failed effort to sustain the Catholic Publication Society.[27]

The book historian Una M. Cadegan has recently observed that while a certain amount of Catholic tracts, devotional books, and periodicals were produced both before and after the Civil War, "newspapers dominated the print culture of Catholic readers" well into the twentieth century. From 1880 to 1920, Catholic newspapers experienced a brief golden age as the American Catholic Church responded to a decree by the Third Plenary Council that each diocese have its own newspaper.[28] Cadegan also notes that in subsequent decades many of these newspapers, which had been focused on political issues of interest to immigrants (particularly Irish issues), rapidly decreased in importance. By 1920, when the American church had lost much of its immigrant identity and became less interested in the kinds of news—such as bulletins about Irish politics—Catholic newspapers had been diminished as a significant vehicle for religious communication among the faithful. As these independent newspapers failed or were consolidated, they were purchased by Catholic religious orders and congregations, and were thus brought under the direct control of the Church. Magazines such as the *Catholic World* became somewhat more prominent, although they were publications without a strong advertising or subscription base and were of necessity supported by religious orders and congregations "for whom publishing was an apostolate—that is, a part of their religious mission rather than a profit-making venture."[29]

Popularity in the print marketplace is of course only one dimension by which to assess Hecker's literary efforts. What was unique about Hecker's evangelical program is that he combined a tendency toward personal asceticism and mystical religion with a more populist desire to spread and reinforce the Catholic faith in the United States, and these competing impulses found rich expression in his published works, even as those public works fell short of his ambitions in reaching truly large numbers of readers. Seeking out such sympathetic works as *Spiritual Doctrine* (1694) by the seventeenth-century Jesuit Louis Lalleman, as well as the mystical writings of St. John of the Cross and St. Catherine of Genoa, Hecker built a course of study during his training for the priesthood that in some respects harmonized with his pre-conversion study of Romantic writers such as Goethe and Schiller. As Hecker's biographer John Farina points out, the effect of much of this reading and study was to reinforce Hecker's inclination to combine private devotion with public service: to seek a reconciliation between a personalized religion and one that required the development of actively virtuous behavior, and to put his mystical insights into conversation with Catholic tradition. Farina summarizes Hecker's theological position around the time of his conversion as being complex: "What the Spiritual Doctrine did more than anything else was to assure Isaac that his confidence in the inner guidance of the Spirit could be reconciled with Catholic teaching. Had he not believed this, he would never have become a Catholic."[30] So it is that Hecker's work in the public sphere included two powerful vectors: a highly personal faith shaped by mystical experiences (which he describes in part during the months leading up to his conversion) and a capacious social vision—amenable to influence by the print marketplace—in which he saw Roman Catholicism playing an important American role.

Mindful of his own experiences as a highly impressionable young reader during his pre-conversion years, Hecker—like Brownson before him—was whipsawed between religious commitments by his intense engagement with religious and philosophical debates of the day and therefore came to see the rapidly expanding print marketplace as a powerful way to spread and reinforce religious doctrine. Having been provided his own intellectual and religious formation by means of a rich, transatlantic course of reading, Hecker could not resist the urge to deploy the force of commercial print culture on behalf of his newfound commitment to Catholicism. Because of its increasingly sophisticated printing technologies and improving distributional networks, print media in the middle years of the century could offer eclectic programs of self-education to religiously inclined readers throughout the continent, potentially allowing ordinary persons the possibility of absorbing the self-conscious spirituality that Hecker himself favored and promoted.

Noting the importance that Hecker placed on the activities of the popular press, Hecker's disciple and biographer, a Paulist Father named Walter Elliott, described Hecker's reverent view of the morally curative properties of an appropriate course of reading in religious doctrine: "To Father Hecker the Press was the highest opportunity for religion. The only term of comparison for it is some element of nature like sunlight or the atmosphere. In the Press civilized man lives and breathes. Father Hecker was as alive to the injury done to humanity by bad reading as a skillful physician is to the malaria which he can smell and fairly taste in an infected atmosphere; and he ever strove to make the Press a means of enlightenment and virtue."[31] Indeed, the intellectual and cultural terrain surveyed and transformed by modern reading and publishing had become so valuable and fraught with potential that Hecker came to see publishing as a crucial religious battleground for the nineteenth century.

Observers of Catholic efforts in the public sphere soon took note of Hecker's attempts to shape the national conversation about religion. For instance, the industrial strength applied to print technology in the nineteenth century is emphasized in James Parton's 1868 *Atlantic Monthly* essay, "Our Roman Catholic Brethren," in which he took wary and yet admiring notice of Hecker's efforts in religious publishing:

> The special work of this [the Paulist] community is to bring the steam printing-press to bear upon the spread of the Catholic religion in the United States. What a powerful engine is this! Suppose the six ablest and highest Americans were living thus, freed from all worldly cares, in an agreeable, secluded abode, yet near the centre of things, with twelve zealous, gifted young men to help and cheer them, a thousand organizations in the country to aid in distributing their writings, and in every town a spacious edifice and an eager audience to hang upon their lips. What could they not effect in a lifetime of well-directed work?[32]

Returning from his journey to the Vatican Council in 1870, Hecker wrote to a fellow priest using language similar to that of Parton, proclaiming: "I felt as if I would like to have peopled [the Vatican] with inspired men and printing presses. For evidently the special battle-field of attack and defence of truth for half a century to come is the printing press," a statement that Walter Elliott interpreted to mean that by means of commercial publishing Hecker felt that "a small band of powerful men could reach an entire nation and elevate its religious life."[33]

Such views were echoed and amplified by John Hassard, a Catholic convert and the first managing editor of the *Catholic World*, whose 1870 essay "Catholic Literature and the Catholic Public" appeared in that magazine around the time of Hecker's trip to the Vatican Council. Hassard concluded that it was more essential than ever before for Catholics to begin buying and reading works sympathetic to its religious principles, since "every Protestant—or we may say un-Catholic—publication contains a drop of poison." After surveying the long-standing alliance between print and religion, dating to the invention of the printing press, Hassard bluntly described the resistless power of mass-print culture by comparison with the traditional medium of the evangelical sermon or the relatively ineffectual mechanism of the weekly Catholic mass: "What preacher ever reached so many minds as a great newspaper which speaks to 200,000 or 300,000 persons and repeats its utterances 300 times in the year?" By contrast, he continues, "the most eloquent of men . . . cannot, by any possibility, be heard by more than 2,000 or 3,000 persons at a time" and "in the course of a year, ye cannot be heard by more people than a newspaper of average circulation addresses every day. Moreover, when his word is once spoken it dies; what is printed remains, and men read it again and again." Hassard, who was already serving as a music and literature critic for Horace Greeley's New York *Tribune*—probably the most influential newspaper of the nineteenth century—undoubtedly was well positioned to see the ways that industrial print culture could have enormous consequences for shaping the nation's morality.

Further evidence of the new print media power emerges during Hassard's subsequent examination of circulation figures for Protestant-oriented—not to mention overtly anti-Catholic—newspapers and magazines. Whereas a number of national magazines at the time had circulations in the hundreds of thousands and the American Tract Society was publishing hundreds of titles per year, the strongest pro-Catholic periodical of the day was the *Boston Pilot*, with a mere 10,000 subscribers out of an estimated 6 to 7 million American Catholics. As for books, Hassard came to the conclusion that although the clergy purchased Catholic works in considerable numbers, "Catholic laymen hardly look at the literature of their own denomination." Catholic publishers therefore derived most of their earnings from such things as prayer books or school textbooks, since "their best customers are devout people of the poorer class, who have generally too little education to take an interest in literature, and for whom books of piety must be manufactured in the cheapest possible way." Demographic changes during the nineteenth century had shifted the American population so that a very substantial minority of the reading public was Roman Catholic, but Hecker and his colleagues struggled to reach them effectively with their own literary efforts.[34]

With John Hassard handling most of the editorial work for the *Catholic World* during the period 1865–88, Isaac Hecker had secured the able assistance of a professional literary critic but also a like-minded, conservative opponent of the latest trends in popular fiction.[35] Hassard, who became a Catholic as a teenager and graduated from Fordham College at the top of his class, is an important but little-studied figure in nineteenth-century New York literary culture, and his work with Hecker and the *Catholic World* was instrumental in elevating the prestige of the journal. Only a year after he took on the managing editor's position for Hecker's *Catholic World*, he was enlisted as a contributor and later managing editor of Horace Greeley's *Tribune*. Hassard wrote frequently for the *Tribune* about literature and especially about classical music, eventually becoming the foremost American music critic of his generation. His views on popular literature are significant as well, and his attitude about women writers especially is very much in line with concerns raised by Brownson and Hecker during this period. Although Hassard echoed and promoted similarly conservative and moralistic literary values, he recognized the power of the print marketplace to shape American culture. Literary representations that deviated from his sense of religious propriety were thus alarming to Hassard, who registered some of his apprehensions in a scathing *Tribune* article about the prolific and popular English writer "Ouida" (Marie Louise Ramé), a feminist whom he disparaged for her work in what he called "the carnal school of literature": "How then shall we account for 'Ouida's' popularity? Well, there are people who love to read of the sins they have yet a little too much conscience to commit . . . and there are people who relish daring language from a woman which they would not tolerate from a man, just because it is contrary to all our instincts of right that women should not be familiar with those particular forms of impropriety."[36] While many reviewers of the male critical establishment opposed the "lurid" and "sensational" quality of her writing, the popular fiction of Ouida would have been of special consequence to Hassard and other Catholic critics of the day not only for her success and influence as a professional writer but also for her tendency to set many of her historical romances in Catholic Italy, where she lived for much of her life. Ouida used the Catholic context of her narrative not to promote religious views—she was an outspoken critic of Christianity in general—but as a technique meant to highlight her radical views on gender and marriage by contrast with the Catholic traditionalism of peasant Italy. Hassard's aversion to Ouida's popular fiction exemplifies the tendency of Hecker and his circle to recognize the literary common denominator by which large reading audiences could be acquired, while illustrating their inability to apply the common touch to their own publications.

With Hassard as the long-term editor of the *Catholic World*, Hecker had secured a reliably conservative Catholic literary professional, but one who, by keeping the magazine's attention focused on the concerns of Catholic intellectuals and the clergy instead of the popular print marketplace, would prevent the magazine from having a significant effect on the broader American Catholic culture. The *Catholic World* would remain a publication that achieved a certain amount of prestige but only modest influence in nineteenth-century literary culture, even in the hands of a skilled professional editor like John Hassard. But magazine publication was only one literary avenue that Hecker pursued in support of his ambitions to move more Americans to embrace his brand of Roman Catholicism.

Hecker's first major venture away from his life as a traveling mission preacher into the world of publication serves, on the one hand, as an index to the possibilities of influence of Catholic priests on American literary and cultural life as new avenues for their writing were opened to them. On the other hand, his *Questions of the Soul* (1855) outlines part of a radically different American intellectual trajectory, one that traces an arc from the early ferment of New England transcendentalism toward objectives far afield from the ones favored by Emerson and his circle. Although Hecker had known Emerson through mutual acquaintances during the 1840s, when Hecker was in residence at Brook Farm and Fruitlands, and had even lectured on Roman Catholicism (against Emerson's wishes) in Concord, they were not close friends because of their disagreement over religion and especially because of Hecker's later role as spiritual advisor for Anna Barker Ward, who converted to Catholicism in 1858 while in Rome.[37] Weighing Hecker's missionary work and sensing danger from the threat of Roman Catholic incursions into American culture, Emerson later wrote in his journal that anti-Catholicism was the only reasonable posture to adopt in light of the Church's deviance from democratic principles: "It is the political character of the Roman Church that makes it incompatible with our institutions, & unwelcome here."[38] In spite of Hecker's and Emerson's vastly differing ideas about religion and politics, the idea of America as a privileged site for generating modern morality and thought—a notion that motivates Emerson's "American Scholar" essay—can be found in *Questions of the Soul*. Departing from Emerson's critique of religious tradition and authority, though, Hecker makes clear his desire that strong religious authority be deployed by an organized church energized by activist clergy and laity.

Although Hecker never produced anything close to a bestseller, he did manage to reach a small audience of intellectually sophisticated readers with *Questions of the Soul*, which appeared in three small printings of one thousand copies each during the first six months of 1855.[39]

Admiration for *Questions of the Soul* came from distinguished Catholic and non-Catholic critics alike. In his review of the book, the eminent historian (and Harvard Unitarian) George Bancroft praised it highly, optimistically asserting that its publication indicated "that men are beginning to look inward and desire with loftier earnestness to solve the great problems of existence."[40] Orestes Brownson, assessing Hecker's *Questions of the Soul* in the pages of his own self-published quarterly journal, sounded a note of literary triumphalism not unlike that of Herman Melville in his famous essay "Hawthorne and His Mosses" (1850) for the *Literary World*. Here, Melville called for an end to European imitations in literature so that the way might be cleared for artists like Hawthorne, who for Melville was preeminent among "those writers, who breathe that unshackled, democratic spirit of Christianity in all things, which now takes the practical lead in this world, though at the same time led by ourselves—us Americans."[41] Brownson, like Melville and many other American intellectuals coming of age during the antebellum years, wrote with confidence and anticipation about America's cultural destiny, albeit with the important difference that Brownson's idea of America's future was inextricable from his plans to advance Roman Catholicism.

Hecker's first book, it seemed to Brownson, constituted one of the first major efforts to enlist for Catholicism the teeming moral and intellectual energy of the United States. Brownson is explicit on this point, opening his review by observing the intellectual freshness and cultural relevance of *Questions of the Soul.* True American identity and values, he argues, had discovered one of their foremost exponents in Hecker. Having already made his mark as an evangelist by founding and leading the first order of American Catholic priests, Hecker was now poised, in Brownson's judgment, to become a major literary figure: "We have in these 'Questions of the Soul' a remarkable work and one of the very few original and genuine American books our country can boast. It could have been written only by an American 'to the manner born,' and is destined, in our judgment, to have a marked influence on American thought and American literature." Perhaps only a man such as Brownson, who wrote so much for so few readers after his 1844 conversion, could imagine that Hecker was truly on his way to an influential literary career.[42]

Questions of the Soul presents Hecker's path to Catholic religion as having been shaped by his eclectic reading of the German Romantics and

American transcendentalists, as well as close study of works by prominent converts such as John Henry Newman. He supports his discussion of Catholic spirituality by citing verse passages from the likes of Emerson, Channing, Goethe, Schiller, Tennyson, Dante, Hawthorne, Wordsworth, Carlyle, Lowell, Milton, Bayard Taylor, Spenser, Bryant, Herbert, Shakespeare, Byron, and Shelley. By thus mining the religious sensibilities of writers drawn mainly from outside the pale of Catholic religious tradition, Hecker argues for the congruency of the deepest poetic and spiritual insights within writers who would seem at first to be deeply divided about matters of religious doctrine and practice. A primary rhetorical tactic that Hecker deploys in *Questions of the Soul* is the juxtaposition of quotations from these apparently antithetical writers. In an early chapter, he sets up an especially strong sense of trajectory between Romantic epistemology and Catholic mysticism by interweaving a number of citations of Romantic poetry. The chapter epigraph sets the tone for this exchange, and, because the lines are taken from Schiller, the affinity between Catholicism and Romanticism is immediately made clear: "Could I find a path to follow, / Ah how glad I were, and blest!"[43] In Romanticism, Hecker thus sees the emergence of weighty questions about destiny and human purpose, but the secular Romantic traditions of poetry then serve as a kind of ladder to what he perceives as a higher level of spirituality. Tennyson next is heard to propose the helplessness of the Romantic quester: "My will is bondsman to the dark, / I sit within a helmless bark,"[44] followed by Goethe, who broaches the issue of human agency in the light of "irresistable [*sic*] fate": "How strangely Fate my feet is leading; / And, ah! I feel it soon or late, / Much more awaits me, all unheeding."[45] Finally, these characteristic Romantic tropes find resolution in what Hecker repeatedly describes as a reasoned capitulation to a "higher power." In short, he proposes that Romantic imagination eventually finds its soul "yielding at length with confidence to its invisible guide."[46]

Hecker also relies on the voice of an eminent poet so that his own assertions can be leveraged by the insights of an elite sensibility, as when he cites a conversion poem by Cardinal Newman:

> I was not ever thus, nor prayed that Thou
> Shouldst lead me on.
> I loved to choose and see my path, but now
> Lead Thou me on!

I loved the garish day, and spite of fears,
Pride ruled my will: remember not past years.

So long Thy power hast blest me, sure it still
Will lead me on,
O'er moor and fen, o'er crag and torrent, till
The night is gone;
And with the morn those angel faces smile
Which I have loved long since, and lost awhile.[47]

As recapitulated by Newman, the Romantic narrative eventuates in Catholic faith rather than at the humanist extremes of despair or optimism and thus is congruent with the American experience of Hecker. Infused with Romantic impulses and inscribed in the register of elite literary culture, Newman's brief conversion narrative in this poem resembles the one suggested by Hecker's path to conversion, in which Hecker, like his English counterpart, followed a course of study in literature and theology that shaped his preference for refined discourse and his ambivalence about literature aimed at popular audiences.[48]

At the vanguard of Euro-American Romantic discourse, Goethe had been an early favorite of Hecker's even before his 1844 conversion. But from Hecker's mature perspective both as a Catholic convert and industrious print evangelist, Goethe's literary and philosophical influence presented serious hazards for readers who might be susceptible to an unholy torrent of subversive forces. Here we can see Hecker's precise alignment with Brownson's patronizing and censorious impulses: the transformative power of the commercial press is at once a signal that it must be either avoided entirely or else be subject to religious control. Goethe's artistic genius in such works as *Sorrows of Young Werther* and *Wilhelm Meister* may have been galvanizing for American thinkers of a transcendentalist bent, especially those transcendentalists, like Hecker, for whom German was a first language. Hecker notes with regret, though, that the energies of German Romanticism would never be suitable for ordinary American readers, for whom a popularized Romanticism tended to place before them a "most subtle and licentious philosophy displayed in a most seductive form."[49] Other European national literatures come in for intense scrutiny by Hecker as well, since they too have been damaged by the "occult affinities" spawned by Goethe's seminal works. French literature, from Rousseau's *Confessions* to the contemporary novels of George Sand, is attacked because of its decadence and immorality, as Hecker complains that the French exemplify the problem that "popular literature is one gross attack upon social virtue and morality, and upon all that is held sacred, holy, and divine." In like fashion, the English literature of Byron and his heirs "presents no flattering picture of the boasted progress of the English nation in civilization":

> What have we in England? Byron, who has the distinguished honor of being the father of the modern satanic school of poets,—if this be not robbing Milton of his glory,—Byron, who would have us believe him when he says:—
>
> "Whate'er
> I may have been, or am, doth rest between
> Heaven and myself—I shall not choose a mortal
> To be my mediator:"
>
> And in the meanwhile blazons his licentiousness on every page of his writings, and makes the whole world the confidant of his crimes and miseries![50]

Like Goethe before him, Byron and his imitators serve in *Questions of the Soul* as impious villains, and their writing exemplifies the danger to true religion within cultures made increasingly susceptible to "the idolatry of women and of self," a deeply provoking idolatry that technologies of modern publication have disseminated by using the voices of "infidel and licentious" European poets.[51]

Singling out one of his companions from earlier days at Brook Farm as a victim of this Romantic trend toward the secular confessional in American literary culture, Hecker points to the case of the feminist writer Margaret Fuller and the literary executors who had published her scandalous memoirs after her untimely death in 1850: "Even those among ourselves who pride themselves on their moral culture and delicate sense of propriety, often publish things, not concerning themselves alone, but their friends, which shock a rightly instructed conscience, and which had been much better hidden and forgotten under the seals of sacramental confession; as for example the authors of Margaret Fuller's life."[52] Hecker emphasizes that the correct alternative to salacious disclosure in the press is the sacramental and private Catholic confession, which has "the divine power to relieve your conscience of sin, and the science and skill to cure your soul of its ravages." He goes further, however, to argue that the dangers of Romanticism and its confessional procedures become more significant with the advent of widely available publications catering to the licentious imagination. The literary marketplace, "flooding society with the details of . . . secret vices and miseries," functions according to the logic of a religious institution, albeit a failed one that leads men to "rid their hearts of the passions and miseries with which they are filled, by infecting the innocent and unsuspecting and by corrupting the pure and virtuous."[53] Fuller's *Memoirs*, an important document for American feminism and the transcendentalist movement, was carefully edited by her friends and family after her untimely death in 1850, but it is nevertheless—because of its acknowledgement of Fuller's giving birth to an illegitimate son—held up by Hecker as a prime example of writing that is toxic to the religious spirit.

Parting with the transcendental/Romantic individualism that he had explored so avidly as a young man, *Questions of the Soul* shows Hecker in middle age advocating a Catholic religious structure that would express itself as masculine, centrally controlled, highly organized, and able to assert its power and discernment according to modern bureaucratic methods and technologies: "Religion must become an everyday business and a public affair if souls are to be saved and sanctified, and the people made peaceable and happy. It must be in the closet but also in the family, in society, in trade and commerce; its spirit must pervade our public assemblies and penetrate our legislation. Its spirit must be everywhere, for out of Christ there is no way, no truth in life. But as this never can exist in our land so long as there are such a number of sects, isms, and schisms."[54] In keeping with this hopeful but patronizing view that it lay within the power of Catholic religion to have "the people made peaceable and happy," the self-reliance at the core of Protestantism, like the extreme, humanist versions set forth by Emerson himself, in Hecker's view constitutes a religious failure along a number of dimensions but largely because of its inability to engender piety and, especially, humility, "the mother of all other Christian virtues." Christian humility, according to this perspective, cannot be nurtured by Protestant religion because of an unmistakable arrogance at the core of its theology: "The beau-ideal of Protestantism, logically developed, is egoism, and the idolatry of self. For its pretended obedience to God, or the Holy Ghost, or its faith in Holy Scripture, is an act which always involves the supremacy of private judgment; consequently, its virtues are but other forms of pride and self."[55]

These faults of pride and self, according to Hecker, result in a number of devastating problems. Just as its adult membership is encouraged to turn inward as a way of examining the spiritual self and often in isolation from other believers, the children of Protestantism are deprived of the guidance and tutelage that Catholicism, rightly configured, can supply. By inverting the traditional criticisms of Catholic ritualism and its historic emphasis on the nondiscursive aspects of religious devotion so that these qualities of Catholicism become desirable in the context of an appeal to the young, Hecker is able to position his Catholicism firmly within the nineteenth-century discourses devoted to the cult of childhood:

> What says Rome to childhood?
>
> Rome says every thing. The Church of Rome is the church of childhood. Lead children into her precincts, and you will soon discover that she pours through every avenue of the mind of childhood treasures of wisdom. The altar, the crucifix, the robed priests, the surpliced acolytes, the pictures and the statues of the holy saints, the stained windows, the organ, the bells,—all combine together to give to the child's picturesque-loving mind, a better and more sublime idea of religion than years of reading and preaching can do.[56]

Rather than attempting to defend Catholic reliance on traditional liturgy as historically authentic or divinely inspired, he turns instead to a defense based upon the utility of these sensory stimuli as tools for attracting believers (albeit the very youngest ones in this case). Childlike piety alone, however, only partially defines the theological position outlined by Hecker. Before the spiritual needs of children can be addressed, a broad submission to authority and guidance must be implemented so that all members of the religious community may develop the skills necessary for the nurturance of the young, whose innocence and simple beliefs in turn become models for adult piety. Once again, Hecker's model for faith development contravenes the ethos of Protestant self-reliance: "Now, how does Protestantism answer [the need for a wise and experienced spiritual guide]? She answers like a step-mother—'Be your own guide.' Or if she tells you to 'read the Bible,' 'look to God,' or 'to pray,' if private judgment be supreme, what else is this but the same answer, only in other words?"[57] "Spiritual pride," then, tends to corrode the familial paradigm necessary for the development of Catholic spirituality, in this instance by replacing parental nurture and unpretentious belief with a sterile, arrogant, and soul-less cult of the self.

By listening to his arguments against self-reliance, we can reconstruct the theory of history and leadership that is written into Hecker's alarm about popular media and his call for censorship. If the ordinary reader and the ordinary Catholic are to be provided with peace and happiness, it will not occur because of their actions alone but because they have been led firmly in the direction of sound religious principles. In shades of Shelley's proposition of the poet/legislator, Hecker issues a call to an elite class of mystics and priests, whose destiny marks them for religious leadership:

> And among those who have a marked destiny, there is a class of souls that cannot satisfy their natures with the common modes of life. A hidden principle leads them to seek a better and more spiritual life. . . .
>
> Many thoughts come to these souls which stretch far beyond the limits of man's reason; noble hopes and aspirations, heroic deeds of sacrifice, and bright dreams of a holy life, awake them in their midnight slumbers, indicating a life beyond mere human strength. Such are the hidden ways of God's providence in preparing that class of souls which he has chosen to do a great work, to live above the race and the common life of men, and to act upon society with a divine energy.[58]

Although he speaks here of Catholic priests, Emerson's notion of the Poet resonates through this passage, which alludes to possibilities of action for an advanced thinker gifted with religious sensibility. But whereas Emerson had suggested a fiercely noninstitutional basis for his transcendental elitism, Hecker's model cleaves to that of the priesthood or the monastic order, a number of which he describes in outline in his chapter on "Special Destiny." More cryptically, though, he marks the presence of the "specially destined" as a function of the broadly conceived progress of Christianity as a national trend, noting that "this class of persons is large, and larger here in the United States than in any other Protestant country" and, more boldly, that "there is scarcely an American family which will not testify to the truth of this statement . . . by the efforts of some one or more of its members to realize such a life."[59]

On the one hand, he notes that these emerging Catholic leaders should be provided with both the physical space and the long stretches of time necessary to organize the suitably spiritualized life. The mystically elect—including members of the laity and clergy alike—should be privileged by the society at large, in direct recognition of their large burden of spiritual and mystical work undertaken on behalf of the Roman Church. On the other hand, though, he calls more directly for "the Church of Christ" to provide her vital sustenance for the "specially destined" class of Catholics. Again, familial metaphors lie at the core of his paradigm for religious nurturance; the guiding persona of the Church is written as piously feminine and profoundly maternal: "She must stretch out her maternal arms and say to them: 'Come to me, children of my heart's life. Here in my bosom is all you seek. Your inspiration, your noble aims and hopes are the whisperings of my Divine Spouse to you souls. Come, here is a mother's heart, a mother's love, a mother's care, a mother's blessing, and a mother's choicest gifts.' Such must be the language of Christ's Church to this class of privileged souls."[60] Family metaphors such as this one also require a national context for correct implementation. While seeking to empower a burgeoning cohort of mystical leaders and priests, Hecker grounded their "special destiny" of faith in national prerogatives that could be more legibly read in terms of another kind, the "manifest destiny" then current in American political ideology. The geopolitical destiny for America, a fashionable topic in the popular press and literary journals,[61] helped to nurture Hecker's proposition that American spirituality could have a kind of destiny as well—one related to both market capitalism and expansive geography.[62] First, Hecker observes that in order to adopt fully the ethos of the Catholic mystic, or what he calls a "higher life" inflected with the "nobler powers of the soul," one requires the kinds of political and economic freedom that are most richly provided in America. Setting aside the compulsory poverty traditionally imposed by mendicant orders, Hecker insists that a suitably American asceticism and mystical life are made possible not by impoverishment and humility but by leisure enhanced with wealth.[63]

It is apparent, from Hecker's pre-Catholic interest in communal life and in his mature references to monastic perfectionism, that the experiences at Brook Farm and Fruitlands had reinforced in him a desire to nurture a small, energetic cadre of the specially devout, from whose beginnings a powerful new version of Catholicism might be built. The figure of the Romantic hero of enormous emotional range is transformed into an inward-looking Catholic endowed with a "special destiny" by merit of personal disposition and intellectual power. Religious force, then, can be traced from this small legion of reflective believers, who subsequently perform the work of evangelizing and regularizing the beliefs of the American population. Strengthening the power of this elite group, of which Hecker himself is a prime example, will be the cultural force made possible by a quickly proliferating world of print. Both *Questions of the Soul* and *Aspirations of Nature* confront the challenge of developing a sinewy band of leaders among the Catholic elite but also situate the training of this small group within the larger nineteenth-century context of an expanding political geography of the United States and its rapid development of commercial print media.

With *Aspirations of Nature*, Hecker purports to be directing his sights toward the spiritual attention of "a large body of our intelligent countrymen."[64] Despite these broadly stated ambitions, *Aspirations of Nature* aims mostly at the same narrow audience he had addressed with *Questions of the Soul*, through an examination of complex philosophical questions related to Catholic spirituality. Striking out on a theological path that diverged from Brownson's in important ways, *Aspirations of Nature* stands as perhaps Hecker's most independently conceived view of American Catholicism. But independent or not, the book failed to enlist uniform support even among the narrowly defined audience of Catholic leaders who most interested Hecker, especially his mentor Brownson. In a review that initiated a severe personal and intellectual rift between the two leading Catholic thinkers, Brownson surprised his old friend by sharply criticizing what he perceived as the overly optimistic and naive gestures that Hecker included in *Aspirations of Nature.*[65] Part of the problem for Brownson was Hecker's boundless enthusiasm for American institutions and values. Declaring in his closing pages the necessity in America of choosing a national religion to correspond with and enhance the brilliance of its political ethos, Hecker asserts directly that Catholicism, more than any other form of religion, uniquely suits both the moral grandeur of the American character and the limitless possibilities of the American intellect:

> The question now pressing itself upon the American people is, to determine their Religion, as our fathers did the character of their political institutions. These, under the guidance of an overruling Providence, were based on Catholic principles, and Catholic views of human nature.
>
> With the free exertion of Reason, with the natural impulses of our instincts, and with the silent influences of our noble institutions, the American people will rise in the strength of its manhood and proclaim itself Catholic.
>
> Brothers of America! you who look for religion agreeing with your intelligence, commensurate with all the wants of your nature, and which presents a destiny worthy of your highest efforts, investigate the claims of the Catholic Religion, and exercise your freedom by paying a loyal homage to its Divine Truth.[66]

Walter Elliott cites similar comments by Hecker near the end of his life, when he wrote that "the controlling thought of my mind for many years has been that a body of free men, who love God with all their might, and yet know how to cling together, could conquer this modern world of ours."[67] Although it is not unexpected that Hecker would issue a rallying cry to his imagined readers, several observations may be made about the particular rhetoric of this closing passage in *Aspirations of Nature*.

First, there is his plain statement about a correspondence between American political values and the religious principles of Catholicism. Hecker buttresses this opinion with a claim that the Founding Fathers, in their wisdom, had produced a legal framework that dovetailed perfectly with Catholic religious principles. Latent in the growth of legislation and the practice of American political life since the Revolution, Catholicism can therefore take its rightful place in the young nation, fulfilling—like geopolitical manifest destiny, another kind of "destiny worthy of your highest efforts"—the imperatives of an intertwined religious and political teleology. Its political adolescence waning since the glory years of the Revolution, the population of the United States, argued Hecker, can now "rise in the strength of its manhood." Just as important, though, the "silent influences of our noble [American] institutions" provide only the political infrastructure for a religious population endowed with highly evolved "Reason" and "instinct"—the two modes of human spirituality that Hecker addresses in his defense of an American Catholicism fitted to the latest discoveries of scientific modernity.

Thanks to deep political structures of the United States amenable to Catholicism, as well as a growing population of immigrant Catholics from Europe, Hecker promises that Catholicism will emerge strengthened in the complex and shifting cultural milieu of the American nineteenth century. England, to be sure, had marked the nation deeply with her earlier generations of immigrants, but that fallen country and culture, no longer "under the healthful influences of Catholicism" and presently "renowned for . . . [s]adness, impiety, ginshops, workhouses, and factories," in Hecker's judgment would now give way to a new population, which would in turn foster a new set of spiritual values drawn from Catholicism. This new cohort of Catholics, although they comprise a seeming diversity of cultural styles, was poised to demonstrate that faith need not drain off the individuality and temperament of discrete populations: "Italy, Spain, Germany, France, Ireland, Belgium, are all Catholic nations, yet how widely different in their personal and national character!"

In predicting the triumph of Catholic religion in the rapidly changing American melting pot, Hecker blends ethnic stereotyping with a confident view of their malleability as prospective church members. By combining new political freedoms, geographic opportunities, and authentic religion, the "passionate, lively, and choleric Italian," "the slow, grave and philosophic German," "the sombre, stately, inflexible Spaniard," "the gay, affable, plastic Frenchman," "the warm-hearted, cheerful, all-enthusiastic Irishman," and "the quiet, steady, sedate Belgian" perpetuate their traditional perspectives on religious practice, while at the same time seizing the opportunity—uniquely available in America—to form and solidify a model of true Catholicism. Given the healthy social and political climate within antebellum America, then, Catholicism as understood by Hecker can give full expression to its synthetic and yet traditionalizing genius since it stood as "the only religion which preserves the individuality of persons as well as the characters of nations." According to this line of reasoning, Roman Catholicism served as a potential solution not only to pressing religious questions but also to issues of politics and national character.[68]

Writing just after midcentury, Hecker also predicts that America will soon find itself experiencing a religious sea change, which will make manifest the seldom-visible but always-latent Catholic character of the nation that previously had been obscured by Protestant hegemony and the legacy of Calvinism. In his view, "What has powerfully accelerated the downfall of Protestantism in this country, is the antagonism which exists between it and the spirit of our institutions. . . . The free institutions of the United States are not based on man's essential depravity, but on his essential goodness." Oddly enough, the adversary identified here by Hecker as the antagonist of American institutions is that of Calvinism, rather than the Unitarianism of his old New England transcendentalist friends. Whereas the severities of Calvinism must be abandoned as inimical to "the natural operation of free American institutions" because its tenets are "hostile to the principles and genius of [American] civilization," Unitarianism undergoes its own critique in *Aspirations of Nature* because of its failure to accommodate the aesthetic and emotional dimensions of human religious experience. However, it is not denominational differences or the particularities of individual churches that make up the most substantial part of Hecker's concerns (and his optimism) about American spirituality. Instead, he points to the Catholic leadership of "a large class of men who cherish the lofty aspirations of their nature, and are loyal to their religious convictions."[69] In an oddly counterintuitive set of claims, Hecker here presumes widespread and popular support for his religious ideas, even as his writing appeals almost entirely to—and was read only by—a small cadre of intellectuals.

Spurious assertions and self-serving hyperbole weaken Hecker's argument about the appeal of his Catholic theology among Americans. Although he cites no verifiable sources and provides no documentation for his claims, Hecker contends from the very outset of his book that "we have it from authentic sources of information, that this class of minds compose more than one-half of our population who have arrived at the age of manhood; and it includes many, if not most of our intellectually gifted and noble-minded countrymen." With an asserted demographic reality featuring this "large class of intellectual men" holding a shared set of religious convictions, all that remains is to reveal to that group the correspondences between their innate sense of spirituality and the venerable teachings of Catholicism.[70] In his biography of Hecker, the Paulist priest Walter Elliott summarized Hecker's ambitions that the divine plan of American Catholic conquest would soon be delivered to this logical conclusion, revealing the truth that "Almighty God, intending a great age and a great people, has put here in America a singular development of nature's powers and gifts, both in man and out of man—with the further will, I have the faith, of crowning all with the glory of the supernatural."[71]

Missing from Hecker's self-deluding argument about the popular appeal of his religious ideas, however, is any sense of how his own writing would be able to connect with ordinary American Catholics or with potential converts. Despite his own (unacknowledged) inability to relate to a popular reading audience, Hecker remains persuaded that the readership for his ideas about Catholic religion is potentially enormous—but not primarily because of the recent tides of European immigration. Noting the evidence of a sacralized American landscape and culture, "the countless churches, the Sunday-school unions, missionary enterprises, Bible and Tract societies, and other religious institutions broadcast over this extensive land," Hecker cites evidence for the progress of religious colonization across the American continent. These material artifacts and emblems of various missionary enterprises Hecker takes to be the tangible evidences of "a large class of men who cherish the lofty aspirations of their nature, and are loyal to their religious convictions," who will in turn comprise a substantial core of a new Catholic leadership.[72]

While he himself was unable to write the kinds of books or publish the kinds of periodicals that would truly make a substantial difference in the religious lives of ordinary people, Hecker never lost sight of how popular media could shape American culture. In *Aspirations of Nature*, for example, Hecker stubbornly cites developments in the popular print marketplace as evidence for his notion that Catholicism, broadly conceived as the best religious expression of reason and human instinct, also helped to lay the foundation of American institutions and culture. For instance, Hecker singles out the popular poem *The Song of Hiawatha* (1855), by Henry Wadsworth Longfellow, then the most popular and highly regarded poet in the United States. Noting its picturesque affirmation of primitive American religious sensibilities, Hecker ties the popular appeal of *The Song of Hiawatha* to the nation's deep-seated religious tendencies. In that poem's reflections on the moral world of Native Americans, Longfellow had allowed for the possibility of primal religious instincts and inchoate moral principles among Indians who had been dispossessed by European peoples: "Even in savage bosoms / There are longings, yearnings, strivings / For the good they comprehend not." This instinctive seeking by aboriginal peoples for a divine principle of human consciousness, what Hecker calls "the First True, the First Good, the First Fair," corresponds in his view to the broadest outlines of the Western intellectual tradition of philosophy and letters. It is an intellectual tradition that Hecker glosses as a search for authentic religion: "It is written on every page and breathed through all the works of genius. The philosophers, from Plato to Kant, vainly strove to sound these secret depths of the soul; the poets, from the author of "Prometheus Bound" [Aeschylus] to the author of "Intimations of Immortality" [Wordsworth], exhausted their gifts to express it; the pencil and the chisel have alike failed adequately to embody this mysterious birth of the conscious soul,—a birth which is the starting point of all philosophy, the ideal of genius, and the basis of all religious beliefs."[73] American poetry, English Romanticism, German and Greek philosophy, and Native American religions are thus arrayed under the rubric of human spiritual striving and perfectionism, which in turn have become increasingly public since the advent of mass publication in Europe and America. As Hecker well understood, one of the implicit possibilities of mass-print culture, with its national marketing and its increasingly sophisticated systems of production and distribution, is that broader swaths of the educated and the intelligent could be exposed to a body of literature calculated to elicit their highest religious impulses. It was not a possibility realized through Hecker's efforts, but this failure does not negate his judgments about the power of print media in nineteenth- and early twentieth-century America. It would, however, require other hands to make the most forceful use of the potentialities for Catholic religion in the American print marketplace.

It is clear enough that in spite of his ambitions, Hecker would never have the adaptability to a literary marketplace and the vagaries of popular piety that would mark the writings of the more successful religious writers of his day. Even among Catholic writers, his influence was rather limited. The common touch of other antebellum Catholic writers, who appealed with some success to a mass readership with their Catholic novels based on popular genres, eluded the grasp of Hecker in his early years as a priest writing for a prospective elite audience, and in his attempts to promote the *Catholic World* as an influential magazine. But it is equally apparent from a reading of each of Hecker's major apologetical tracts that unlike pioneer Catholic priests like Anthony Kohlmann, who sacrificed any sense of the popular appeal of religion to the rigors of intellectual analysis and in his writings took to the perceived high ground of engaging Protestantism at the highest pitches of theological analysis, Hecker made certain to allow (albeit briefly and in the abstract) for the possibility of various and wide-ranging human needs and preferences within a single religious denomination. In this matter of the apparent self-contradictory character of Catholicism, Hecker's writing also reads at times like that of a hybrid thinker in debt to both nineteenth-century Emersonian secular individualism and today's theoretical models of religious creativity and partial or provisional religious practices. Seeing diversity, authentic spirituality, and tolerance where anti-Catholic polemics had found only authoritarianism, mysticism, and idolatry, Hecker remained perennially confident that "the Catholic religion, so far from crushing man's individuality and independence, is wonderfully calculated and adapted to call forth, sustain, and perfect the tastes, propensities, and peculiarities of human nature."[74] The creation of Catholically inflected American writing that would truly speak to these tastes, propensities, and peculiarities, however, would not occur for several more decades, when certain non-Catholic Americans began to turn elements of Roman Catholicism into aspects of their modernist literary practice.

3

Entering the Mainstream

The Fiction of Jedediah Huntington and Anna Hanson Dorsey

> Young Catholics are, by nature, like other human beings, they have imaginations which require food, and a craving for mental stimulus equal to a thirst in the desert. The mind needs relaxation and amusement perhaps more than the body and if all this is not provided for them inside the Church, they will seek it on forbidden grounds, as thousands of them do, and will continue to do, so long as the dearth of agreeable reading suitable to their need continues.
>
> Anna Dorsey, letter to Father Daniel Hudson, June 18, 1879

Although the religious activism of Hecker and Brownson was acknowledged and even admired in some quarters of the educated Catholic elite, it would be misleading—given the rather limited audience for their work—to construe their literary production as anything like a comprehensive guide to nineteenth-century popular Catholic thought. Their ill-fated eclecticism and conservatism, however, should not be mistaken for a wholesale failure of their insights about print media, because both men understood very well the growing importance of the commercial press in American media, and they both took steps to shape the

American religious literary conversation over the course of their several decades in the public eye. Ever the keen student of nineteenth-century industrial print culture, Brownson in particular knew from his early days as a freelance critic that the popular novel figured as a powerful literary genre for describing and adjusting the nation's social and religious preferences. Indeed, as much as any of his Catholic contemporaries, he would have been aware of the unprecedented commercial success achieved by popular novelists such as Lydia Maria Child, James Fenimore Cooper, Harriet Beecher Stowe, Maria Cummins, and Susan Warner. Brownson's awareness of how commercial print was increasingly leveraged to shape the national imagination helps explain his own interest in writing popular fiction, which led to such uneven efforts as his semi-autobiographical *Charles Elwood, Or the Infidel Converted* (1840) and the fictional *The Spirit-Rapper* (1854), neither of which was popular enough to be called a commercial success. Despite his personal shortcomings in drawing truly substantial attention to his fiction or most of his other writings,[1] he was attentive to the evolving habits and preferences of American readers, an increasing number of whom were women. However, in his anxious criticism of women's writing and what he saw as an overly feminized popular literary culture, Brownson was very much out of step with trends in commercial publishing.

Revisionist scholarship in recent years has fostered a substantial and illuminating reexamination of nineteenth-century literature for women in the United States. Much of this scholarship has paid special attention to re-examining "sentimental" texts created by American novelists, resulting in important new understandings of women's fiction in nineteenth-century America and providing a great deal of new context for the political import, social complications, gender paradoxes, and racial construction of these novels. Once dismissed by scholars (and male authors) as subliterary writing, these novels, which in some respects drew on the example of British fictional models from Samuel Richardson's *Pamela* (1740) and *Clarissa* (1747–48) through Charles Dickens's *A Christmas Carol* (1843) and *Little Dorrit* (1857–58), have recently been described as "the most radical popular form available to middle-class culture."[2] Leslie Fiedler's sharp critique of the alleged artistic impoverishments of these books has been abandoned by feminist scholars since the 1960s, who, bypassing or modifying the aesthetic imperatives of Fiedler and other early twentieth-century critics, now prefer to ask pointed questions about the "cultural work" that these books have performed within

American society.[3] Serious consideration of long-neglected works such as William Hill Brown's *The Power of Sympathy* (1789), Susanna Rowson's *Charlotte Temple* (1791), Hannah Foster's *The Coquette* (1797), Susan Warner's *The Wide, Wide World* (1850), Maria Cummins's *The Lamplighter* (1854), and Louisa May Alcott's *Little Women* (1868–69) has provided newly complicated views of nineteenth-century reading culture, while pointing the way toward a broader consideration of literary sentimentality and, more broadly, the place of women in American fiction. Moreover, Nathaniel Hawthorne's notorious dismissal of these popular women writers as nothing more than "a d——d mob of scribbling women" appears at the present critical moment to have provided not merely a point open to debate, since many sentimental writers have been male, but an irresistible challenge for analyses of the remarkable power of mass-print sentimental culture in nineteenth-century America.[4]

For example, the current view of nineteenth-century American sentimental culture, in one of its more impressive critical formulations, has been articulated as what Karen Sánchez-Eppler has called "bodily bonds": the problematics of race, class, and gender as they intersect in sentimental discourse, and as they operate on and around the bodies (promiscuous, chaste, resistant, mobilized, caricatured, sympathetic, suffering, repressed, engendered, politicized, racialized, enslaved, nurturing, etc.) in these texts.[5] In similar fashion, as Shirley Samuels has suggested, the recent project of analyzing American sentimental culture has devoted itself to a category of texts that work inevitably to "expose bodies."[6] In the case of writers committed to the cause of Roman Catholicism, the bodies included in their stories were also deeply involved in religious activities that set them apart from most of their American contemporaries.

When considering the production and circulation of books by Catholic novelists of this period, it is important to understand that a variety of writers made attempts to capitalize on the commercial and evangelical potential of the American print marketplace, but there was no more consensus among Catholic writers about how to write a Catholic novel than there was theological agreement among authors who evangelized on behalf of Protestant religion. As a consequence of these diverse approaches to writing fiction, literary historians have been somewhat divided in their assessment of the antebellum Catholic literary tradition.[7] It is possible to observe certain patterns in Catholic publishing circles, though, which were analogous to developments on the American commercial publishing scene as a whole. These patterns show Catholic writers and publishers awakening to the evangelical potential of large-scale publication and distribution of books, becoming more attuned to the commercial aspects of the book business, and responding to powerful market trends that were placing female authors and readers—producers and consumers of popular fiction—at the center of American literary culture.

The popular novel would seem to have been an ideal medium for systematic exploitation by Catholic writers, given that best-selling novels had shown by midcentury that fiction by Protestant writers could serve as a uniquely powerful medium for promoting moral, political, and religious ideas.[8] Indeed, Catholic novels and even Catholic devotional books and catechisms were thematically in step with the tide of literature, much of it moralistic in tone, produced during the nineteenth century. As Jane Tompkins has argued about the importance of popular American religious texts and their relationship to sentimental literary themes, "The implantation of virtue was the primary goal of everything nineteenth-century Americans read: textbooks, novels, poems, magazine stories, or religious tracts." Although until fairly recently the predominance of modernist aesthetic standards has worked to devalue women's writing (including the sentimental genre) of the nineteenth century, Tompkins and other feminist scholars have persuasively asserted the centrality of these works to an accurate understanding of the period: "The very grounds on which sentimental fiction has been dismissed by its detractors, grounds which have come to seem universal standards of aesthetic judgment, were established in a struggle to supplant the tradition of evangelical piety and moral commitment these novelists represent. In reaction against their world view, and perhaps even more against their success, twentieth-century critics have taught generations of students to equate popularity with debasement, emotionality with ineffectiveness, religiosity with fakery, domesticity with triviality, and all of these, implicitly, with womanly inferiority."[9] To the extent that their fiction depicted scenes of romance and sentiment in ways calculated to appeal to American women readers, Catholic novelists were thus full participants in the literary culture of the nineteenth century, which so frequently relied on Christian religious principles to supply compelling moral parameters in its narratives.

As shown by David S. Reynolds, one of the few recent critics who have paid heed to American Catholic fiction of the nineteenth century,

Catholic authors were moving "away from theology toward sentimental fiction," a trend confirmed by the fact that "[during] the 1840s novels displaced doctrinal works as the most lucrative product of Catholic publishers."[10] What Reynolds sees here as a fairly narrow window of opportunity for considering generically something called the "Catholic novel" itself suggests that the scant few decades that he focuses on in his study of Catholic fiction should be understood as a brief and transient development of American Catholic writing. Indeed, with the ongoing development of the print marketplace and professionalization of authorship, novelists with a deep investment in Catholicism (like novelists with other religious commitments) began to broaden the scope of their writing considerably beyond the didactic or tutelary modes to create more subtle religious presentations within their narratives. The isolation of purely doctrinal works as representative of the category of Catholically religious fiction functions to delimit perhaps too rigorously the boundaries of this movement in American letters, which can be seen in a variety of forms throughout the century, with only a portion of those forms adhering to the didactic mode that Reynolds identifies in his discussion of the antebellum Catholic novels. In addition, Reynolds's assertion that, by 1855, "the Catholic novelist had decided to conform to the culture he had been wooing for nearly three decades" deserves re-examination because of the complex ways that Catholic fiction writers pressed for the advancement of religion even as they adapted their work to the commercial realities of the print marketplace.[11]

Like their Protestant contemporaries, Catholic writers were awake to the evangelical possibilities offered by the emergence and national reach of industrial publishing, as evidenced by the emergence of American Catholic novelists and publishers in the nineteenth century, beginning with the pioneer bookman Bernard Dornin of Brooklyn, an Irish émigré who opened a Catholic book store on Pearl Street in Manhattan and soon thereafter brought out a Bible for Catholics in 1805. Other Catholic publishers soon followed suit in understanding that money could be made from American Catholic readers. By midcentury Catholic writers were well positioned to take advantage of the many exciting new developments in the print marketplace. American Catholic publishing houses, most of them led by businessmen of Irish descent, like Patrick O'Shea (New York), Patrick Donahoe (Boston), Denis and James Sadlier (New York and Montreal),[12] John Kenedy (New York and Baltimore), and John Murphy (Baltimore), brought to market many of the era's most important and widely disseminated Catholic novels. The D. Appleton publishing house of New York, while not an avowedly Catholic publisher, also seems to have been friendly to that cause in fiction, having published not only a large number of Catholic authors but also a very substantial Catholic encyclopedia.[13]

That Catholic writing and publishing grew during the nineteenth century is a function of the large numbers of new readers who populated the print marketplace during these years, but this growth is also related to the increasing influence of print as an efficient and profitable means of religious communication. To some extent, the expansion of commercial publishing also shaped the lived practice of Catholic religion. As Jay Dolan's study of the nineteenth-century Catholic experience has shown, print media was a major factor in the steady transformation of what he calls the "plain style of Catholic piety" focused on the sacrament of the Mass to "devotional Catholicism" that featured popular devotions, prayers, and meditations distinct from the sacramental Mass.[14] The historian Daniel Walker Howe and others have noted that while oratory and preaching were important aspects of nineteenth-century religious discourse—especially during the early national and antebellum period—the retailing of religious morality by midcentury was tied powerfully to industrial print culture, in which "[the] writers of America's literary renaissance took advantage of the improvements in communications technology to market their art and their moral values to larger and more widespread audiences than writers had ever before enjoyed." Inexpensive books, newspapers, and religious tracts became staples of industrial print culture in the United States by the antebellum period, and the wide distribution of these products, which increased along with the western expansion of the frontier, gave a new generation of professional writers an audience that was truly national in its distribution.

Despite its promise as a medium for evangelism, though, the popular novel as a medium for spreading Catholic faith was never very successful in the United States, at least not on the commercial scale of best-selling works produced by the most popular American writers of the day. Nevertheless, a number of Catholic writers produced novels that were aimed at bringing Americans into the Church while reinforcing the beliefs of the faithful. Until recently the work of nineteenth-century Catholic writers has been neglected or dismissed as irrelevant to American literary history, much in the way that women's writing generally had been marginalized by scholarly opinion until the later twentieth century.

In *The Catholic Spirit in Modern English Literature* (1922), the Catholic critic and editor George N. Shuster voiced a forceful version of this attitude, asserting that American Catholic fiction had been both a commercial and aesthetic disaster: "Catholic fiction has suffered from the same ailments that have afflicted the American novel in general. Obsessed by abstract ideas, schemes of reform, and a theory that art is designed for our weaker-minded sisters, we have given, at best, only a mediocre version of American life, a version that has satisfied so well the tastes of a great majority of readers that nothing else is likely to be commercially successful. The great bulk of American Catholic fiction is unreadable."[15] Despite Shuster's dismissal of these works of fiction as fit only for "our weaker-minded sisters," the efforts of Catholic novelists to write popular novels with sympathetic portrayals of Catholic life do in fact comprise a fascinating aspect of nineteenth-century literary culture, much of which was grounded in structures of moralism borrowed from the evangelical Christian movement as a whole and therefore was produced with aspirations toward mass publication as a means of promoting religious faith. These novelists also figure as a prologue to American writers of a subsequent period, in the later nineteenth century and early twentieth century, when for a variety of reasons the overtly didactic Catholic novel (like the overtly didactic Protestant novel) fell out of favor in the print marketplace.[16]

Taking a cue from Brownson and Hecker's concerns about the powerful role of fictional narratives in shaping American religious, familial, and political culture, this chapter examines some of the directions traveled by Catholically inflected fiction during the mid-nineteenth century, when the anti-Catholic novel had already provided an anxious and aggressive literary discourse about the role of Catholic values in American culture. This was a period when the lists of best-selling novels included salacious anti-Catholic potboilers such as Rebecca Reed's *Six Months in a Convent* (1835), Maria Monk's *Awful Disclosures of Maria Monk* (1836), and Ned Buntline's *The Jesuit's Daughter: A Novel for Americans to Read* (1854), all of which described Roman Catholicism as morally dangerous, politically subversive, and threatening to Protestant religious hegemony in the United States.[17] The following examples of Catholic novels are not meant to demonstrate mere opposition to anti-Catholic fiction or to provide a comprehensive history of the American Catholic novel. Instead they are presented as examples of how some mid-nineteenth-century Catholic fiction asserted its religious appeal for American readers by elaborating Catholicism as a luxurious or exotic realm and by placing women at the center of its concerns.

Two of the most interesting novelists active during the middle and later years of the nineteenth century are the Catholic convert Dr. Jedediah Vincent Huntington (1815–62), best known as the author of *Lady Alice; or the New Una* (1849), and Anna Hanson Dorsey (1815–96), also a Catholic convert and author of many novels, including *Coaina, The Rose of the Algonquins* (1867). These works serve as instances of the ways popular literary themes could be adapted for Roman Catholic audiences but also as texts in which writers sensitive to trends in the literary marketplace adapted their writing for purposes of print evangelism. These writers are significant figures both as participants in an underappreciated dimension of antebellum culture and also as convert novelists whose relationship to Catholic religion is frequently more artful and less preoccupied with religious controversy than most overtly evangelical writing of the period. Both Huntington and Dorsey resemble their non-Catholic literary counterparts in their focus on the moral and religious world of women characters. Representations of romantic-but-virtuous womanhood are emblematic of the attempt by these writers to produce works of fiction that would remain true to both Catholic religious principles and American national values. Finally, they are writers who resemble Orestes Brownson and Isaac Hecker in their adult conversions to Roman Catholicism, and as such demonstrate the extent to which nineteenth-century Catholic literary culture was strongly shaped by religious converts. The careers of Huntington and Dorsey demonstrate the zeal and influence of American Catholic converts in the nineteenth-century literary sphere, while at the same time serve as examples of the way convert novelists to a certain extent avoided exploration of the complex but humble lives of ordinary Catholics, such as the immigrants who had become the largest cohort of the American church.

Huntington in particular and to some extent Dorsey as well placed many of their fictional narratives far from the contemporary realities of American Catholic life: Huntington's *Lady Alice* portrays Anglo-Catholicism among a set of wealthy individuals, situating them in exotic European locations. Dorsey's *Coaina* develops the story of a pious Catholic Native American girl, based on an account provided to Dorsey by Armand-Francois-Marie de Charbonnel (1802–91), a French-Canadian missionary priest who became bishop of Toronto in 1850. By using Roman Catholicism as a prevailing theme but not as part of an adversarial posture toward other religions, these novels demonstrate something of the complexity of antebellum Catholic literary culture while anticipating to a certain degree the way that non-Catholic modernist writers of the later nineteenth and early twentieth century would use Catholicism for purposes not overtly connected with evangelism.[18]

Evangelical Christian themes are a crucial element of the nineteenth-century American literary canon, as is evident from that period's most notable and enduring works of fiction. Protestant writers set the tone for antebellum literary culture and set terms for the American print marketplace that Catholic writers of later generations would inevitably encounter. Three of the most religion-obsessed American novels of the nineteenth century—Nathaniel Hawthorne's *The Scarlet Letter* (1850), Herman Melville's *Moby-Dick* (1851), and Harriet Beecher Stowe's *Uncle Tom's Cabin* (1851–52)—were composed by famous writers from Protestant backgrounds and yet were published during a decade of large-scale Irish immigration to the United States, whose arrival made the status of American Catholicism a controversial issue for many readers. As Hawthorne was working out his relationship with the Puritan history of New England through the story of Hester Prynne, as Melville was using a fictional whaling voyage to sort out the particulars of Calvinist belief, and as Stowe was advancing the abolitionist cause by means of her tale of African American slaves whose authentic Christianity validates their full humanity, Roman Catholic writers were beginning to produce works of fiction that spoke to a dimension of American religious experience made increasingly visible because of Irish immigration to the United States. Social tensions caused by the arrival of so many immigrants from Catholic Ireland combined with a long-standing American tradition of evangelical Christian publishing to create conditions that were ripe for exploitation by religious novelists. The extent to which these important novels by Hawthorne, Melville, and Stowe were infused with concerns central to Protestant Christianity provides a useful index to how receptive American readers were to novels that were unapologetic about taking up overtly religious issues. In addition, the mid-nineteenth century was a volatile political crossroads during which Catholics and Catholic novels were already under siege in American culture, the former by nativist harassment, political propaganda, and caricature in anti-Catholic fiction, and the latter by the literary establishment.

One of the first nineteenth-century professional novelists to embrace Catholicism, Jedediah V. Huntington—New England blueblood, scion of a prominent Connecticut family, former Episcopal minister, and editor of a St. Louis Catholic newspaper—was immediately attacked in print for his work as a Catholic fiction writer. Like his contemporary and fellow New Yorker Herman Melville, Huntington came from a wealthy and distinguished family that had played important political and military roles during the Revolutionary War. A grandson of Judge Benjamin Huntington (a member of the Continental Congress and the first elected congressman to represent Connecticut) and also of storied Revolutionary War general Jedediah Huntington, Huntington came of age firmly ensconced in the security and comfort of the American upper class. Educated at Yale, the University of the City of New York, and the University of Pennsylvania (where he earned a medical degree), Huntington worked as a schoolteacher for several years before being ordained as an Episcopal priest in 1842. In 1846 Huntington left the Episcopal congregation he had been leading in Middlebury, Vermont, and journeyed to Rome and the papal city, where he apparently first began writing fiction in the company of his brother, the American painter Daniel Huntington.[19]

Jedediah Huntington became a Catholic in 1849, at a time when the Oxford Movement was inspiring numerous high-profile conversions from the Anglican Church to Roman Catholicism. As a novelist who came to prominence during the antebellum period, Huntington soon drew the attention of Orestes Brownson, who was a colleague in his effort to promote American Catholic fiction and criticism, and reviewed Huntington's fiction in pages of his own magazine. Very much a professional man of letters with an interest in the commercial side of his literary work, Huntington was also widely known during his career as an outspoken advocate of international copyright, which was then being proposed in order to protect the livelihood of professional writers in an era of reckless transatlantic piracy of novels and other printed works.[20] Joining his contemporaries Hecker and Brownson as a religious journalist, Huntington also made attempts at leading two short-lived periodicals, the *Metropolitan Magazine*, which was based in Baltimore, and the *Leader*, a St. Louis newspaper.[21]

While at various times during his career he tried his hand at poetry, translation, teaching, and editorial work, Jedediah Huntington's first attempt at writing a specifically Catholic novel produced *Lady Alice; or, the New Una* (1849), the same year that he and his wife, strongly influenced by the religious ferment of the Oxford Movement and John Henry Newman's turn to Rome, abandoned the Episcopal Church and converted permanently to Catholicism. Huntington now began a distinguished career as a Catholic novelist, producing a body of work that set him apart, in Willard Thorp's view, as "certainly the most worldly of the Catholic novelists . . . and the most talented."[22] *Lady Alice* is interesting not only for its favorable representations of Roman Catholicism but also because its narrative uses Catholicism as an appealing aesthetic dimension used to heighten the narrative romance. Avoiding any engagement with specifically American Catholic issues, *Lady Alice* features a complicated love affair between a Catholic Englishman (Frederic Clifford) and the beautiful young English woman (Alice Stuart) whom he pursues romantically after saving her from drowning during a holiday in southern Italy. Huntington's easy and cosmopolitan familiarity with English customs and manners were such that some reviewers of the novel's English edition believed its author to be British. In the cheaply bound thirty-eight-cent edition of *Lady Alice* published later in that same year, Huntington included a prefatory note explaining that he was in fact an American.

The events of the novel unfold in a series of adventures in exotic European locales such as Italy, England, and Switzerland, and after a long and elaborate courtship the couple finally weds after confirming their love and their shared Catholic faith. Most of the novel, however, is not concerned with the nuances of theology or the particulars of faith. These are well-educated, and wealthy, English Catholics who luxuriate in the aesthetic experiences of their faith, and whose expensive accoutrements, candles, crucifixes, and chalices signify their religious commitment, even as their overindulgent activities are concerned mainly with romance and courtship rather than substantial discussion of religion.

Because of its aesthetic treatment of Catholic religiosity and its purportedly lax morals, *Lady Alice* was met with hostility in long, anonymous reviews in the *Southern Literary Messenger* of Richmond and Boston's *North American Review*, both of which were influential arbiters of taste for American intellectuals. For example, an anonymous Protestant reviewer for the *North American Review* found that although the risqué eroticism of Huntington's fiction was infused with an aura of Roman Catholic piety, the novel was in fact nothing more than a vehicle for immorality that barely disguised its invitation to sinful behavior behind a cynical tissue of religious pretension. The reviewer was particularly scandalized by a bizarre sequence in the novel that features the abduction of Alice Stuart, who subsequently is forced to cross-dress as a man in order to avoid recognition. Still later, Alice continues voluntarily to dress in male disguise so that she can pursue her love of painting, and the discovery of her disguise by various male characters, including Frederic Clifford, becomes a device for putting her into erotically charged situations. For the Boston reviewer, though, these scenes of gender instability are deeply troubling, as are other scenes in which the symbols of Catholicism are used to sanitize temptations and immoral behavior. "The leading personages of the novel," the reviewer complains, "are kept from yielding to temptation, not by religious faith or principle, but by the presence of influential symbols. Alice's purity under her masculine attire is ascribed chiefly to her keeping a crucifix on her bed."[23]

The anonymous reviewer for the *Southern Literary Messenger* was similarly antagonistic to the blending of religion and romance in *Lady Alice*, protesting that Huntington's novel failed to offer a true portrait of Roman Catholicism and that its main effect was titillation rather than instruction: "We . . . dismiss this book by saying that as a theological exposition it is a slanderous caricature of Catholic Christianity. As a moral treatise it is licentious and corrupting in the extreme. As a work of art, professedly upholding a theory, it is a wretched failure."[24] The harsh reviews in both journals address their comments to the moral shortcomings of a plot centered on characters whose chastity is made ambiguous. However, it should be pointed out that *Lady Alice* also presents a narrative containing subtle issues of theology and scenes of upper-class social life that likely would have made its appeal rather limited among ordinary American Catholic readers. The profound disparity between the scenes presented in *Lady Alice*, which pivot on the question of whether High Church Anglican or Roman Catholic modes of belief are most appropriate, and the real-life situation of ordinary Irish Catholic immigrants is a reminder that writers like Huntington were *not* creating books that were immediately relevant for a truly popular American audience. It is difficult to imagine that substantial numbers of immigrant Irish readers, for instance, would readily identify with the elite styles of Catholicism that Huntington chooses to portray. The novel's cosmopolitan narrator moves its characters and situations far from the immediate concerns of ordinary American Catholic readers and creates a pleasurable fantasy milieu in which Catholicism itself serves as the context for a romance conducted among a wealthy European social set. All of these factors may have contributed to Huntington's relative success among English readers and the limited appeal his novels held for American Catholics.[25]

The affluent social world created in *Lady Alice* was precisely the literary opposite of what Father Isaac Hecker had in mind some decades later, as he was considering ways of promoting American Catholic fiction. Nearing the end of a long editorial career and perhaps finally recognizing the shortcomings of his own publications when it came to reaching out to the ordinary American Catholic reader, he prevailed upon the prolific Irish-Canadian-American novelist Mary Anne Sadlier to write fiction that would create appealing representations of Irish Catholic immigrant women in domestic service. Sadlier, an Irish-born author who would eventually produce about sixty pious and overtly pro-Catholic novels, responded to Hecker's request by dutifully publishing her tale of a devout young Irish servant girl in *Bessy Conway: The Irish Girl in America* (1885), a book very much in keeping with her concern about Irish immigrants and the religious and educational issues facing the Irish in nineteenth-century America.[26] Mary Anne Sadlier's tendency to write heavily didactic Catholic fiction that represented and sought to influence the quotidian lives of immigrant Irish Catholics was counterbalanced to a certain extent by writers like Huntington, who took a broader and more cosmopolitan approach to religion in their novels. Characters such as Sadlier's pious Catholic servant girls are nowhere to be found in the wealthy and sophisticated milieu created in *Lady Alice*, which presents a social world in which Catholic religion serves as a marker of wealth, taste, and intellect rather than immigration, exile, and poverty.

Despite some reservations the always-unpredictable Orestes Brownson had expressed about Sadlier's writing (he had published a review of her work in *Brownson's Quarterly Review*), surely it was Mary Anne Sadlier who answered Brownson's perennial call for religious fiction suitable for the American public. In the preface to her novel *The Blakes and the Flanagans* (1850), Sadlier wrote that her fiction was indeed something other than the kind of "novel" then current in the print marketplace, and she shared Brownson's oft-expressed dislike for novels that did not accord with Catholic religious values. "I do not profess to write novels," she insisted. "I cannot afford to waste time pandering merely to the imagination, or fostering that maudlin sentimentality, which is the ruin of youth both male and female. No conscientious Catholic can write a story wherein the interest depends on the workings of passion. One who has Eternity ever in view, cannot write mere love-tales; but simple, practical stories, embodying grave truths, will be read by many, who would not read pious books." Plainly moralistic views like this were doubtless received well by Brownson, who after ceasing publication of his own *Review* in 1864 began writing contributions for Mrs. Sadlier and her *New York Tablet.* Nevertheless, Huntington felt free enough in his literary craft to express himself in novels that deviated from Sadlier's call for "grave truths" and indulged in the kinds of narrative sentimentality and erotic tension that so troubled Brownson in his reviews of other popular books.[27]

Whereas it might be expected that a Roman Catholic novelist of the mid-nineteenth century would have been at least moderately concerned to structure his writing in ways calculated for appealing the many new Catholics who had immigrated to the United States, Huntington admitted privately to Brownson that in fact he disliked foreigners. Furthermore, as a proud New Englander he also sympathized with anti-immigration views in Nativist politics.[28] Huntington's elite sensibility combined with a tendency to avoid the grittier realisms that he might have selected for his fiction; his neglect of the immigrant Catholic ethnic and religious experiences central to the work of highly popular writers like Sadlier helps explain the limited success of his fiction in the print marketplace. At the same time, though, his method of constructing sophisticated romantic fiction in which religion is presented in the form of supple context rather than adamant dogma supplies an artistic precedent for American fiction writers of subsequent decades. By the late nineteenth century, after the sharp decline in popularity of the controversial religious novel, Roman Catholic representations continued to appear in American fiction, but their appearance was less frequently accompanied by the assertive rhetoric of evangelism or controversy.

Among the benefits of considering Huntington's place in nineteenth-century Catholic literary culture is the opportunity to consider his own reflections on the role of fiction, and especially the usefulness of romance, in shaping the national conversation about religion. In his preface to *Lady Alice,* Huntington comments defensively about what he perceives to be a sharp distinction between his own approach to religious fiction and the putatively immoral novels then available to American readers. Like his friend Orestes Brownson, whose views of religion and literature were infused with a harsh critique of feminine sensibility, Huntington also situates gendered emotion and piety within the main currents of his fiction, but by contrast with Brownson's injunctions about resisting impulses to create an overly feminized version of Catholicism, Huntington remained consistently attuned to the emotional and material world of women. Or, as the Catholic historian James Walsh has written, drawing on the recollections of Patrick John Ryan (1831–1911), bishop of St. Louis, Missouri, "While Huntington was a strong character and had a mind of a distinctly philosophic bent, there was something rather effeminate about his manner and some strikingly feminine mental qualities. These were particularly exhibited in the tendency of his novels to give ultimate details of feminine dress, and a clerical friend once said that Dr. Huntington would never think of introducing a young woman into one of his stories until he had told just the number and kind of flounces that she wore not only on her outer, but also on her under garments."[29]

In his discussion of Huntington's later novel, *The Forest* (1852), Walsh returns to the relationship between Huntington's apparently unstable gender identity and his choice of narrative techniques in the course of describing yet another scene of cross-dressing in that novel, which like the one in *Lady Alice* had led to condemnation by critics. Speculating that Huntington's poor judgment in presenting such scenes might by due to "Huntington's own super-refined and overdelicate nature," Walsh asserts that Huntington "lacked many of the virile qualities, and seems to have been deficient as well in certain of the passional associations." All of this is to imply that, although Huntington set his characters within scenes that appear to solicit inappropriate sexual activity, his own dormant heterosexuality prevented him from writing narratives that cross the line into pornographic representations. The course of reading in which Huntington had indulged, continued Walsh in a line of argument that might have been written by Orestes Brownson, also had something to do with Huntington's tendency to create salacious scenes: "Something of his failure to realize ordinary impropriety undoubtedly was due to his practice of reading French novels, to which he devoted to the greater portion of his spare time." Stopping just short of the pornographic tendencies that had made contemporary French fiction a scandal, wrote Walsh, Huntington apparently drew upon the risqué situations of those popular works in order to shape his own narratives: "He was constantly supplied with the latest editions from the French presses, and, while he did not introduce the objectionable features of French passionistic literature, some of the situations depended on to produce effects in his own novel writing were consciously or unconsciously borrowed from them." In any case, Huntington's writing was considered by his Catholic contemporaries as highly accomplished literary work, but there was concern among some critics that his romantic situations too often veered away from piety into suspect moral terrain.[30]

Huntington shaped the mild didacticism of his writing to conform with the tastes of a reading public grown accustomed to tales featuring not only the popular themes of local color, frontier adventure, and social reform but also feminine perspectives on romance and the relationship between women and pious morality. At all points, however, Huntington would claim that his fictional representations of romance and his depictions of women occupied the most lofty religious terrain. Although he had been accused by the *North American Review* of contriving overly provocative romantic episodes in *Lady Alice*, such as scenes of unchaperoned youths of both sexes frolicking on a beach, Huntington responded by distinguishing his depiction of romance from that of other religiously interested popular writers: "The passion of love may be made interesting, I think, without those conflicts which the moderns love to paint, and which suppose a degrading anarchy in the soul. Nothing has been done more to confuse the distinction between virtue and vice than modern English sentimental fiction, particularly that which claims to be moral, if not religious; and one object which I have had in view in my former, and I have pursued in my present work, has been to make the lines sharp and distinct."[31] Whether Huntington's romantic fiction managed "to confuse the distinction between virtue and vice," it is nonetheless certain that his fiction used the erotic leverage of romantic situations typically found in nonreligious novels to advance his own notions of Catholic religion.

For Huntington, as with other advocates of Catholicism in nineteenth-century print culture, trends and developments in novel-writing presented major obstacles to religious principles and individual probity, even as the American novel was evolving into a major tool for the transmission of ideas into culture, thanks to the rise of industrial scale printing, distribution, and marketing of books. Romantic episodes, realistically portrayed, obviously figure as a major component of nineteenth-century fiction, but Huntington readily saw the tension between the romantic scenes he chose to depict and the traditionally censorious dimensions of Christian religion. Huntington's critics would later complain that such scenes, written for books whose readership was largely female, created an unmistakable tension between his work and conservative religious attitudes about courtship and sexuality. In his preface to *Lady Alice*, Huntington anticipates such criticism by attempting to argue for the chastity and virtue of his heroine and the higher pretensions of his own artistry, even though she will be depicted in a variety of sexually charged scenes:

> [C]ertain persons . . . may strongly except to the plot in general, and to many of the incidents, and to the dénouement, as essentially connected with a species of interest that breathes through all the Plastic Arts, that was the soul of ancient Poetry, and makes still the inexhaustible charm of our old Poets, but which the moderns, for some reason or other, have generally agreed to avoid. To be "simple, sensuous, passionate," was once the definition of Poetry; it is so no longer; and people say that the age is become *subjective*! . . . Poetry, and *every* Art, while it does not ignore the actual state of the world altogether, must, if it would not abdicate its office, treat its main figure as if Paradise had not been forfeited, and human nature still were all radiant with its first glory.[32]

Such high-minded protestations notwithstanding, even Orestes Brownson, who admired his friend's attempts at writing fiction sympathetic to the Catholic cause and frequently wrote in support of that fiction, had sharp words for Huntington's tendency to eroticize his female characters and complained that "we think it repugnant to the laws of true art for the writer, every time he has occasion to introduce a woman, to stop and give us a full-length portrait of her, the color of her hair, the form of her eyebrows, the cast of her features, the pouting or not pouting of her lips, the shape of her bust, the size of her waist, and the working of her toes."[33] Once again, Brownson and a chorus of critics asserted that while his favorable and skillful representation of Roman Catholicism put him in the forefront of Catholic novelists, Huntington's writing was to some degree unseemly because of his failure to show a suitable degree of modesty about sexual matters.

One of the dangers that accompanied narratives focused on women and femininity, according to conservative critics like Brownson and Hecker, was that such a focus left open the temptation to pander to the popular audience through overtly sexualized, even pornographic, depictions of women. Ironically, just as one of the standard techniques of nineteenth-century anti-Catholic propaganda, such as the convent exposés that were among the first American best-selling books, was to show priests as sexual predators and young Protestant women as their victims, so too did some pro-Catholic novelists—broadly didactic though they usually were—eroticize their narratives by emphasizing the passionate dimensions of romance and the ways that women could figure as both pious and desirable. Such narrative tactics, perfected by Huntington, thus drew criticism from critics like Brownson, who would have preferred less provocative tales, but more especially from the *North American Review*, which deplored the exotic aristocratic trappings and aestheticism of *Lady Alice*. Even worse, in their view, was the matter of Huntington's steamy descriptions of men and women dancing and even participating in a frolic at the beach:

> Our author makes religion a perquisite of the aristocracy. . . . But follies of this class are a slight blemish compared with the thoroughly licentious character of the novel before us. Our reading in this department of literature is, indeed, very limited, both in extent and kind; but we doubt whether, in the whole of it, we have found so much that seems adapted to minister to the lowest passions, and to justify the loosest style of manners and opinions, as in this single volume. Every opportunity for a voluptuous picture of personal charms is eagerly embraced. The details of seduction and concubinage are described . . . with a minuteness of indecency, for which we know not how to give expression to our abhorrence. . . . The waltz is [Huntington's] favorite dance, and, in describing it, he takes good care to group around it every association of sensuality that can appertain to it.[34]

The complaint of the *North American Review* critic, like the anti-sentimental gender-jeremiads of Orestes Brownson, describes Huntington's literary failings as a function of his mishandling of gender identities and sexual situations. Moreover, by associating Catholicism with the privileged classes and because he "makes religion the perquisite of the aristocracy," Huntington also unsettles the usual view that impoverished immigrants, like the Irish American multitude, presented the most significant aspect of American Catholicism.

The critic went on to lament this shift, observing that in Huntington's work "there is but one characteristic of Romanism that we miss [in Huntington's novel],—its spirit of humane and tender regard for the poor and lowly. . . . Plebian worship and piety are beyond his conception."[35] Once again, the critical objections to Huntington's work turn on a paradox: Huntington's inclination to write novels about the leisure classes, featuring refined individuals whose affluence and taste are meant to be attractive and engaging for men and (especially) women readers, combined with the tendency of his novels to conjure a rather flexibly Catholic atmosphere in which theology is secondary to the romantic life of the protagonists. Unlike the reliably pious Catholic novels of contemporaries like Mary Ann Sadlier, which frequently delineate the humble yet devout world of the Irish and Irish immigrants to America, Huntington had discovered in Roman Catholicism a luxuriant aesthetic palette for expressing his rather progressive ideas about both religion and romance.

The substance of Huntington's next novel, *Alban: A Tale of the New World* (1851), is likewise instructive in this regard and extends the themes and issues elaborated in *Lady Alice* but allows them to play out in New England rather than in Europe. Exemplary as an early instance of New England local-color narrative and set in the fictional town of Yanmouth on the Connecticut coast, *Alban* tells a romantic story of the eponymous hero's journey from enervated Presbyterianism to robust happiness in Roman Catholic marriage. In what Huntington would later describe as "the mental history of a young Puritan," Alban Atherton himself (very much cut from the cloth of Huntington's biography) is the scion of a wealthy and prominent Connecticut family, one that has produced a succession of distinguished prominent ministers, along with a "President to Congress, Governors to States, Judges to the Supreme Bench, Generals to the army of the Revolution, and, brightest distinction of all, a 'Signer' to the Declaration."[36] Famous male progenitors notwithstanding, the novel's specific concern for women's role in religious life is apparent from the very first pages of the book, when the narrator, observing the Sabbath meeting in picturesque Yanmouth, laments that the New England churches are in spiritual decline.

Evidence of this declension may be found in the attitudes of its modern Protestant women, for whom "the downcast looks and formal composure of the females that marked the old congregations have disappeared." By contrast, Alban comes from sound New England stock, and he is brought up by righteous New England churchwomen. Noble specimens of American humanity, the Atherton women are benevolent and pious to a fault. They preside over their households and burnish their inherited good reputations, or as Huntington writes, "the family was always conspicuous for the piety of many of its female members," whose pious Christian memoirs "enriched the hagiography of New England." Feminine moral influence, in the shape of "maiden aunts," forms the basis for Alban's progress to adulthood, as "the virgin sister of his mother had watched over his childhood; the virgin sister of his father was to preside over his incipient manhood; for it is somewhere, we think, from twelve to sixteen that young Americans begin to be men."[37] Thanks in part to the example and ministrations of the good Presbyterian women, Alban Atherton grows up with an appreciation for Christian religion and also for the incipiently feminine dimensions of his own personality. During his boyhood, Alban appears as a normally active and energetic youngster, but with a difference that Huntington maps along gendered lines and describes as a "peculiarity of his position" in the family. As a male child raised mostly apart from the influence of sisters, "he had the sweet recollection of his aunt, and he knew the reserved tenderness of his mother; but apart from these influences, it was a hard, a boisterous, and a far from refined society in which he lived. Yet all agreed that Alb Atherton, though foremost in sports, *for innocence of manners and sweetness of temper was the girl of the school*."[38]

By the time Alban reaches college age and departs for Yale, he has been immersed in Christian evangelical culture and become the pride of his Presbyterian and Episcopal female relatives, all of whom admire his work on behalf of the "Tract cause" and his stature as "President of the Juvenile Foreign and Domestic Missionary Society, and Corresponding Secretary of the Babylon Auxiliary of the American Sunday-School Union."[39] But the galvanizing intellectual experience for Alban occurs while he is at Yale, during a literary society debate, for which the question of the day is "Does the probable increase of the Roman Catholic religion in the United States, by conversion and immigration, threaten the liberties of America?"[40] Thus primed for consideration of his nation's fate in light of Catholic evangelism and immigration, Alban begins his long journey toward religious conversion. Alban later meets the beautiful and chaste—and wealthy—Mary De Groot, with whom Alban falls in love. Raised by her Harvard-educated father as a Unitarian (her mother was an Irish Roman Catholic), Mary De Groot emerges as the strongest influence of all, inducing Alban to turn, with her, toward Catholic conversion. Much of the novel, ostensibly intended as a history of Alban, is given over to a lengthy description of the beautiful Mary's strong attraction to the religion of her Irish mother, rather than that of her father, who is described as a transcendentalist and thus by definition opposed to the traditionalism of the Roman Catholic church. Although her father was a substantial religious figure in his own right—"one of those splendid Unitarians whom their own circle nearly deified, and whose daring transcendentalism, although not accepted as sound by the body at large . . . was nevertheless listened to by them all with something of that reverence which the Orientals pay to the utterances of the insane"—her mother's Catholic faith ultimately carries the day for the young converts. As we observe this romantic arrangement, in which an attractive young man and woman who both have feminine traits adopt an Irish mother's religion, it is possible to conclude that Huntington is expressing certain dimensions of his own gendered self. But much more importantly, by creating a romance within a religious but feminized narrative, Huntington shapes his novel in ways that seem calculated for a print marketplace that itself was becoming increasingly influenced by female writers and readers.[41]

The version of Roman Catholicism presented by Huntington in *Alban* is notable for its association with luxurious but feminized domestic spaces. For instance, Alban's meeting with the De Groot patriarch, late in the novel, comes as a revelation and surprise for the genteel New Englander, who recognizes in the magnificent Fifth Avenue quarters and connoisseur's art collection a deeply pleasurable and yet paradoxically reserved sense of wealth and sex as foundations for the Catholic religiosity of his daughter Mary:

> Ideal busts of lovely female personifications, placed on pedestals of buhl or precious marble, flanked the doors; statues sparkled like snow in front of the lofty mirrors. Tables of buhl and pietra dura, cabinets of inlaid work, and etageres of rosewood and ebony, supported vases and other curious objects; here gleaming solitary, as if too rare to be otherwise; there grouped in orderly confusion; of porcelain, of Etruscan pottery, of half-gems, even of gold and silver. The wilderness of sumptuous seats astonished him. The corresponding richness of the window-curtains was enhanced by the style of the shutter-panelling in dark wood, and by the massive stone balconies seen between. A line of rich chandeliers consummated an effect which was not of mere splendor, for besides the grand effect of space, a certain simplicity presided over all. . . . While Alban yet stood admiring it (for he was afraid to sit on the rich chairs) the soft rustle of female garments made him turn. It was Mary's simple garb, and the same beautiful, ingenuous face, bright with friendship. (206)

In Mary De Groot, Alban recognizes the physical and moral manifestation of all that he has found lacking in the rigid Calvinism of his Presbyterian family and Yale seminary training: chaste purity commingled with exoticism, religious sincerity tempered and yet magnified by luxury and wealth.

Huntington's bold literary stroke, administered in an era dominated by virulent attacks on working-class Catholics and by widely held perceptions of young Catholic women as members of a servile and impoverished class of menial workers, uses the familiar techniques of regional fiction writing while infusing his romance with representations of Catholicism as sophisticated, feminine, and suitable for the monied classes. Constructed according to the conventions of New England local-color narrative, the spiritual biography of Alban the "young Puritan," whose austere yet benevolent Protestant female relatives take on such work as Christianizing the local Mohegan Indians, shows him turning away from the sensual privations and threadbare gentility of his family's provincial Calvinist legacy. Eschewing his own religious legacy thus allows him happily to be attracted to Mary De Groot, and in so doing he strives zealously not so much to conform with religious doctrine as to enjoy the colors of her money and the comforts of her Catholic luxury.

The pleasures of Roman Catholicism are thus knit into a narrative relationship with pleasures of the flesh that Huntington had focused on in his previous novel, *Lady Alice*, to which American reviewers had responded so harshly. His latest novel produced a similar reaction, scandalizing the anonymous reviewer for the *Southern Literary Messenger*, who pronounced himself utterly shocked that a reputable New York publisher like George P. Putnam would allow his imprint to be associated with *Alban* and the "flagrant immodesty" of Huntington's writing. Along with the repetition of criticisms on the basis of immodesty, though, what is most telling in the reviewer's remarks about Huntington is his conclusion about religious fiction—"theological novels are generally dull"—combined with his grudging admission that Huntington's romance is salacious but not boring: "For although Mr. Huntington is dry as an Oxford Tract wherever he is decent, there is some piquancy in other passages where he gives play to his very impure imagination. Where he is proper he is stupid, and where he is not stupid, he is marvelously improper." But once again, in spite of this grudging admiration, Huntington's frank sexual implications summon the wrath of the reviewer, who asserts that *Alban* is a book whose unseemly qualities surpass even the productions of Lord Byron or George Sand. Anxious about the deleterious effects of such works, the reviewer insists: "We would not think of placing the novels of George Sand in the hands of a young female friend." Further, he writes, "There have been other writers of the class dangerous, who are 'tabooed' in good society. But the author of *Alban* has left them all behind. The little colporteurs of the devil who furtively sell yellow-covered romances at every street corner, have nothing secreted in their baskets, so utterly vile and abominable as [Huntington's] fictions."[42]

There is much to be said about this reviewer's lacerating critique of Huntington, including his concern about the salacious European literary tradition represented by Sand and Byron and his patronizing defense of women novel readers. But perhaps most revealing is his vivid citation of the urban pornography vendors who "furtively sell yellow-covered romances at every street corner." It is intriguing to consider this reviewer's gimlet-eyed assessment of the chaotic and increasingly profitable nineteenth-century print marketplace, in which high-minded professional literary men writing for the intellectual magazines are always several steps behind the purveyors of pulp fiction and other dangerous reading materials.[43] From the perspective of cultural gatekeepers like this non-Catholic anonymous reviewer for the *Southern Literary Messenger*, but also from the vantage point of Catholic conservatives like Orestes Brownson, Mary Anne Sadlier, Isaac Hecker, and John Hassard, activist writers who were vigilant about what they saw as the dangers of mass-print culture in nineteenth-century America, there is an obvious tension between popular reading culture's religious and sensational dimensions. It is they for whom the literary freedom exercised by Huntington, even as it claimed strong religious principles, represented a profound cultural disruption and an existential threat to Catholic norms of behavior. In the reviewer's critique and dismissal of *Alban*, a raw and important cultural paradox is exposed: the tension between the evangelical potential of popular religious books and the moral damage that popular books, in the hands of immoral or misguided authors, could inflict.

His reception among Catholic readers was considerably more positive, even as Huntington's brief but very productive career as a Catholic novelist concluded with the publication of *Rosemary, or Life and Death: A Tale of Our Own Time* (1860), an intricately plotted romance centering on the life of a talented young sculptor, Rory O'Morra. It appears that *Rosemary* was about as popular among readers as *Lady Alice*, and the novel garnered a positive review from Orestes Brownson, who was relieved to announce that although the novel dealt with the affluent classes of New York City, the story nevertheless retained its proper moral bearings. Catholics who opened a novel like this, the crowning achievement of Huntington's career, wrote Brownson, "may read *Rosemary* without fear of having their modesty, or their prudery shocked." In creating *Rosemary*,

Brownson went on, Huntington had attained the status of being "one of the first literary men of the country, and decidedly the first purely literary man Catholics in the United States can boast." Later in his review, Brownson reflected on Huntington's accomplishments as a way of appraising the overall state of American Catholic fiction in 1860:

> Let us see if we have literary taste and American feeling enough to sustain him; for it is only through a common language and a genuine American literature that the variety of races and nationalities of which our Catholic population is composed, can be moulded into a uniform whole, with common sympathies and true brotherly feelings as a people. If *Rosemary* does not meet a wide circulation and become popular with our Catholic public, we shall despair of a Catholic American literature, and advise our literary men . . . to throw down the pen, and take up the shovel and the hoe. Hitherto no literary work from an American pen has met with what can be called a moderate success in our Catholic community. Our booksellers drive a fair business in Bibles, Prayer-Books, and school-books, but scarcely a book of any other description,—no purely literary work, pays. . . . With this indifference to intellectual and literary culture how are we to meet the objections every day brought against our holy religion?[44]

Huntington's *Rosemary* sold moderately well and was reprinted, despite its length and its extremely complex plot, although it never attained the kind of wide readership that Brownson knew would be necessary in order for a book of Catholic fiction to have made a significant intervention into the national religious conversation. Still, in Brownson's estimation, Huntington's work was of sufficiently high quality that it could be recommended to all readers on the basis of its religious dimensions and its artistic achievement. But how to solve a more significant problem outlined by Brownson: that of the American Catholic "indifference to intellectual and literary culture"?

Perhaps even more important than the popularity of a Catholic novel like *Rosemary*—or the particulars of its labyrinthine romantic plot—is the candor with which Huntington expresses his larger aims as a religious fiction writer. In an aside to the reader, he differentiates his own work from that of the writer of ordinary devotional books: "We have not undertaken to talk like a prayer-book, in order to prove that we may be read with profit. [*Rosemary*] is not a prayer-book, but a story written expressly to win the attention of those who will read nothing but stories, and sensational ones at that; and if we succeed in adding to the species that literary merit in which most specimens that we have seen are notably deficient, we shall be content." Here, Huntington had arrived at the firm conviction that Catholic religion was a suitable theme for his novels, but not if its teachings interfered with its attainments as literary art. Whatever the shortcomings of Huntington's work as a fiction writer—and there is no avoiding the judgment that a reading of his novels today shows that they lack the depth and expressive power of his better-known contemporaries—he made a number of important, even visionary, statements about how serious literary artists should deal with religion in their work.[45]

Near the end of his life (he died of tuberculosis in 1862), Huntington arrived at conclusions about Catholic fiction that were both clear-minded and prescient. In an unpublished review manuscript intended for the pages of the *Catholic World* and probably composed just before the 1860 publication of *Rosemary*, Huntington confronted directly what he called "one of the living questions" facing Catholic fiction—the seemingly intractable problems facing a Catholic literary practice that aspired to be both popular among large cohorts of readers while at the same remaining time true to its religious principles. He asked, "Can romantic fiction be imbued with Catholic faith and morality, so as to serve the interests of religion? Where this question is resolved in the negative, another arises: Can Catholics write romantic fiction as a simple art-creation? In other words, if Romance cannot be Catholicised, is it lawful for Christians?" These queries go directly to the heart of criticisms of popular writing that both Brownson and Hecker had been voicing for a generation, and Huntington's answer to these criticisms is surprisingly affirmative, both about the value of fiction itself and about the possibility of Catholic fiction. With a statement that Brownson might have found troubling, Huntington voices his sincere appreciation of fiction as a genre amenable to the highest artistry: "The love of fiction is a universal passion. Being the imitation of human life, fiction belongs to the great class of the poetic arts: it is impossible to deny its legitimacy without at the same time impugning that of sculpture, painting, music and poetry; of the wonders of architecture." At this point in his argument, however, Huntington turns to a remarkable dismissal of didacticism in religious fiction, in which he anticipates developments in American modernist fiction that would not occur for nearly half a century.[46]

The major problems with most Catholic writing of the day, according to Huntington, were associated with its preoccupation with doctrine and its inability to delight: "The failure of the controversial novel is essentially inartistic. Its failure does not at arise at all from the want of charm in modern Catholic life, which is, on the contrary, the most beautiful thing that exists, and the only thing that is divinely beautiful and thoroughly pathetic. . . . The failure, we repeat of the controversial novel arises from not confining itself to its proper sphere, which is to create the beautiful imitation of real human life, not to convince, not to refute even the most real and the most lamentable human errors." With these brief, clear-minded remarks from a professional man of letters and a faithful Catholic, Huntington provided his generation's most incisive critique of religious fiction, Catholic or otherwise. Willard Thorp rightly points out that *Rosemary*, for all of its faults as an overly complex and mordant novel written when the author was himself seriously ill from tuberculosis, conveys its religious themes with considerable subtlety: "As in his other novels, Huntington manages to keep the Catholic rationale of the action before his readers without resorting to tract-like passages, exhortations, or sermons."[47] Modern readers, as Huntington was beginning to understand, were becoming more sophisticated in their literary tastes and could no longer be presumed to be passive consumers of heavy-handed religious instruction.

Even more remarkably, Huntington in the same unpublished review advances a theory of how religious fiction might be constructed so as to provide inspiration for the faithful. Not only could romantic fiction be amenable to Catholic values, he argues, but because of its embrace of both natural and supernatural realms, "the Catholic novel, ideally considered, is the highest, truest and most beautiful species of romantic fiction, and . . . ought to commend itself not only to Catholics, but to all other readers." Using the example of Walter Scott's novels, which were written by a non-Catholic and which did not intend to promote Catholic religion and yet had the effect in England of reviving interest in Roman Catholicism, Huntington makes a case that "those are not necessarily the best Catholic novels, which are written by Catholics who set out with the intention of writing novels of a Catholic kind . . . on the contrary, some of the best Catholic novels (in our sense of the word) have been written by non-Catholics, or at least without any design on the part of the writers of doing what they did":

> I define a Catholic novel as one that represents human life, in the present or in past ages, as interpenetrated by the supernatural element im-

> parted to it by the Catholic faith. This is the way [Sir Walter] Scott came to be, in effect, a Catholic fictionist: he described human life as it was in the ages of faith, in the ages when Europe was Catholic, when society rested on the supernatural basis of Christianity; and being learned in antiquities and at the same time an appreciative artist, he could not but describe it on the whole truly; and describing it truly, his work was unconsciously Catholic; relatively to a Protestant public, to a fallen society, he rendered a fascinating picture of a Catholic age, the more effectual because unintended and unsuspected.[48]

In citing Scott as a significant (albeit unintended) voice for Catholicism, Huntington had reached an important conclusion about the function of literature as a vehicle for religion.

While devotional publications such as missals, Bibles, catechisms, and Sunday school readers would continue to serve as a lucrative staple of Catholic publishers during the later nineteenth and early twentieth century, those same publishers never succeeded in creating anything even remotely like what antebellum critics like Brownson and his colleagues had proposed: a Catholic American literature. All of which is not to say that Roman Catholicism disappeared from American writing. To the contrary, American writers of that time frequently created works that were centered on cultures of Roman Catholicism, but there was a steep decline in their reliance on the controversial and evangelical rhetoric that had grown out of the various Christian tract publications of the earlier nineteenth century and had infused much Catholic fiction of the antebellum period. As the century proceeded, American novelists with an interest in Catholicism applied their evangelism with a lighter touch and sometimes avoided religious controversy, even as they persisted in associating the world of Catholicism with the discourse of gender.

The Baltimore novelist Anna Hanson McKenney Dorsey (1815–96) was a contemporary of Jedediah Huntington's but one whose career as a Catholic writer was much longer and more prolific (she wrote poetry, numerous stories and sketches, and about thirty novels).[49] A comparison of their novels demonstrates the substantial difference between their approaches to creating fiction for Catholic readers, while illustrating some of the diverse ways used by nineteenth-century American writers to describe faith in fiction. Whereas Huntington typically averted his gaze from the experiences of Catholic immigrants in the nineteenth-century melting pot in favor of a much more sophisticated and cosmopolitan set of literary characters, Dorsey published numerous works of fiction that spoke directly to the lived religious experience of ordinary people, especially that of the Catholic immigrants to the United States who formed the largest portion of her readers. As such, Dorsey's work is a helpful index to the kind of fiction published in serial and book form and in periodicals such as *Ave Maria*, the *Boston Pilot*, and the *Catholic World.* Dorsey's fiction writing was a major staple of American Catholic literature both before and after the Civil War, and she had an especially prolific period during the years 1848–60. Over those twelve years, Dorsey serialized six novels in the *Boston Pilot* (owned by the noted Catholic publisher Patrick Donahoe), a widely circulated paper that is estimated to have had about 100,000 subscribers by 1860. Because of the commercial leverage provided her by newspaper publication, and with the possible exception of Mary Ann Sadlier, Anna Dorsey was likely the most widely read American Catholic writer of her generation.[50]

Born in 1815 to an American navy chaplain and Chloe Lanigan, Anna McKenney converted to Catholicism in 1840 along with her husband, Lorenzo Dorsey. Her successful first novel, *The Student of Blenheim Forest* (1847), was followed by four decades of fiction writing aimed to serve the purposes of American Catholicism. Clarity of religious purpose, combined with the practical and economic advantages of professional authorship that emerged during the midcentury, allowed her the opportunity of writing fiction full time. Addressing her friend and editor of the Catholic periodical *Ave Maria*, Father Daniel E. Hudson, CSC,[51] in the introduction to her next novel, *The Oriental Pearl; or the Catholic Immigrants* (1848), a tale featuring sympathetic depictions of German American immigrant farmers, Dorsey makes clear that her fiction finds its motivation in an explicit desire to foster Catholic religious ideas: "The object of this little narrative," she wrote, "is to eulogize and assist in sustaining the great Catholic truth, that confidence in the mercy and wisdom of God is the best preservative from temptation and despair, amid the tearful and sudden mutations of life."[52] This is a novel that, in the view of the historian Jay Dolan, is typical of American Catholic literary culture at midcentury when "Catholic fiction . . . idealized poverty and resignation to God's will."[53] Much in the tradition of Huntington, Anna Dorsey viewed herself essentially as a designated promoter of the organized Roman Catholic Church in the United States, a perspective that she apparently passed along to her daughter, Ella Lorraine Dorsey (1853–1935), a professional author and advocate for Catholicism.[54] Catholicism is not incidental to Anna Dorsey's fiction and, to an even greater degree than the luxuriant romances of Huntington, her protagonists are given over to displays of religious piety and devotion, which are undiminished by hardships and dangers on the frontier. Prolific and popular like her Catholic novelist contemporaries Mary Ann Sadlier and Christian Reid (Frances Fisher Tiernan), Dorsey shared with Reid the admiration and friendship of a young archbishop from Baltimore, James Gibbons, who personally presented editions of her novels to the pope during a visit to Rome. Dorsey's fiction often had international reach, with German translations of *The Oriental Pearl* making their way into the hands of the Austrian royal family of Franz Josef. Later in her long career, after she had become a prominent novelist and short-story writer in Catholic periodicals, she also drew the admiring attention of the English Cardinal Nicholas Wiseman and the Earl of Shrewsbury.[55]

Although less adventurous in style and subject than the New England patrician Jedediah Huntington and less doctrinaire in her Catholic evangelism than the Irish immigrant novelist Mary Anne Sadlier, the moderate devotional flavor of Anna Dorsey's melodramatic novels situates her as a middle-class benchmark for American Catholic novelists. She is also a transitional figure in a number of respects. Because of her long career as a writer, it is possible to trace in her works a movement away from overt didacticism toward a self-conscious attempt to entertain her younger readers in a lively way. As she wrote to Father Daniel Hudson at the University of Notre Dame in 1878, "Young Catholics need relaxation and amusement. If this is not provided inside the Church, they will seek it on forbidden grounds. The Mediaeval literature and the lives of the Saints will hold the attention of some readers, but in order to hold the attention of the young I have endeavoured to blend religion with strong dramatic incident." In the same letter to Hudson, Dorsey remarked that she felt herself alone in the world of Catholic fiction, especially since the once-prolific Mary Anne Sadlier was now publishing so infrequently. Five years later, Dorsey expressed once again her view that the best sort of religious fiction had the ability to balance piety and morality with a light touch: "Healthy reading combining amusement as well as information and a Catholic spirit without . . . sentimental piety is what a person in the Church needs."[56]

In his study of Anna Dorsey's role in Irish American literary culture, David Jerome Callon has observed that Dorsey was twice awarded medals by Pope Leo XIII in recognition of her religious writings and that during a very long career her novels were widely read by upwardly mobile

Catholics in the United States: "In the latter half of the nineteenth century, one could hardly grow up in a literate Catholic household and not encounter a Dorsey novel as part of one's formation."[57] Dorsey's fiction was especially sensitive to women readers, and the popularity of her work must have been strongly connected to her deft adaptation of sentimental themes that had proven to be the hallmark of so many of the best-selling novels of her generation. Callon states that women readers were important for Dorsey's literary project, noting that in novels like *Nora Brady's Vow* (1869), "the future of Catholicity in America in many ways rested squarely on the shoulders of working women."[58] The adaptation to and conformity with popular literary trends, which were crucial for her commercial success, were nevertheless applied within moral limits, as she wrote to Baltimore Archbishop James Gibbons during the prime of her career: "I take comfort in the thought that governed by a high motive, I have declined *liberal* offers which have been made by secular—no, that is not the word—godless publishers, to write sensational romances to suit the times. I could have done it, but refrained from purely conscientious considerations." This kind of self-conscious restraint provides ample evidence of Dorsey's awareness of her position in commercial print culture, just as her friendship with Gibbons demonstrates her close relationship with Catholic clergy who understood the power of novels to sway religious opinions. Less audacious than Jedediah Huntington in her treatment of romantic subject matter, Dorsey's was a literary career that would be conducted with a self-conscious piety that served to keep her writing always within the bounds of religious propriety. Dorsey thus resigned herself to writing for the Catholic press exclusively, even if it meant perennial wrangling with the Irish Catholic publishers who, she repeatedly complained to Father Hudson, as a rule were sharp dealers and cheats who consistently fleeced her of her publishing royalties.[59]

One of Dorsey's most intriguing novels demonstrates her application of Catholic themes to a framework of sentimental writing aimed primarily at an audience of women. *Coaina, The Rose of the Algonquins* (1867) is constructed as a true-historical narrative in which Dorsey creates a doubly idealized Virgin Mary figure who bears all the religious signs of the Madonna combined with those of a chaste and beautiful Native American maiden. This hybrid characterization presents her readers with a double displacement of Dorsey's invented Catholicism. First, by setting her tale on the Canadian frontier, far from the East Coast of the United States, Dorsey lays aside the problems associated with urban assimilation by the Irish. Second, Dorsey redirects the matter of Catholic ethnicity in the United States (usually associated with Irish and German identities) by nominating a Native American woman as her protagonist. Published just after the Civil War but set in 1838 near Montreal, Dorsey's *Coaina* creates an unusual blend of narrative effects by combining the perfected religious self of Mary with the imagined perfections of an indigenous Native American woman, whose piety is knit together with the experience of displacement and exile in ways that must have seemed familiar to the immigrant Irish Catholics.

In exploiting the popular American interest in Indian life—which was most intense during the years of their active removal from tribal lands—Dorsey was far from alone among American novelists, but in *Coaina* her application of Catholic devotional writing to the historical romance of Native life marks a significant development in the American tradition of novels about the indigenous peoples of America. For well-known authors like James Fenimore Cooper, Lydia Maria Child, Herman Melville, Mark Twain, and scores of other nineteenth-century writers who recognized the dramatic potential of tales set on the American frontier, Native American life (and its relationship to non-Native American culture) held extraordinary resources for the fictive imagination and ripe opportunities for the print marketplace.[60] Academic historians contributed as well to the documentation of a Native American Catholic presence in America and the creation of a market for fiction with Native American themes. For example, Dorsey's Algonquins play an important role in Francis Parkman's *The Jesuits in North America* (also published in 1867), a classic history that stands as the most important historical statement of the period in terms of describing the range of seventeenth-century Catholic missionary activities. Whereas Parkman's account centered on the failure of early Jesuit missions to win converts among the Native American population, and their related failure to spread Catholic religion across the continent, Dorsey turns in *Coaina* to an idealization of the Catholicized remnant of the Jesuit missions, insisting on the existence of the highest Christian virtue and feminine piety in the exemplary person of Coaina.[61]

Dorsey's narrative in *Coaina* crafts a fictional elaboration of a historical incident related by her acquaintance, Bishop Armand Charbonnel, a Sulpician missionary serving as bishop of Toronto who had returned from exploits in Canada to work in a seminary in Dorsey's home city of Baltimore.[62] According to Dorsey's introductory note to *Coaina*, the true story of the pious young Indian girl derived from Charbonnel's recounting of the events at her home in Baltimore and from a brief manuscript, signed by Charbonnel himself, which appears at the end of the novel as proof of both the tale's historical accuracy and its sanction by Church authority. It is apparent, however, that Dorsey has provided a substantial fictional supplement to the historical account. In an introductory note, after acknowledging her debt to Father Charbonnel and citing her own reading of the *History of the Indian Missions in North America*, Dorsey allows that "the names of the characters—except Coaina's—are fictitious, and so are some of the trivial incidents and embellishments."[63] Perched athwart the attractions of fictional narrative and the pressure to provide a "true" account from authorized Catholic sources and testimony, Dorsey frames her text as the "history of Coaina." Even so, her embrace of historical accuracy must be interpreted alongside her ability to present religious orthodoxy according to trends in the literary marketplace. Avoiding an arid retelling of Canadian missionary history, Dorsey shows an obvious sensitivity to developments in contemporary print culture by constructing a tale that includes a range of popular literary themes and techniques: pious femininity, local color and provincial setting, moral didacticism, and the sentimental motifs of slow death and unrecognized virtue.

Coaina opens with a richly picturesque description of Algonquin life in Canada, with an emphasis on the lingering tension between residual traditions of pagan belief and the newly adopted beliefs of Catholic Christianity. At all points, though, the Indians are represented as essentially sincere, rustic characters who have for the most part turned to the fervent religion of the missionaries. But the Natives are not simply Westernized; as Dorsey notes, "Religion has stripped these children of the forest of none of their simple enjoyments or innocent customs; . . . it has transformed them from worshippers of idols to worshippers and adorers of the one true God. . . . Thus, by an easy transition it became a strange but devout pleasure to these primitive people, instead of offering sacrifice and libations to the great Wendigoes (giants), to propitiate [God's] favor whenever they engaged in any enterprise of hardship and peril and to invoke the protection of the Blessed Virgin, and ask the assistance of the prayers of the saints."[64] Following the tendency of local-color fiction to dwell on the subtleties of landscape, Dorsey introduces her characters only after providing a pastoral view of the Algonquin village, with its central shrine to "Our Blessed Lady of the forest," as it stood in 1838:

> Something is in progress in and around the rustic chapel, into which the slanting rays of an August sun fall in trembling showers of gold through the quivering leaves, which indicates an approaching festival. Young Indian lads, with blossom-laden boughs from the forest, with trailing vines bedight with flowers of tropical hues, with baskets of mosses, with branches of wild roses, with great clusters of golden-rod, asters and the wood anemone, with wicker cages containing birds, with clusters of wild grapes, still clinging in purple richness to the graceful vines, and garlands of ground myrtle, glowing with thousands of coral berries, were grouped here and there around the chapel doors . . . their low converse interrupted now and then by a burst of innocent laughter, which sounded in sweet accord with the rustling of leaves overhead, the wild notes of the caged birds, the drowsy hum of bees, and the distant murmurs of the dancing waters of the lake.[65]

It is difficult to imagine a landscape more different from the ones inhabited by the vast majority of American Catholics in the post–Civil War era, and yet Dorsey, like Huntington before her, chose to locate her tendentious vision of American Catholicism at the farthest provincial reaches of the nation. Opting to privilege aesthetic viewpoints drawn from local-color narrative, decades before the more general turn to realism and naturalism in the closing years of the century, Dorsey encodes Catholicism with the idiom of a frontier picturesque: exotically historical, humbly virtuous, and ultimately unthreatening.

Physical descriptions of the ill-fated and yet virtuous and beautiful young Coaina only serve to reinforce these patterns of Catholic representation: "Her skin was like the pale, amber-colored satin; her forehead low and broad; her nose straight, with thin expanded nostrils; her mouth, small and exquisitely formed, was rendered more beautiful by the white, even teeth, which the slightest smile revealed; her eyes full of intelligence and spirit." Coaina (an Algonquin name for "Catherine"), it soon becomes clear, is meant to be understood as an iconic Madonna; or, as Dorsey explains, "Coaina was very beautiful, and I am particular in describing her, because her young life was so fully offered to Him who fashioned and formed her wonderful loveliness, and modelled so perfectly on the virtues of her, whom . . . He had predestined to be the Mother of His Divine Son.[66] In drawing links between morality and physiognomy, Dorsey adopts a popular and familiar Dickensian technique, one that Harriet Beecher Stowe, for example, had used to great effect in *Uncle Tom's Cabin*, in which characters' appearance and racial traits can be related quite easily to their moral stature. Moreover, Dorsey's idealized young woman combines Madonna-like virtue and beauty with a Christ-like capacity for suffering.

Some indication of the relation between sincere piety and the capacity for suffering emerges in the early part of Dorsey's tale, when an old Algonquin tribesman describes his grandmother's part in the execution of a French Jesuit: "She was a Huron. When he was dying under the torture; when his fingers and thumbs were cut off; when he was pierced with lighted splinters, torn with scourges and hacked with hatches, many of the prisoners around him, who had likewise been tortured all night, begged him for baptism. . . . She had helped torture him, but she was a woman. She gave him [some wet cornstalks and] he signed the cross in the air over their heads with the maize, and so they were baptized with the dews of heaven and his own blood."[67]

Dorsey thus presents her Catholic readers with a beleaguered Madonna Coaina, whose impeccably virtuous reputation—embellished by six months of training in a Montreal convent—is eventually destroyed by a termagant aunt and a jealous female cousin. After spreading rumors that Coaina has been seeing lovers other than the young and Christian Algonquin chief who has been chosen for her, her scheming aunt tricks her into being kidnapped by a rival Iroquois chief, who attempts to seduce the heroine. Dorsey uses the opportunity of this capture to show once again the ardor of Coaina's Catholic piety, but also to separate Coaina's Catholicism from accusations of idolatry, one of the primary charges leveled against Catholicism in anti-Catholic fiction. Refusing the pagan chief's sexual advances and crushing the Iroquois ceremonial pipe beneath her heel, Coaina piously announces, "In the name of Christ, I trample on all idolatry!" thereby answering that typical attack on Catholicism with the voice of a martyr while symbolically reaffirming her virginity and her ideal Christian femininity.[68]

Eventually, the Catholic community realizes Coaina's intact virtue, but not before she undergoes a ritual humiliation before her community, who had previously seen her as a flawless example of devotion, a woman "who was, after the Blessed Virgin, the purest model of womanly and Christian virtues they knew on earth." When Coaina becomes subject to the most punishing slander and community sanction, Dorsey as novelist appears to be adjusting her narrative to reflect important literary precursors, especially the numerous sentimental fictions that featured passively tearful heroines in moments of social crisis. But there is an even more explicit link between the beset heroine of Dorsey's now-forgotten tale and well-known fictional characters like Hester Prynne of Nathaniel Hawthorne's *The Scarlet Letter*, a link that shows yet another enterprising way that authors of nineteenth-century Catholic fiction patterned their work according to popular literary trends.[69] Huntington and Dorsey availed themselves of a range of local-color devices as they crafted their representations of Catholicism for American women, but in *Coaina*, Dorsey's heroine treads the same path of juridical examination, harsh sentencing, and public scorn that Hester Prynne experienced. The following passage shows immediately the way that Dorsey has adapted, for Catholic purposes, the opening scene of Hawthorne's novel, in which the adulterous Hester undergoes the harsh and punitive gaze of her (Puritan) community:

> Coaina was sentenced:
>
> "*First.* To live alone in a hut adjoining her aunt's lodge.
>
> "*Second.* To perform such servile offices for her as might be needed.
>
> "*Third.* To seek and encourage no intercourse with the young people of the mission.
>
> "*Fourth.* To wear the garb of a public penitent.
>
> "*Fifth.* To have her hair cut close, and wear a coarse veil.
>
> "*Sixth* (and most terrible of all to her). She was to be deprived of the sacraments, and was forbidden to enter the chapel, but was to kneel in her penitential dress at the door, during the celebration of all the sacred rites, offices and ceremonies of the Church, with the title of hypocrite printed in large letters and suspended upon her breast."
>
> On the same day she was invested in her robes of humiliation. Crowned with ignominy, she knelt at the door of that chapel of which she was the angel, receiving, instead of homage, the cold sneers, the cruel whispers, the open condemnation, the mockery and scorn of all who passed her by.[70]

Once again, nineteenth-century Catholic writing can be seen to absorb and refashion certain themes and representations from popular fiction, revamping the Puritan historical themes of Hawthorne's fiction in order to promote Catholic piety. Significantly, Dorsey's tranquil frontier scenes of rustic Catholicism, in which all the motifs of local-color writing have been evident, also evolve into the even more familiar Hawthornian theme of community surveillance—and religious control—of female sexual morality and agency.

Coaina is eventually vindicated and restored to her status as tribal Madonna, a status strengthened by the assistance she provides to her community during the ravages of a cholera epidemic. Her experience of humiliation and unwavering piety lead her not to the marriage for which she had been destined but to a life of prayer and solitary contemplation. Rejecting the hand of the handsome young Algonquin chief, Coaina claims: "I have found my true and constant Lover, He not only comforted and sustained me, when all else failed, and the world abandoned me; but He also suffered and died for me." When Coaina herself later succumbs to cholera, her role as martyr and exemplary Catholic woman becomes clear; just before her death, her religious devotion remains undiminished and all of her desires are sublimated into a pious regard for her "Divine Guest," to whom she cries, "Come sweet Jesus, it is now that my wedding feasts are about to begin, never to end."[71] In a sense, this kind of portrayal of Catholic femininity responds to the kinds of concerns about American womanhood that Orestes Brownson had voiced in his own reviews of nineteenth-century fiction and critiques of popular culture. The imagined terrain of American Catholicism, in Dorsey's narrative hands, shifts sharply away from domestic life, urban tensions, and sexual dangers of the sort often recounted in anti-Catholic fiction of the day. Whereas the novels of Jedediah Huntington presented the attractions of Catholicism as a luxuriant and sophisticated alternative to genteel Protestantism, Dorsey's complex heroine appears as a secular nun, a profoundly feminized martyr figure drawn according to the deepest patterns of American frontier mythology and representations of Indian culture as spiritually innocent. However, what ties Huntington and Dorsey together in a mutual project of American religious portrayal—their turn to history and to the national margins made legible through local-color writing—works to sustain a literary tradition in which Catholicism can be presented as a set of ideal aesthetic qualities and moral virtues (especially the virtues of women) so long as they exist in an exotic and yet tangential relation to contemporary culture and the perceived centers of national life.

Even though their fiction was written with the bold ambition of advancing Roman Catholic religion in the United States, Huntington and Dorsey shared with non-Catholic writers a preoccupation about the appropriate place of women as readers and writers in an unprecedented American culture of print. Historians of the decades following the Revolution have frequently been impressed by the new representations of women in the early republic and the antebellum period, representations that focused on the importance of American women as moral and religious stewards of their families. Inscribed as key elements in the transition from province to nation, the politically restorative and morally corrective force of idealized bourgeois women, as depicted in countless novels, essays, and images, quickly became a fulcrum for elevating and codifying the new republican ethos of virtue, character, and order. In very basic terms, and as many historians have observed, to the extent that women had primary responsibility for the conduct of their children and supervised their moral education within the home, they were performing the significant work of educating virtuous citizens for the new republic. Conspiring with steady developments like the rise in popularity of the sentimental novel and a labor field increasingly split along gender lines, rapidly improving print distribution networks and production methods during the first half of the nineteenth century amplified the national fascination with a variety of female roles—as seduced lover, chaste ingénue, oppressed slave, idealized mother, honest laborer, or even a writer of fiction—in American culture. Accounts of this important development vary widely in their emphases and ideological grounding, but there is no question that the study of nineteenth-century fiction will continue to be tied to the problems and pressures of gender identity and the role of women as a strong social force in the new republican nation. We may now include Catholic writers as full participants in the American conversation about women's part in its political, literary, and religious culture.[72]

Idealized representations of women during the antebellum period, given extra momentum by the political upheavals during the Revolutionary and early national periods, exerted tectonic social force within both secular and religious spheres. Writers advocating American Catholicism in fiction, as with the numerous scribes working for and among Protestant groups, turned their literary lights directly on the role of women as agents of religious morality and virtue. In part, this practice extended the political desire to suggest models for republican womanhood and for domestic life for women in the increasingly distinct women's sphere produced by industrialization, urbanization, and other factors. It is well known that women during these years increased in importance as readers and purchasers of popular books.[73] Added to all of these factors, antebellum Catholic modes of devotionalism (habits of prayer and piety) maintained a "feminine character" until late in the century. This devotionalism, which manifested itself through church attendance figures and participation in religious festivals and other rituals, lends some support to Jay Dolan's assertion that in nineteenth-century America, "devotional Catholicism was especially attractive to women." Similarly, attempts by religious novelists to promote appealing representations of Catholic women during this period are a logical response to women's centrality in Catholic devotion and their increasing importance within the print marketplace as a whole.[74]

The most successful literary efforts at representing a Catholic America during the nineteenth century were consistently framed in terms of women's lives and directed mostly at women readers, even though it is incontestably obvious that male dominance of the ecclesiastical structures of the Catholic church have to this day remained firmly in place. Inevitably, men controlled many developments in literary matters as well; the influence held by male religious activists like Brownson, Hecker, and Hassard gives ample support to views of literary Catholicism as an inherently male-dominated aspect of the religion itself. Yet all of these important male literary figures understood—and sometimes criticized harshly—the centrality of femininity and women to the practices of piety, prayer, and social fabric of Catholicism. Unsurprisingly, a careful reading of their work, and the work of the novelists treated in this chapter, reveals a large amount of anxiety about the role of women in American Catholicism. Of even more interest is their tendency to show a deep sensitivity to the fact and potential usefulness of women as producers and consumers of popular books during a period of immense growth and transformation in American print culture. Therefore, it is clear that without a precise concept of the ways that Catholic women were described in these books, it is impossible to compile an accurate account of Catholic literary culture within the context of a broader American literary history, a history whose past constructions have tended to elide or to marginalize Catholic writing.

Finally, religious novelists of the nineteenth and early twentieth centuries should be considered not in isolation from one another but in consistent dialogue, and as elements of what should more properly be described as a culture of literary Catholicism. Reinforcing this particular strain of religious literary culture, a network of publishers and editors contributed in significant ways to allowing these works to be disseminated.[75] Even more importantly, these novelists can be tied directly and indirectly to the other subjects of this book: Brownson was a friend of Jedediah Huntington's and reviewed his novels favorably; Hecker lent his support and encouragement to Anna Dorsey's fiction. All of them conducted their literary work with a conviction that the commercial print marketplace held tremendous evangelical promise for the advancement of Roman Catholicism.

As the nineteenth century unfolded, Roman Catholicism as expressed in American literature would show far fewer direct ties to the institutional church and would eventually become a more subtle presence in popular fiction according to models of what the literary critic Thomas J. Ferraro has organized under the rubric of "cultural Catholicism." This concept is essential for understanding the ways that religion seeps into an artistic or literary culture, for as Ferraro observes, cultural Catholicism "suggests the development and deployment of Catholic ways of knowing and habits of being outside the official precincts and sanction, if not the purview, of the Church."[76] Put another way, Roman Catholicism as represented in American literature did not disappear but instead declined as a program of self-conscious religious propaganda written exclusively by Church members. Deployment of Catholicism in harmony with "official precincts and sanction" had frequently been a concern of those nineteenth-century literary evangelists who implicitly took up Brownson's challenge to create a body of fictional narrative suitable for the great republic. At other times and places, however, and especially toward the turn of the century, literary Catholicism appeared in the work of American writers whose official relationship with the Church is tenuous at best but whose work bears the unmistakable moral and aesthetic marks of Catholicism. These legible signs are aspects of the "Catholic ways of knowing and habits of being" that Ferraro has in mind when he refers to cultures of Catholicism, and they are the signs that persist as an important residue in American literary culture by the early twentieth century.

Catholicism in American fiction has showed itself to be a viable set of narrative modes, even as the authors who eventually deployed its ways of knowing and habits of being outside or at the outermost margins of a relationship with the institutional church—one that had been an object of fear and loathing for much of the nineteenth century. The American Catholic mind—contested and reshaped as immigrant groups continued their renovation of demographic reality in their adopted nation—offered multiple perspectives in fiction during the late nineteenth and early twentieth century, even as the role of women in American Catholicism remained a consistent preoccupation of its writers, publicists, and even its priests. Prominent Catholic clergy in the United States, in some instances, appear to have been attuned to the religious narratives extant in the literary marketplace, and in at least one major example brought powerful themes from popular fiction into accord with the Catholic catechism itself, with notable results.

4

Sentimental Catechism

James Gibbons and Literary Devotionalism

Every impartial student of history is forced to admit that woman is indebted to the Catholic Church for the elevated status she enjoys today in family and social life.

James Gibbons, "Relative Condition" (1886)

Novels that addressed Christian religious experiences were an extremely important aspect of literary culture in the nineteenth century, but a broader view of religious writing is necessary in order to follow the ways that Roman Catholicism adapted itself to the literary tendencies of the period. Turning from analysis of fiction to consider a widely distributed catechism, this chapter follows another avenue of nineteenth-century sentimental literature and considers its relationship to Roman Catholicism by analyzing *Faith of Our Fathers: Being a Plain Exposition of the Church Founded by Our Lord Jesus Christ* (1876), written by the American Catholic missionary and bishop James Gibbons (1834–1921). Gibbons's catechism perpetuates the traditions of European Catholic sentimentality and devotionalism while borrowing from a variety of the newer versions of literary sentimentality found on the American scene.

As such, it is a prime example of religious writing produced in response to popular literary themes and yet adapted to specific Roman Catholic theological ends. A striking bodily consciousness lies at the heart of Gibbons's book, which follows the metaphorical contours of what the religious historian Ann Taves has described as a pious "household of faith."[1] In Gibbons's hands, this "household" is a fictive construct that allows the devoted Catholic to participate in a religious domestic scene in which Mother Church, Jesus the Spouse, and the infantilized believer perform a starkly physical version of sentimental domestic bliss.

For the purposes of developing the larger debates concerning nineteenth-century sentimental culture, Catholicism in America (and its encounter with Protestant hegemony) provides several important components: vast numbers of Catholics, who will read sentimental culture through the filter of Catholic teaching; a systematic missionary effort, which rapidly came to understand and to implement the power of mass-print culture in America; and finally a centuries-old post-Tridentine tradition of devotionalism, in both print and iconography, of bodily discourses.[2] The objections made by Orestes Brownson to sensational and sentimental texts, especially those written by and for women, are important evidence of how the most influential American Catholic intellectual of the period failed in significant ways to account for women's experiences of reading and religion. However, Brownson's reservations about the nineteenth-century culture of sentiment that James Gibbons adapted for his catechism should not prevent us from seeing the relationship between American Catholic writers and their responses to popular works inflected with sentimental themes.

Gibbons's *Faith of Our Fathers* shows the extent to which the popular sentimentalism of American mass-print culture, combined with a legacy of sentimentality drawn from European devotional writing, provided a textual method for negotiating tensions between American Catholic evangelical efforts and Protestant hegemony. Gibbons's creative and successful use of European and American models of religious/literary sentimentality, tempered by his personal experience as provincial missionary, points toward a better understanding of the ways and means by which the expression of Catholic dogma was conditioned by contemporary literary trends. In addition, the success of his catechism sheds brighter light on nineteenth-century Catholic literary culture and the ways that Catholic writers like Gibbons advanced their religious cause with an acute awareness of the commercial print marketplace and the sensibilities of ordinary American readers.

> The night I arrived in Wilmington, there was a torch-light procession of emancipated slaves, many of them now holding office and domineering over their former masters. If one can imagine an enormous crowd of negroes, most of whom were intoxicated, all of whom were waving torches in the blackness of the night, one can very easily imagine the first impressions of a new and very young Bishop.[3]

With this diary entry from 1868, a thirty-four-year-old Irish American Catholic bishop named James Gibbons marked the beginning of his missionary experience in North Carolina and started a process of evangelism in the Protestant South, with its smattering of Catholic residents. His work would culminate nearly a decade later in Baltimore with the publication of his popular and widely distributed Catholic catechism, a "manual of devotion" titled *Faith of Our Fathers* (1876). Thrust into an overwhelmingly rural state during one of the most difficult periods of Reconstruction,[4] Gibbons faced a challenging missionary project made even more daunting by his isolation from urban centers of Catholicism, an impoverished population that included large numbers of freed African American slaves, a new and completely untested state constitution (passed in January 1868), rampant crime statewide, and a tiny diocesan budget. Gibbons quickly understood the many obstacles for Catholic proselytizing in the postbellum American South. In particular Gibbons felt acutely the serious shortage of books of religious instruction that he might share with his small flock of faithful Catholics as well as with the innumerable prospective converts spread across the rural reaches of the state. As an itinerant bishop, he was learning through firsthand experience the importance of bringing prospective converts into immediate personal contact with Catholic teaching. At the same time he was realizing the difficulties of doing so solely through his preaching and that of his limited number of missionary priests.[5]

Other than the long-standing Catholic community of Baltimore and eastern Maryland, the census of Roman Catholics had always been low in the South, and especially in North Carolina. At the time of his appointment as bishop for North Carolina, there seem to have been less than a handful of priests at work in that region, and their primary charge was the estimated thousand or so Catholics spread across the state. Still, Gibbons was an energetic missionary to his small Carolinian flock. Commentary by a nineteenth-century historian of Catholicism gives a sense of the new responsibilities that the young bishop was shouldering: "[Gibbons] traveled night and day, and by all modes of conveyance, new and obsolete. His visitations were incessant. He knew all the adult Catholics in North Carolina personally and called them by name. He administered the sacraments in garrets and in the basements of houses, preached and lectured throughout, always ready and prepared for every emergency."[6]

Despite his zeal and energetic work among the faithful of North Carolina, by February 1869 Gibbons was already expressing his fears for the loss of faith among his widely dispersed flock. In a letter to his superior in Baltimore, Archbishop Martin Spalding, he reported that what truly was needed in the thinly populated provinces of the South were books of religious instruction, inexpensive catechisms outlining Catholic dogma in a simple way. Gibbons reached the conclusion that in order to overcome the problems of achieving an effective rural mission in North Carolina, "my one remedy is the circulation of books." Books alone, however, would be insufficient unless those made available to the faithful contained suitable Catholic doctrine. John Hassard, the prominent New York writer and editor of the *Catholic World*, had warned of this "drop of poison" only a few years before the appearance of Gibbons's remarkable catechism (see chap. 1): "We cannot afford to take it without also a corrective [of Catholic literature]. Little by little it will extinguish our fervor if it does not undermine our faith. . . . For the present, until we are far stronger, we cannot avoid the poison; let us be careful to take the antidote."[7] Although it is not certain that Gibbons was aware of these comments by Hassard, they are in keeping with numerous pronouncements made by Gibbons's hero, Orestes Brownson, in his published book reviews of the preceding decades. It is possible to imagine Gibbons reacting to this kind of literary summons, published in the leading Catholic intellectual journal of the day, when he began to conceive of a book that might remedy the stronger currents of American Protestant writing during the postbellum years.

James Gibbons had been assigned to his first significant church leadership position at an auspicious moment for Roman Catholic evangelism. Gibbons's early years in preparatory school and seminary during the 1840s and 1850s in Baltimore coincided with waves of Catholic immigration into the large and rapidly growing cities of the eastern seaboard (with accompanying Nativist antagonism against the immigrant Catholics, especially from the Know-Nothings in cities such as Baltimore). From an urban perspective, Gibbons would have seen the immense prospects for growth within the American Catholic Church and must have felt the intimidation of forces arrayed against Catholicism by even the more liberal and tolerant Protestants.[8] Gibbons's understanding of his missionary work, shaped and modified by his position as an evangelist for a minority religion, necessarily grew even more complicated because of changes occurring in Protestant culture in America during the period 1820 to 1875. During these years, when many northeastern Protestants were enacting a gradual transformation by moving from strict and conservative churches to much more liberal ones, the withering of a formerly rigorous Calvinism in America was matched by a corresponding social transformation. As cultural historian Ann Douglas has noted, during this period, "American culture seemed bent on establishing a perpetual Mother's Day,"[9] a widespread phenomenon for church members and clergy in which theological rigor gave way to more secular forms of religious instruction.

In Douglas's influential but controversial opinion, much of this secular "teaching" took the form of the popular novel or story (written largely by women) rather than the sermon or argumentative tract (traditionally written by men) and began from premises based on the value of matriarchal virtue. Yet, the literary impulse toward matriarchal virtue subsequently devolved into the literature of sentiment, what Leslie Fiedler had earlier lamented as a mere "Sentimental Love Religion" in which the "Pure Young Girl replaces Christ as the Savior."[10] Perhaps even more significant in this development is the way that sentimental themes constituted an aspect of evolving gender politics. As Nina Baym has shown in her study of nineteenth-century woman's fiction, "the story of young women discovering and asserting their powers, thereby wresting respect and recognition from a hostile and indifferent world, was immensely pleasurable to a huge number of American women."[11] And indeed, Gibbons's catechism demonstrates very well his comprehension of this aspect of nineteenth-century writing for women.

In an age that continued to cherish high hopes for the power and efficacy of orderly domesticity while relegating ministerial roles and status (at least within Protestantism) to levels similar to those of the middle-class woman, Gibbons conceived of his own Catholic ministry through the prism of American sentimental culture and its European analogues. Paradoxically, though, Gibbons's initiation into his first serious provincial assignment in North Carolina had also provided him with a troubling vision of dysfunctional (and decidedly unsentimental) social structures: subversive nocturnal street-corner politics, intemperate and threatening black bodies, disordered families, and collapsed hierarchies of master and slave. For a man endowed with a decidedly "domesticated," even sentimentalized, moral compass, such disorderly events were anathema, contravening his vision (later formalized in his published catechism) of a harmonious Roman Catholic religious community, one operating at every level according to the paradigm of a pious and cohesive bourgeois family.

Despite the moral anxiety accompanying his first glimpse of the profound social and familial disruptions of North Carolina during the Reconstruction years, Gibbons would later find reason to believe that many of the faithful "children" of his flock were truly exemplifying and embodying the domestic ideal, one expressed vividly within the largely, but not exclusively, Protestant tradition of domestic fiction. Like other sentimental writers, Gibbons's notion of ideal domestic space (inflected spiritually through religion or materially in daily living) implicitly defined and articulated itself through discourses of class status and racial identity. As in nineteenth-century fiction with antislavery themes, race becomes an important conceptual locus of sentimental morality. And while Gibbons's later catechistic writing is largely silent on the matter of racial difference and Reconstruction-era politics, his presumption of the necessity for intact nuclear families would, at least conceptually, preclude many blacks from his efforts to domesticate the Catholic religious sphere promulgated in his *Faith of Our Fathers*. Although he would remain a lifelong believer in the inferiority of negroes, by 1872, when he left North Carolina for new assignments in Richmond and Baltimore, Gibbons shifted his cultural gaze away from racial politics altogether, apparently preferring to nurture a less disempowered group of social outsiders.

Leaving his southern mission for new responsibilities in Baltimore, he praised his growing flock of predominantly white Carolinian believers, remarking in his final sermon in the small Wilmington church that "I would be doing violence to my own feelings, if now on the eve of leaving you, I did not bear testimony to yr. unfeigned piety which always edified me; to your spirit of obedience which consoled me, & to your unbounded liberality which encouraged me in my difficulties. In future times, the best tribute of praise I can pay to other congregations, is to tell them they are as pious, as docile & as generous as the people of Wilmington."[12] He admires in his congregation some of the same traits (piety, docility, generosity) one might find in Harriet Beecher Stowe's descriptions of Little Eva and Uncle Tom in her sentimental masterpiece, *Uncle Tom's Cabin.* Like Gibbons's Carolina Catholics, Stowe's best characters endure patiently through all adversity; exemplars of ideal Christianity, they demonstrate the guiding principles of gentleness, piety, obedience, liberality, docility, and generosity—all values crucial to the spiritualized subservience and ritual passivities necessary within a sentimentalized family structure. Linking him rhetorically to Christian writers like Stowe, his sermon's moral barometer shows the extent to which Gibbons follows a theological path not unlike that of his Protestant ministerial peers, who were "increasingly joining middle-class women and becoming part of a special subculture" that conjoined the interests of clergy and those Christian women.[13]

Like many an evangelical minister stationed in a remote provincial mission, Gibbons viewed his Catholic followers, and especially the newly converted believers, as children in need of guidance by a parental figure, by a father-priest in Gibbons's case. He is explicit on this point as well in his final sermon to the church in Wilmington: "Like an absent father who reads with nervous hands the letters of his devoted children far away, I will watch you my spiritual children, for such you still remain."[14] From the perspective of his imminent departure, then, the historical narrative of his southern mission has taken on a decidedly domesticating trajectory. A number of the "bodily bonds" of sentimental culture appear in the narrative: from the harshly disrupted families of riotous and newly freed slaves, to the Catholic missionary's invocation of the nurturing Mother Church, and finally to the reinforcement of family imperatives, the social organization of faithful bodies as written into his final exhortation. The progress of his provincial missionary work along this trajectory thus builds a sentimental correspondence between the solidification of domestic values and the growth of a church.

Later, his theory of spiritual/material domestication would become central to a number of chapters in *Faith of Our Fathers,* in which he would also maintain that the Catholic home should not only be a space for a certain kind of family but also that the household itself could and should be a place suitable for study and worship. Indeed, Gibbons continued, "not only are Catholics instructed in church on Sundays but they are exhorted to peruse the Word of God, and *manuals of devotion*, at home."[15] Here again Gibbons adapts some of the domestic themes of nineteenth-century woman's fiction for the purposes of Catholic evangelism, while showing that women's power could predominate in both home and church. As Nina Baym has asserted, the extended reach of domesticity in American literature of this period was a sign of women's expanding social influence: "The domestic ideal meant not that woman was to be sequestered from the world in her place at home but that everybody was to be placed in the home, and hence home and the world would become one."[16] That a feminized church and home overlap extensively in Gibbons's catechism surely explains some of its appeal among nineteenth-century readers.

Blurred boundaries between home and church played a prominent role in many nineteenth-century sentimental fictions, such as Susan Warner's hugely popular *The Wide, Wide World.* In this runaway best-seller, published in 1850 and reprinted through the end of the nineteenth century, tearful and sobbing female sympathy supplies the emotional accompaniment to a didactic tale featuring Protestant female self-denial and the forceful construction of a rigid domestic sphere. Both home and church provide representational spaces for a range of sentimental experiences. For example, when Warner's heroine asks for permission to go alone to church for a second time on Sunday, not because she must but "for pleasure," she provides a link between domesticity, tearful sentimentality, and the traditionally sacred space of the church, sinking into the pew "with a curious feeling of quiet and of being at home."[17] The tears of domestic sentiment find their way into the church as well, while the church provides a respite from the peculiar discipline of domesticity: "She was no sooner seated . . . than leaning forward as much as possible to screen herself from observation, bending her head upon her knees, she burst into an agony of tears. It was a great relief to be able to weep freely; at home she was afraid of being seen or heard or questioned; now she was alone and free, and she poured out her very heart in weeping."[18] Enacting the devotional procedure modeled by women writers of the day and later endorsed by Gibbons, the heroine of *The Wide, Wide World* shows fictional women rehearsing sentimental impulses within the mutually disciplinary spaces of home and church, deploying emotional expression according to the overlapping rituals of domesticity and liturgy.

Much of the emphasis that Gibbons places on domestic devotions and the construction of a sentimentalized "household of faith" follows the European Catholic model of sentimentalized devotional texts.[19] In particular, *Faith of Our Fathers* resembles the contemporary devotional writings of the English hymnist and popular theologian Frederick W. Faber in its emotional appeals to the faithful and its reliance on the model of a filial bond between believer and divinities. Along with Alphonsus Ligouri, a devotional writer and missionary to rural Italians, Faber's writings exemplified the nineteenth-century Euro-American Catholic "resurgence of affective spirituality."[20] Drawing on the earlier, more restrained lay devotions of the German bishop Francis de Sales, seventeenth-century author of *Introduction to the Devout Life*, both Ligouri and Faber (a Catholic convert and missionary priest among the Irish poor in London) wrote popular and widely disseminated devotional books that drew upon the highly emotional style associated with ultramontane Catholicism. Specifically, as Ann Taves has observed, they "used meditations to form affective bonds between human and supernatural beings."[21] Writing in his popular *All for Jesus; or, the Easy Ways of Divine Love* (1854), for example, Faber outlined his version of the Catholic spiritual household: "The blessed Lord God is our Father; His dear Majesty is our affair; our Elder Brother created us, and has our own nature; Mary is our mother; the angels and saints are all the kindest and most familiar of brothers; so we go up and down stairs, in and our, and to each other's rooms, just as it may be; there is no constraint about it at all."[22] With precursors such as Faber, then, Gibbons was able to frame his own catechism with reference on the one hand to American sentimental writing but on the other to the vivid traditions of affective piety drawn from European Catholicism.[23]

In addition to its discussion of the infallibility of popes (which had recently been written into Catholic dogma during the Vatican Council of 1870), the sacrifice of the mass, the invocation of saints, and the Catholic sacraments, *Faith of Our Fathers* is fundamentally a book centered on, and invested heavily in, the figure of the nurturing Mother in all her manifestations. Gibbons would remain convinced of the centrality of maternal nurture in the development of pious Catholic youth, and he wrote frequently on the subject in later years, notably in an historical essay about women and the Christian tradition published in 1886 in the *American Catholic Quarterly Review*: "On [Christian mothers] devolves the duty of directing the susceptible and pliant minds of their children, and of instilling into their youthful hearts the principle of piety." In a similar way, and adapting in specifically Catholic terms a long-standing iconographic tradition within medieval Christianity, Gibbons's catechism relies heavily on maternal metaphors and symbolism, dating from at least the twelfth century, in which the fleshly symbols of female breasts, the mouth, and menstrual blood depict catechistic instruction by the Church as a distinctively maternal outpouring of love.[24]

The catechism conjoins the gendered discourse of medieval Christianity with nineteenth-century literary gestures that address and privilege the social and moral world of women. By enlisting powerful vectors in American mass-print culture, especially those in popular sentimental novels and poetry, Gibbons encoded his catechism with sentimental/domestic values central to Protestant culture, while at the same time attempting to show the congruence of Catholic teaching with similar notions of family morality centered on ideal womanhood. In so doing Gibbons was participating in a broader, transatlantic conversation about women's social role. As with similar developments in Europe during the century following the French Revolution, modern motherhood and the corresponding cults of domesticity functioned in the processes that gradually replaced aristocratic female role models with conceptions of ideal republican womanhood. Noting that the idealized maternal figure in nineteenth-century France, for example, had been influenced by economic development that caused much of women's productive labor to become unnecessary, Bonnie G. Smith has suggested that the "sweet vocation" of motherhood resulted directly from the separation of women's sphere of work from that of men during the Industrial Revolution. Consequently, beginning in the early part of the nineteenth century in Europe, "the home could serve the political purpose of highlighting aristocratic wantonness. Sexually faithful and morally upright, the inhabitants of the middle-class home laid their claims to social leadership."[25] Gibbons's devotionalism follows the general outlines of changing European domestic ideology, as exemplified by the changing role of women in France, while blending that ideology with the emotionalism of Faber and the literary cross-currents of American sentimental themes.

Clearly, Gibbons was no religious or literary isolationist. Paul Giles has argued convincingly that a consideration of Gibbons's career as a whole shows him seeking to integrate Catholic ideas into American culture and politics well into the twentieth century (with his support first of the Knights of Labor and later of the labor union movement). Like other Catholic leaders, Gibbons understood that maximum growth in the Catholic Church would never occur in America so long as the

Church relied strictly on maintaining its role as "a refuge for impoverished immigrants seeking escape from the pressures of harsh Protestant materialism."[26]

Faith of Our Fathers appeared just prior to Gibbons's 1877 appointment as archbishop of Baltimore, in the midst of a wave of revivalism among nineteenth-century American Catholics. These revivals mirrored in many ways Protestant movements during the same period and also played a significant role in the dissemination of religious books in the maturing American publishing industry.[27] Jay Dolan speculates that the primary means of distribution for Gibbons's catechism was through the parish mission movements, otherwise known as Catholic revival meetings. The immense popularity of these meetings provided a large market for both religious devotional material and Catholic books. Through this marketing and distribution method, whereby priests served as drummers for book sales, Gibbons managed to produce and sell one of the more popular books on religion in the English language.[28] But the development of Gibbons's catechism should not be understood only as a contribution to the culture of the religious revival or as a product solely of urban Catholic necessity. Having worked as a missionary in some of the least hospitable parts of the United States for a Catholic evangelist, Gibbons viewed the publication of *Faith of Our Fathers* as the distillation of his religious teaching, modified somewhat by his familiarity with popular literature and informed by his experience of Catholic missionary work in the American South.

The text of *Faith of Our Fathers*, whose "object is to present in plain and practical form an *exposition* and *vindication* of the Catholic Church," readily shows its purpose and design as a missionary document. Not only does it intend a statement of catechism for the Catholic faithful, but it also aims to evangelize the "separate brethren" who follow Protestant teachings and who refer to Scripture primarily, or exclusively, as a source of spiritual authority.[29] From a thematic perspective, though, the reference to "separate brethren" aligns the text with discourses relating to sentimentality and domesticity. At the most obvious level, the notion of "separate brethren" attaches itself to the time-honored parable of the Prodigal Son, an important paradigm for the construction of the ideal Christian family and a staple in the repertoire of popular late nineteenth-century Protestant urban preachers. One such was the fabled evangelist Dwight L. Moody, of whom Gibbons would have been well aware, as Moody was then approaching the crest of his international popularity and influence.[30] But the invocation of family space in Gibbons's catechism does not end simply with his use of this familiar parable or with general notions about the "family feeling" that accompanies membership in a religious denomination. The entire text is permeated with suggestions that the Catholic Church is a kind of mother, one who will function maternally and protectively for her children, the faithful. So it is that the rhetorical space that Gibbons constructs through his catechism persistently follows the contours of the modern nuclear family, the model of domesticity that had become so familiar from the popular fiction of the period.

Faith of Our Fathers situates itself in both defensive and evangelical rhetorical postures. It suggests to the reader that its publication may mark the first occasion of an accurate account of Catholicism being printed in America; self-consciously, Gibbons logs the importance of his catechism in the history of religious publishing in the United States. As Gibbons puts it, in tactile terms: "Perhaps this is the first time in your life that you have *handled* a book in which the doctrines of the Catholic Church are expounded *by one of her own sons*."[31] In a single stroke, then, Gibbons indicates that his writing will function not only as a theological document to be read but as a physical artifact and concrete manifestation of authoritative Catholic dogma. Text here becomes instant holy relic, forming a part of the distinctively Catholic habitus of sentimentality.[32] This catechism, Gibbons insists, will be seen by others and "handled"—and not merely studied. This reassuringly tactile mode, in which the book becomes a material part of the domestic sphere for Catholics and potential converts, supports the theme of domesticity by emerging from a religious teacher who is more than just a priest—he is "one of her [the Catholic church's] own sons," a man who understands both religious teaching and discourses of domesticity.

Faith of Our Fathers was aimed at educating the faithful and evangelizing a nominally Protestant country, the work that Gibbons would call a missionary effort in America. For one thing, it is a catechism that conforms to Protestant expectations about the centrality and importance of scripture itself in religious pedagogy.[33] Gibbons recognizes this relationship to scripture on the part of the "separated faithful . . . who generally accept the Scripture as the only source of authority in religious matters" and so documents his catechism with copious footnoted scriptural references, much in the same way a formal Protestant sermon or religious treatise would be documented.[34] Gibbons's sense of the importance of scriptural documentation and his sensitivity to Protestant concerns came not only from efforts to convert Protestants but also from his missionary experience of having preached in a number of Methodist and Episcopal churches in North Carolina, as well as in court houses, public halls, and Masonic lodge rooms.[35] As one of his biographers has noted, Gibbons's preaching in unusual missionary contexts and circumstances gave him ample exposure to non-Catholic thought during the period of his mission in the American provinces: "Although the circumstances were sometimes strange, nonetheless the bishop gleaned a wealth of experience and knowledge of the non-Catholic mentality from these visits through rural Virginia and North Carolina and it was this enrichment of mind that gave to his first and most famous book, *Faith of Our Fathers*, an approach and a tone which rapidly made it the vade mecum of so many non-Catholic Americans whose interest had been aroused in the doctrine of the Catholic Church."[36] The biographer may here be somewhat optimistic about the actual audience of *Faith of Our Fathers*, because he provides no evidence to support his premise that non-Catholics were reading this book in substantial numbers. It is clear, though, from a reading of his catechism that Gibbons adapted much from Protestant religious discourse that he would later use in framing his lessons.

Gibbons weaves into his catechism an astonishingly sensitive grasp of American secular and religious history. But such historical consciousness and sensitivity, if surprising in their effectiveness, also emerge predictably from standard accounts of other missionary endeavors in which secular and sacred content of the mission are paramount for its success at conversion or religious colonization. What separates this particular catechism from others, though, is its extraordinary rewriting of and immersion in the cultural dynamics of sentimentality and domesticity. As he announces his intentions to revise misguided histories of the Catholic Church, Gibbons offers a reminder that "it is to me a duty and a labor of love to speak the truth concerning my venerable Mother, so much maligned in our days."[37] Religious mission overlaps with sentimental domestic ideology at such points in his text, merging spirituality with social formations and responsibilities within an appropriately moral and nuclear family. Referring to the popular representations of Catholicism in America found in "pamphlets," "romances," "the [Protestant] pulpit," and in "a large portion of the press,"[38] Gibbons turns the usual anthropomorphic female identity of the Roman Catholic Church into a fiction partaking of both domesticity and sentimentality in their nineteenth-century popularized iterations. "I have imbibed her [the Catholic Church's] doctrines with my mother's milk" announces Gibbons in his introduction to the catechism, continuing his opening figuration as a child of the faith, within a household ruled benevolently by a nurturing Mother of vast proportions.

The role of Jesus, within a Catholic understanding of the Trinity, Gibbons domesticates and sentimentalizes just as he sentimentalizes the function of the Church/Mother. While the problematic Holy Ghost will be assigned the role of moral guide for the Church/Mother, who "in her teachings [will be] preserved from error by the special guidance of the Holy Ghost," the figure of Jesus takes on a crucial persona in the construction of the spiritual family.[39] In the fictive sentimental world of Gibbons's catechism, Jesus is figured as an ideal Husband—he is the "Divine Spouse" of the Church/Mother, one who devotedly burnishes her image as exemplar and source of Christian morality.[40] Always working in service to the maternal, domesticating force, "[Jesus] was pleased to stamp upon His Church certain shining marks, by which every sincere inquirer could easily recognize her as His only Spouse."[41] As parents, Jesus and the Catholic Church represent a welcoming family, even for the poor, who may "find refuge in the bosom of their true Mother, the Catholic Church, who, like her Divine Spouse, claims the afflicted as her most cherished inheritance."[42] "Walking in the footsteps of her Divine Spouse," the Church/Mother "never repudiates sinners nor cuts them off from her fold," always striving "to weaken their passions, if she cannot altogether reform their lives";[43] with the assistance of Jesus, the Divine Spouse, familial order will be maintained against the onslaught of "double warfare, one foreign, the other domestic—in foreign war against Paganism and infidelity; in civil strife against heresy and schism fomented by her own rebellious children."[44]

At times in *Faith of Our Fathers*, sentimentality merges with the sensational and the lurid, but always with the intent of more powerfully re-inscribing the inevitable virtue of the Church/Mother. In Gibbons's chapter 6 ("Perpetuity of the Church"), the Catholic Church once again is written into a bridal role; enduring a tide of heresy and Protestantism over the centuries, "she" remains permanently youthful and maternal: "Is not her very survival the greatest of prodigies? If you beheld some fair bride with all the weaknesses of humanity upon her, cast into prison and starved and trampled upon, hacked and tortured, her blood sprinkled upon her dungeon walls, and if you saw her again emerging from her prison, in all the bloom and freshness of youth, and surviving for years and centuries beyond the span of human life, continuing to be the joyful mother of children, would not you call that scene a miracle?"[45] Through virtue, then, the young woman representing the Catholic Church, the sentimental and sensational narrative survives intact. Although chastened by her experiences of bodily mutilation, even the gravest difficulties do "not bring a wrinkle on the fair brow of the Church."[46]

The narrative trajectory of much nineteenth-century sentimental literature leads directly to the deathbed, a traditional locus for the tears of profound emotional experience, as well as for the vivid display of suffering and pain. At the same time, however, Philip Fisher reminds us that sentimental deathbed scenes are primarily scenes concerned with loss, instead of death, and that "to use death as the central image for suffering is to strengthen the passivity within sentimentality."[47] In creating a sentimentalized domestic model of Catholicism for his readers, Gibbons—who proved himself throughout his career to be a reactionary antifeminist who strongly favored traditional roles for women[48]—emphasizes the protective capacities and the wisdom of the Church/Mother; always her advice "mothers" her children, guiding them spiritually and in practical matters. Gibbons's chapter 7 ("Infallible Authority of the Church") features such a wise and culturally informed mother, one conscious of the potential snares awaiting the unsuspecting Catholic believer, so that "neither Mormons nor Millerites, nor the advocates of free love or of women's rights, so called, find any recruits in the Catholic Church. She will never suffer her children to be ensnared by these impostures, how specious so ever they may be."[49] Mormonism figures as the obvious enemy of conventional domesticity, and Mormons come in for criticism at several points in the text, and always in relation to the blatant threat to nuclear families that their agitation in favor of "abominable polygamy" represented.[50]

Reassuring potential converts and sensing the importance and credibility of his maternal construct, Gibbons systematically details the correspondence between Catholicism and nourishing motherhood. "In her nourishment there is no poison; in her doctrines there is no guile" he concludes, after recounting the tale of "a recently converted Minister of the Protestant Church," for whom conversion had been tantamount to a kind of childhood regression. According to Gibbons, the former Protestant "became as a little child, and rushed like a lisping babe into the arms of [his] Mother."[51] And no children will be refused entry into the maternal sphere of the Church, an infantilizing space in which sentiment for the nurturing mother conflates with sentiment for a nurturing faith in the mind of the believer. The argument for faith is not theological here, but strictly in the register of sentimentality and gendered morality: "If she is our Mother, where is our love and obedience? When the infant seeks nourishment at its mother's breast it does not analyze its food. When it receives instructions from its mother's lips it never doubts, but instinctively believes. When the mother stretches forth her hand the child follows unhesitatingly. The Christian should have for his spiritual Mother all the simplicity, all the credulity, I might say, of a child, guided by the instincts of faith."[52] The inseparability of religious faith and domestic sentiment is reinforced vigorously at moments like this in the text, in passages that borrow heavily from the idiom of sentimentality as expressed through women's fiction, another popular nineteenth-century genre in which women enacted a familial role of moral guide, object of desire, and center of bodily and cultural nourishments. Although the final arbiter of power in sentimentalized depictions of domestic space remains the patriarch (father, priest, bishop, pope, God the Father), since "even in every well-ordered family, domestic peace requires that someone preside," the Church/Mother will provide the coherence for the pious Catholic family.[53]

Given the ambivalent preoccupation with the cult of true womanhood manifest throughout Gibbons's book, it comes as little surprise that by far the most lengthy of the thirty-one chapters in *Faith of Our Fathers* is chapter 14, "Is It Lawful to Honor the Blessed Virgin Mary As a Saint, to Invoke Her As an Intercessor, and to Imitate Her As a Model?" It is here that Gibbons presents his reader with a mediating figure between the Church/Mother and the earthly woman. His teaching about Mary, the mother of Jesus, shades over into a lesson in domestic values supported in part by sentimentalized notions of Mary from popular literary texts. The mother of Jesus, the "Divine Spouse," has been honored and admired by Protestants as well as Catholics. In opposition to Protestant teaching that would deny the perpetual virginity of Mary, but citing William Wordsworth, he notes that Mary "united in her person 'a mother's love with maiden purity'" and suggests that Mary's chaste maternity not only indicates her honorable position but also, paradoxically for ordinary humans, the advantages of imitating the Mother of God, whom the Canon of the Mass "speaks of . . . as the 'glorious *ever Virgin*.'"[54] Turning to historical narratives, Gibbons recalls that veneration of the "Blessed

Virgin Mary" has been intrinsic to the cultural discourse of American settlement and colonization as well: "It is interesting to us to know that the Immaculate conception of Mary has been interwoven in the earliest history of our own country. The ship that first bore Columbus to America was named Mary of the Conception. This celebrated navigator gave the same name to the second island which he discovered. The chapel erected in Quebec, when that city was founded in the early part of the seventeenth century, was dedicated to God under the invocation of Mary Immaculate."[55] By thus reclaiming colonial American history for Catholics, Gibbons enacts a displacement of Protestant hegemony in the field of history while suggesting that American history showed the early imprint of Mary, a prototypical sentimental figure.[56]

Along with this kind of historical displacement of Protestantism in his crucial chapter on Mary, Gibbons also deploys the tactic of excerpting various British and American secular or Protestant writers, such as Wordsworth. The effect of these references and citations is to illustrate the high esteem that Euro-American culture has shown for Mary, and by extension the model of domesticity that she epitomizes, and so to shape his argument to the concerns of potential converts from Protestantism or secularism. Disturbed by the failure of many Protestants to pay proper tribute to Mary, Gibbons appeals to their Anglo-American sentiments about ideal motherhood, observing that "the piety of a mother usually sheds additional lustre on the son, and the halo that surrounds her brow is reflected upon his."[57] Citing Oliver Wendell Holmes as "one who made little profession of Christianity" but who still understood the sanctity of Mary, Gibbons inserts some verse from Holmes that illustrates the currency of even nonreligious accounts of Mary's honorable spiritual position:

> Is thy name Mary, Maiden fair?
> Such should, methinks, its music be.
> The sweetest name that mortals bear,
> Were best befitting thee.
> And she to whom it once was given
> *Was half of earth and half of heaven.*[58]

A range of selections from nineteenth-century poetry is excerpted in Gibbons's chapter 14 in support of the Catholic view of Mary, and it is one of the few chapters in which this device of quoting secular poetry is used.[59]

Gibbons provides scriptural citations in support of this part of the catechism, as in the other chapters, but the mustering of these literary quotations, along with the length of the chapter itself, indicates that Gibbons knew that this lesson, with its alignment of formal teaching about the Blessed Virgin Mary with secular teaching through literature, held the potential to strike deeply into cultural traditions and discourses about the role of women. Elsewhere, Gibbons quotes an entire sonnet from William Wordsworth, claiming that appreciation for Mary knows no denominational bounds. Wordsworth, the icon of elite European culture, "though not nurtured within the bosom of the Catholic Church, conceives a true appreciation of Mary's incomparable holiness in the following lines."[60] And on the American historical front, Gibbons points to George Washington as a figure venerated by Americans, thus refuting the Protestant claim that the Catholic veneration of Mary constituted a transgression of true Christian faith while maintaining that "no one was ever suspected of loving his country and her institutions less because of his reverencing Washington, so no one can reasonably suppose that our homage to God is diminished by our fostering reverence for Mary."[61] Although wishing to avoid "being accused in certain quarters of Mariolatry,"[62] Gibbons returns repeatedly to the centrality of Mary within the Catholic experience, emphasizing sentimentally her prototypical motherhood. "Never does Jesus appear to us so amiable and endearing as when we see Him nestled in the arms of His Mother," that is, the feminine spiritual and moral role model who embodies all the highest forms and religious force of the ideal virginal woman, the domestic angel "who never tarnished her white robe of innocence by the least defilement."[63]

In Gibbons's catechistic model, the Catholic faithful and converts to Catholicism become, in a variety of ways, members of the family of Mary, the prototypical domestic angel and sentimental heroine: "She it was that wiped the stains from His brow when taken down from the cross. Now we are the brothers of Jesus. He is not ashamed, says the Apostle, to call us His brethren. Neither is Mary ashamed to call us her children by adoption."[64] As a prototype of the sentimentalized Mother in popular culture, representations of Mary are found by Gibbons in both likely and unlikely places. The "fireside poets" Holmes and Henry Wadsworth Longfellow (in two substantial excerpts from his *Golden Legend*) are included in this chapter on Mary, indicating once again the congruence of theme and tone between the sentimentality of Gibbons's catechism and mainstream Protestant writers.[65] The depiction of Mary embellishes the existing image of motherly purity then current in American culture, in which "that hallowing influence which a good mother wields over the Christian family" had become a kind of sentimental fetish.[66] The sources Gibbons uses show his consistent preoccupation with this attempt at alignment of Catholic teaching with the cultural values of his potential converts, even to the point of reaching far beyond the Catholic pale. Always alert for incipient conversions and sympathies among the popular writers of American mass-print culture, Gibbons notes that "*though not of the household of the faith,* Edgar A[llan] Poe did not disdain to invoke Our Lady's intercession, and to acknowledge the influence of her patronage in heaven"[67] in his poem "A Hymn," which Gibbons quotes in full, except for a missing title.[68]

The differences in the conceptions of piety between Gibbons, with his highly sentimentalized and always welcoming "household of the faith," and Poe, author of morally questionable and domestically troubled tales such as "The Fall of the House of Usher," would seem to have militated against Gibbons's use of Poe in the context of a catechism. Nevertheless, the fact that he did so indicates the lengths to which Gibbons was willing to travel in order to incorporate secular versions of domesticity and womanhood under the rubric of Catholicism, in which Mary functions "as a beautiful pattern to those that are called to rule a household."[69] As with the previous examples of Gibbons's appropriation of writings from Longfellow, Holmes, and Wordsworth, the recruitment of non-Catholic writers for the Catholic missionary cause allows his catechism to show points of contact between the differing religions and thereby open a space for potential conversions. By Americanizing the European traditions of ultramontane devotional sentimentality in this way, Gibbons in effect customized his text for an audience that comprised both immigrant and American-born readers. While acknowledging and praising the Catholicity (if not the Catholicism) of these non-Catholic literary figures, Gibbons situates himself as both literary critic and priest, but one who praises American sentimental writing for its highest religious impulses while offering a detailed handbook for full conversion and belief.

Both literally and figuratively, Mary embodies the prototypical model of sentiment for the female adherents of sentimental culture, who will also then strive to enact her virtuous behavior as they supervise domestic life, as well as the increasing "domestication of death."[70] "Consolation literature," that peculiar but extremely popular nineteenth-century genre that Douglas extended to include "obituary poems and memoirs, mourner's manuals, prayer guidebooks, hymns, and books about heaven," can be extended even farther in the case of the Gibbons catechism.[71] In discussing the importance of prayer for the dead and dying in his chapter "Purgatory and Prayers for the Dead," Gibbons related the following scene in which a daughter (not a Catholic) was attending to the bodily needs of a terminally ill parent: "Many an anxious day and sleepless night did she watch at his bedside. She moistened the parched lips, and cooled the fevered brow, and raised the drooping head on its pillow. Every change in the patient brought a corresponding sunshine or gloom to her heart."[72] As is so often the case with Gibbons's catechism, the emotional impact of religious experience is its most important characteristic and its most marketable aspect for a readership saturated in popular sentimental literature. More than simply offering a lesson in charity and prayer for the infirm, this passage, with its allusion to moistening "parched lips," "rais[ing] the drooping head on its pillow," and the fine gradations of pain for the sufferer, whose fluctuations engender "corresponding sunshine or gloom," has a powerful affinity with death scenes in popular sentimental fiction, in which the suffering victim is attended by a household saint endowed with a repertoire of pious Christian gestures and sentiments.

The ultimate chapter of *Faith of Our Fathers* ("Matrimony") recapitulates the ethos of the catechism as a whole and reinforces the importance of the Catholic nuclear family's spiritual and social structure. And it concludes by suggesting that although Protestants have done rather well in terms of a low divorce rate, preserving the sacred integrity of matrimony, nevertheless their success in that regard was likely "in no small measure due to the presence among them of the Catholic religion, which exercises a beneficial influence even over those who are outside the pale of her communion, like the sun, whose benignant light and heat are felt even in those secluded spots which his rays can but obliquely and dimly penetrate."[73] Mormonism, Gibbons's archenemy of conventional domesticity and the monogamous family, once again comes in for a harsh critique in this chapter. Because Mormons espouse polygamy, they represent for him the antithesis of pious womanhood. As Gibbons insists, the very fabric of the family, the household of the faith, is placed in jeopardy by polygamy, which "cannot fail to be a perpetual source of family discord and feuds,"[74] and threatens the sanctity of marriage, not to mention the sanctification of woman that marriage in its nineteenth-century iteration represented: "Christian wives and mothers, what gratitude you owe to the Catholic Church for the honorable position you hold in society! If you are no longer regarded as the slave, but the equal of your husband; if you are no longer the toy of his caprice and liable to be discarded at any moment, like the women of Turkey and mormon wives of Utah; but if you are recognized as the mistress and queen of your household, you owe your emancipation to the Church."[75] By contrast, Gibbon's particular brand of Roman Catholicism provides the essential moral guidelines not just for instructing women about their roles in church and family but also for delineating the limited sphere in which Catholic women's religious and social power could be expressed.

"A good book is a powerful ally," Gibbons would later remark in reflecting on his missionary experience, noting that one of the most powerful methods of winning and keeping converts was the development of mission libraries in the rural areas of North Carolina.[76] Gibbons's cultural positioning of *Faith of Our Fathers* is evident in his introduction to the catechism when he notes various misrepresentations of Catholicism that have been disseminated by Protestants through mass-market books, beginning with John Foxe's *Book of Martyrs*[77] and continuing to the popular pulp fiction published during his own historical moment in the years following the American Civil War. Like his fellow Catholic bookmen from a previous generation, John Hassard, Isaac Hecker, and Orestes Brownson, Gibbons was concerned about the harmful effects of promiscuous reading and offered suggestions for less dangerous texts such as Catholic devotional literature. Singling out such works as *Following of Christ* by Thomas à Kempis, *Christian Perfection* by "Rodriguez," and the writings of St. Francis de Sales as nonscriptural works that might be read with profit by Catholics and prospective converts, Gibbons frames his recommendations for Catholic study by pointing out the sentiments that these works engender in the reader. Much of the appeal of Catholic writers will thus be not strictly doctrinal, but emotional: "You will search in vain outside the Catholic Church for writers comparable in unction and healthy piety to such as I have mentioned. Compare, for instance, *Kempis* with *Bunyan's Pilgrim's Progress*, or *Butler's Lives of the Saints* with *Foxe's Book of Martyrs*. You lay down *Butler* with a sweet and tranquil devotion, and with a profound admiration for the Christian heroes whose lives he records; while you put aside *Foxe* with a troubled mind and a sense of vindictive bitterness."[78] Noting the increasing power of ever more widely circulated books, Gibbons concludes that it is no longer enough for Catholics to refute the inaccuracies and blasphemies of the anti-Catholic press. "The antidote often comes too late to counteract the poison" when it comes to the contentious arena of modern publishing, and the misrepresentations in easily reproducible image and text, "the most powerful vehicles of information."[79]

Gibbons's nurturing Mother (the Catholic Church) had been under assault in the American print marketplace, and the arms raised against her are brandished under the auspices of the burgeoning popular press: "She is assailed in romances of the stamp of María Monk and in pictorial papers."[80] Moreover: "In a large portion of the press, and in pamphlets, and especially in the pulpit, which should be consecrated to truth and charity, she is the victim of the foulest slanders. Upon her fair and heavenly brow her enemies put a hideous mask, and in that guise they exhibit her to the insults and mockery of the public; just as Jesus, her Spouse, was treated when, clothed with a scarlet cloak and crowned with thorns, He was mocked by a thoughtless rabble."[81] But the damage to the "Mother's" reputation, once enacted in print, would not be undone by rational, dispassionate refutations in painstakingly documented theological tracts. The limited circulation of theological writing would never be able to undo the damage of, say, the "Rev. M. Hobart Seymour's 'Nights Among Romanists' and similar absolutely unreliable compilations."[82]

As Gibbons discovered, fictions sometimes displace "rational theological discourse" as eminently consumable popular books convey religious views to a voracious reading public. Foxe's *Book of Martyrs* figures as a prominent example of this situation for Gibbons, and his use of Foxe's text in illustrating the problems of popular culture also shows his sensitivity to his own reading audience: a mixture, he reckons, of Protestants and Catholics, each of whom would react powerfully and contrarily to the significance of Foxe's "historical" project. Once again, for Gibbons, the central problem for Catholic evangelism emerges as a contest of representations and misrepresentations in the world of print: "The Church is misrepresented in so-called Histories like Foxe's *Book of Martyrs*. It is true that he has been succesfully [*sic*] refuted by Lingard and Gairdner. But, how many have read the fictitious narratives of Foxe, who have never perused a page of Lingard or Gairdner?"[83]

Continuing with a scathing reminder to his Southern readers, many of whom were still reeling from the devastation wrought upon the South only a decade earlier, Gibbons reflects on the role of the popular press during the Civil War, showing once more his self-conscious involvement in a narrative of "right" representation and finding in a secular issue the same dynamic of propagandizing as will be found in religious discourses: "Suppose that I wanted to obtain a correct estimate of the Southern people, would it be fair in me to select, as my only sources of information, certain Northern and Eastern periodicals which, during our Civil War, were bitterly opposed to the race and institutions of the South? . . . Instead of taking these publications as the basis of my information, it was my duty to come among you; to live with you; to read your life by studying your private and public character."[84] Characteristically, Gibbons concludes this part of his introduction, this primer on the power of mass-print culture, with a return to the themes of maternity, domesticity, and sentiment, emphasizing the role of the Catholic church as Mother and the role of believers and converts as loving children: "Ask not her enemies what she is, for they are blinded by passion; ask not her ungrateful, renegade children, for you never heard a son speaking well of the mother whom he had abandoned and despised."[85]

Gibbons perceived his early missionary efforts in North Carolina as a success, but more specifically a success that could be connected to the development and reinforcement of a strong nuclear family: father, mother, and worshipful children, each with clearly defined roles. For example, describing the life-long influence of the Roman Catholic sacraments (from baptism to extreme unction) on the lives of the faithful, Gibbons explains that, like an immortal mother, "the Church accompanies us from the cradle to the grave, supplying us at each step with the medicine of life and immortality."[86] Even Catholic nuns, the Church's "consecrated virgins" (although much-maligned in the lurid convent exposés circulating in nineteenth-century antebellum America), will play a signal part in the modeling and construction of religious/domestic space for the faithful.[87] Expanding from their traditional roles of service, prayer, and meditation, these "sisters" are performing charitable works amounting to a form of "domestic conversion" in their communities: "In every large city of Christendom, [they] are daily reclaiming degraded women from a life of shame, and bringing them back to the sweet influences of religion; [they] snatch the abandoned offspring of sin from temporal and spiritual death, and make them pious and useful members of society, becoming more than mothers to them."[88]

By the time Gibbons was appointed Archbishop of Baltimore in 1877, his preaching and writing had been shaped largely by his sense of an enormously challenging project of religious colonization in the

South, as well as by a continuing immersion in Protestant literary culture, with its prevailing themes of gendered domesticity, sentimentality, and didacticism.[89] Apart from the effects of American Protestantism and the legacy of European Catholic devotionalism and piety, both of which marked his later writings as well, there was a provincial Catholic cultural milieu that shaped Gibbons's sensibilities in significant ways: the personal contacts that Gibbons made among the small but apparently hardy Catholic flock in North Carolina.

One of his closest friends during the missionary years and later, was Frances Fisher of Salisbury, North Carolina, the daughter of a Confederate colonel who had been killed in the first days of the Civil War. Fisher, who had also visited Gibbons in Baltimore before his arrival in North Carolina in order to "receive instruction in the faith" and whose family home was used for Catholic services performed by Gibbons, was a woman with a powerful sense of commercial fiction during those years.[90] Writing prolifically both during the years of Gibbons's mission in North Carolina and until the time of her death in 1920, Fisher published more than forty popular sentimental novels, a drama, numerous short stories and poems, and several novellas. A few, like *Valerie Aylmer* (1870) and *Morton House* (1872) appeared anonymously, while many others, such as *Nina's Atonement* (1873) bore the pious pseudonym "Christian Reid."

Although her precise sales figures are elusive, the novels Frances Fisher published regularly under her nom de plume appear to have been widely read. As one historian of Catholicism in Georgia and the Carolinas enthused, "Her works are read in every part of the English-speaking world—far away in Eastern lands and far away in the West, where the sun sets beyond the boisterous summits of her own loved Carolina."[91] Fisher's many novels drew the attention of a considerable national readership, and she became well known to the American Catholic intelligentsia through her book publications as well as her many short stories and serialized novels that appeared in prominent Catholic journals such as *Ave Maria* and the *Catholic World*.[92]

Fittingly enough, the entire Fisher family—including twenty-two-year-old Frances Fisher—were baptized and confirmed as Catholics by Gibbons not in a church but in the parlor of their colonial residence in Salisbury, North Carolina, on December 15, 1868.[93] An admirer of the handsome young bishop, Fisher would also praise his domestic sensibility: "No convert ever found a gentler or more winning guide nor one who more quickly made the newcomer feel at home in her Father's house."[94] While not a great deal is known about the relationship between Gibbons and the young female novelist in postbellum North Carolina, it is tempting to speculate that his contacts with a person like Fisher and her milieu, particularly in light of her highly developed command of the conventions and idiom of the sentimental novel, may have had some influence on Gibbons's catechistic project. Gibbons, a sworn celibate and ascetic missionary who "slept on cots and ate from a table of rough boards" during the early days of his mission,[95] likely drew upon the cultural resources and knowledge of his novelist confidante Frances Fisher, who would have been able to provide information about the practice of commercial authorship while supplying her family home for his lodging.[96]

In summary, *Faith of Our Fathers* repeatedly depicts religious faith in a variety of terms representing domestic tranquility, re-inscribing aestheticized Protestant descriptions of the Catholic Church as archetypally maternal within a catechism intended, in part, for their conversion. The paradoxical nineteenth-century Protestant relationship to Catholic iconography, dogma, and ritual (particularly those with a Roman or Italianate character), which the literary historian Jenny Franchot has persuasively shown to be manifested in antebellum Protestant writing as a troubled dialectic between the "demonized formulation as Whore of Babylon and [the] sentimentally divinized image as the 'bosom of the mighty mother,'" appears to have motivated Gibbons's effort to demonstrate the ways in which *his* version of Catholicism might conform to the contours of American Protestant discourse about maternality and families.[97] His catechism metaphorically sensationalizes the Mother Church when he describes the "fair bride . . . hacked and tortured, her blood sprinkled upon her dungeon walls." But while the sensationalism of such descriptions provides the shock value, and therefore marketability, of a convent exposé, Gibbons's catechism consistently returns to the intact image of the Catholic church as ever-nurturing sentimental mother.[98] The reward will be a maternal caress for the Prodigal Son. After the conversion or the renewal of faith, writes Gibbons, "the garment of joy is placed upon you, the banquet of love is set before you, and you receive the kiss of peace as a pledge of your filiation and adoption."[99]

Although Gibbons's Catholic God is patriarchal (he functions as the father in the household of the faithful), "one hearty embrace of your tender Mother will compensate you for all the sacrifices you may have made."[100] Inviting the "separated brethren" into the nurturing space of the Catholic Mother, Gibbons tries to refute a commonplace slander against the mother church: "Ah! my dear friend, if you saw her as her children see her, she would no longer appear to you as typified by the woman of Babylon. She would be revealed to you, 'Bright as the sun, fair as the moon;' with the beauty of Heaven stamped upon her brow, glorious 'as an army in battle array.' You would love her, you would cling to her and embrace her. With her children, you would rise up in reverence 'and call her blessed.'"[101] In his study of antebellum religious fiction, David S. Reynolds described the extent to which the Catholic novel became sentimentalized during the period from 1830 to 1850, shifting from a generally stark and logical didacticism in narrative to a style more in keeping with that of Protestant novelists. A landmark continuation of this development may be found in the rhetoric and thematics of Gibbons's *Faith of Our Fathers* that borrows heavily from popular fiction. With its generic confusions troubling any attempts at clear distinction between the appropriate idiom for catechism versus fiction, Gibbons's book indicates new ways to understand the rise and development of sentimental literature in American culture as a transdenominational phenomenon. Popular religious texts like this one serve as evidence about the ways and the extent to which Catholics participated in discourses of sentimentality in America. Gibbons's writing also shows the extent to which Catholic readers and evangelists could bring their influence to bear on the development of American literary culture by advancing and absorbing a legacy of European Catholic devotionalism and reshaping that legacy according to their own religious and social priorities.

Literary historians have persuasively shown that as the nineteenth century progressed, fiction in the form of inexpensive tracts or novels became a dominant method for mass inspiration in American religion. From this perspective, Gibbons's guiding premises of sentimentality and domesticity in *Faith of Our Fathers* become more coherent; his premises and corresponding rhetoric are additional evidence that the weight of the popular press had indeed progressed dramatically toward surpassing theological writing in its influence among ordinary people. As David S. Reynolds has observed, antebellum works of fiction stylistically "replaced rigorous exposition of dogma with diverting narrative in which outward secular crises and consummations supplanted inward self-analysis and contemplation as the center of faith."[102] *Faith of Our Fathers*, while not a work of fiction per se, nonetheless forms part of the changing tradition of religious discursive practice, defined transdenominationally, in a secularizing society in which morality was increasingly enculturated through fictional(ized) narrative. Gibbons's catechism belongs, at least in part, to the genre of pious fiction, even as it adopts the highly traditional form of the religious manual or catechism. As such, it provides at least a partial answer to the larger historical question that Reynolds sketches with regard to defining a "popular religious aesthetic" in nineteenth-century America.[103]

In his review of Catholic fiction from 1829 to 1865, Willard Thorp described early nineteenth-century Catholic fiction as primarily "exemplary, written to show how good Catholics lived and practiced their religion," remarking that despite the well-known cautions against novel-reading, the prefaces of these early Catholic novels often took up something like the following attitude: "Young Catholics will read novels and romances anyway. Let them have their own novels."[104] Reynolds has noted further that after early attempts by Catholic fiction writers (beginning around 1830) to elevate their writing to intellectual and theological levels above the popular sentimentality of Protestant novels, these novelists eventually began to utilize the "secular props" that had proven so successful for Protestant fiction writers.[105]

As the century wore on, Catholic novelists were increasingly willing to sacrifice didactic theological rigor and logical proofs for texts that used more popular devices for attracting large numbers of readers. And Gibbons, with his Catholic catechism, faced much the same challenge in attempting "to win the sympathy of predominantly Protestant readers who were apt to dislike not only Catholicism but authoritarian religion of any sort."[106] Like the novelists in Reynolds's discussion, but using a catechistic form not usually associated with fictional tropes, Gibbons the provincial missionary and urban bishop may have been persuaded to "adopt several of the fictional techniques popularized by his Protestant opponents."[107] *Faith of Our Fathers* displays a conjunction of Protestantism and Catholicism within the forum of religious devotionalism; complicating the ongoing assessment of nineteenth- and twentieth-century American mass-print culture, it provides substantial evidence for the role of Catholicism (Catholic readers and Catholic legacies) in the production of American sentimental representations. Moreover, in its powerful representations of Church as mother and its veneration of the Virgin Mary, it shows the extent to which its author was aware of and responsive to the increasing importance of women as members of the faithful and as readers in nineteenth-century literary culture.

The success of *Faith of Our Fathers* also demonstrates that while the general trend in the nineteenth century was away from didactic theological writing and toward popular fiction as a vehicle for religious ideas, a resurgence of the popular theological tract made a significant mark on post–Civil War American culture. Popular novels, a perennial source of concern for religious leaders who deplored their immorality (at worst) or their laxity in morals (at best), could thus be partially displaced by a widely disseminated religious text, in this case an authorized catechism, complete with papal imprimatur, which craftily embodied the narrative and thematic methods of mainstream sentimental writing.

5

Trading Religion for Feminism

Kate O'Flaherty Chopin's Bayou Catholics

> The Catholic novel that fails is one in which there is no genuine sense of place and in which feeling is by that much diminished.
>
> Flannery O'Connor, "The Catholic Novelist in the South" (1963)

A striking but seldom examined aspect in the fiction of Kate O'Flaherty Chopin (1850–1904) is its linkage of Catholic themes and characters with the picturesque conventions of local-color-writing: her religiously tinged evocations of regionally specific dress, mannerisms, dialect, patterns of thought, and geography. Chopin's proto-feminist representations of expanded autonomy for women, made indelibly famous by her short novel *The Awakening* (1899), were written in keeping with the highly popular "local color" regionalist style then fashionable in American novels and short fiction. In staging her stories with infusions of the distinctive regional dialects and exotic settings of Louisiana, Chopin was following commercial literary conventions of the day, which placed a high value on representations of distinctive subcultures in various American regions, while at the same time advancing progressive ideas about gender roles. Although her works spent decades languishing in obscurity and beyond the notice of most American literary scholars, the timely republication of her collected works in 1969 made her a canonical figure.[1] The feminist critical energy that has canonized Chopin's fiction, and especially *The Awakening*, has fostered much attention to that work, which has been praised for containing important literary and political documentation related to the history of American women's psychology and sexuality. In *The Awakening*'s protagonist Edna Pontellier, for example, scholars of American literature have identified a presciently modern heroine, one whose resistance to traditional familial roles and erotic norms constitutes a welcome disruption of Victorian patriarchy.

However, some implications of her writing have been given less weight than is proper, for in seeing her as primarily an icon of proto-feminist discourse, students of Chopin's writing have directed less attention to other aspects of her work, such as her religious aesthetic, evidenced in a large number of her works. For example, one influential feminist critic has observed that Chopin's work is notable mainly for a progressive view of gender politics rendered in mythical terms: not for its tinges of Catholic religiosity but instead for its inclination toward "an imaginary world beyond the restrictive culture of the nineteenth century, a world in which women might be as free as the mythic Aphrodite was." Taking this argument by Sandra Gilbert to its logical conclusion, whatever Christian religion exists in Chopin's work should be understood as merely incidental and is presented only as an occasion for its repudiation in favor of pre- or post-Christian frames of reference.[2] Recognition of Roman Catholicism in Chopin's writing should supplement nonreligious analyses that have generally been applied to her fiction, that is, interpretations that for the most part (and for good reason) see in Chopin's writing a precursor to later, twentieth-century feminist values. By contrast, attending to Chopin's choice to infuse some of her fiction with Roman Catholic significance enriches our understanding of the ways that a Catholic religious aesthetic formed key elements of her fiction. In this way, Chopin can be seen not only as a proponent of an emerging feminist sensibility in American literature of the late nineteenth century but also in relation to evolving representations of Roman Catholicism in American fiction.

That local-color writing, or what Carlos Baker has described as a late nineteenth-century American "regionalist impulse," encompassed scenes of American Catholicism should come as no particular surprise since, as Baker notes, this regionalism was consequential first in New

England literary circles but also "in one form or another accounted for the emergence of almost every prominent writer in the Middle Atlantic states and the Deep South in the last quarter of the [nineteenth] century."[3] Just as domestic-sentimental fiction opened doors into commercial publication for antebellum women, there were now new opportunities for women as regionalist local-color fiction writers. Richard Brodhead has taken a similar view of regionalism as the ticket to commercial success for postbellum American writers, but he goes even further by asserting that "the genre did not just create a place for writers: in the later nineteenth century, regionalism was so structured as to extend opportunity above all to groups traditionally distanced from literary lives. . . . Regionalism made the experience of the socially marginalized into a literary asset, and so made marginality itself a positive authorial advantage."[4] Chopin's writing supplies as assets at least three "marginal" perspectives well suited for regional fiction: a setting in the Louisiana hinterlands, the voices of women who have unequal social power compared to men, and a minority religion favored by recent immigrants to the United States.

American writers of all secular and religious persuasions took part in the extended conversation about regional difference during the years following the Civil War, when the richness of American sectional diversity was increasingly stitched into narratives that implicitly addressed the idea of national unity. Regionalism is important to Chopin's writing, but notably striking as well is the consistency with which local-color fiction by Chopin makes use of Catholic scenes and characters. Although Chopin was by no means using her fiction for evangelical purposes, she was educated in Catholic schools and was raised in a religious family with easy access to works by Catholic evangelical writers. She doubtless would have been familiar with the writings of those evangelical Catholic novelists such as Anna Hanson Dorsey, Christian Reid, Jedediah Huntington, and Mary Ann Sadlier. Their novels and stories laid considerable thematic groundwork for Chopin, who in her gradually lapsing faith chose to use religious themes and images as aesthetic supplements to her mostly secular fiction.[5]

The strategic deployment of religious motifs in her fiction is one of the most freighted but least studied dimensions of Kate Chopin's feminism. Some of the ways that Chopin used markers of the Catholic religious tradition within her regionalist aesthetic suggest that the local-color mode, in her hands, had such utility for articulating for her readers the presence and implications of Roman Catholicism in America. In turn, the Roman Catholic register of her fiction set out a traditional and patriarchal background that created productive tensions with her very progressive ideas about women's experience and agency. While her work is characterized by the local-color aesthetic that typified much commercial fiction writing of her generation, Chopin's use of religious motifs is a significant departure from the aims and method of most earlier nineteenth-century Catholic novelists, who while diverse in style and subject shared a strong commitment to church membership and worked to ensure that their fictional premises corresponded closely to principles of Catholic theology.[6] By contrast, in the literary career of Kate Chopin we can trace a creative life and incipient feminist politics shaped by her lapsing but never entirely abandoned Catholicism; disaffected with the pieties and practice of Roman Catholic faith, she held onto her Catholicism to the extent that it remained an effective device for framing her stories. Perhaps more important, though, her body of work demonstrates the new and more subtle uses available for religious themes in modern American fiction. Avoiding the evangelical project of nineteenth-century Catholic fiction writers, Chopin deftly arranges her writing in ways that describe aspects of Roman Catholicism but never urge church membership, conversion, or even faith.

Although studies of her fiction have generally neglected its religious dimensions, Chopin's biography invites consideration of the ways her literary career might have been influenced—obliquely or acutely—by her childhood experiences as a Catholic. Kate Chopin was born Kate O'Flaherty into a French-Irish Roman Catholic family in St. Louis. While in St. Louis, she attended the Academy of the Sacred Heart, where she earned a reputation as a creative writer and talented pianist. Reared in a devout and prosperous Catholic family—her father was a successful businessman and a founder of the Pacific Railroad—Chopin had ample opportunity to absorb the religious motifs that would contribute to her literary career. Religious education was more than incidental to her upbringing, as her biographer Emily Toth has shown. The students at the academy received a rigorous education from Sacred Heart nuns, some of whom were young enough to provide significant role models for the teenage students. Chopin's most influential teacher at the academy, a young nun only six years her senior, was a charismatic and gifted Irish immigrant named Mary O'Meara. In addition, Chopin's dearest Sacred Heart friend and intimate writing companion, Kitty Garesché, herself eventually joined Mary O'Meara as a Sacred Heart nun. Both of these women were lifelong nuns who would remain Chopin's close friends and correspondents throughout her literary career.[7]

For Chopin's part, although she did not follow her mentor and close friend into the convent, she brought her knowledge of Roman Catholicism to bear on her creative work. Chopin consistently resorts to types of religious characterization and imagery, which link her in important ways to an earlier, more overtly Catholic generation of writers from the middle decades of the nineteenth century. Like them, she is adept at rendering American landscapes and narratives in which Roman Catholicism is deeply embedded and indeed naturalized. But it is equally apparent, however, that Chopin's literary assertion of Catholicism emerges in an entirely different register than those earlier writers, who not only were outspoken advocates of institutional Catholic religion but also published their writings almost exclusively with Catholic publishing houses or Catholic periodicals.

Chopin's commonplace book, a writing project begun as an assignment at Sacred Heart, and which she continued to maintain for years after her high school graduation and into the early part of her marriage, records a good deal of her concern with the religion into which she was born. For example, one undated entry from the diary book includes a passage transcribed from T. B. Macaulay's "Ranke's History of the Popes," after which she appears to claim rather firmly a Catholic identity. Macaulay writes: "There is not and there never was in this earth, a work of human policy . . . so well deserving of examination as the Roman Catholic Church. The history of that church joins together the two great ages of human civilization. No other institution is left standing which carries the mind back to the time when the smoke of sacrifice rose from the Pantheon, and when camelopards and Tigers in Florian amphitheatre. . . . The papacy remains, not in decay, not a mere antique, but full of life and useful vigor." Chopin responded rather defensively, "It is to me a subject of wonder that a mind such as Macaulay's, so enlightened and free from bigotry, should have considered the Catholic Church a mere work of 'human policy.' He yields however to this politic work a superiority and primacy, in which we (Catholics) see every evidence of a divine Institution." What is most remarkable in this recently published fragment from Chopin's papers is first of all her teenage defense of Catholicism as a "divine Institution" but also her firm statement of personal identity as a Catholic in her own right.[8]

In 1870, two years after her graduation from Sacred Heart, twenty-year-old Kate O'Flaherty married a high-rolling, French-Catholic cotton broker named Oscar Chopin in a Roman Catholic service at Holy Angels Church in St. Louis. For most of Chopin's life before her turn to professional literary work after about 1890, she lived the life of a conventionally pious Roman Catholic woman whose religion was important enough to her that she can be seen wearing a large crucifix in portraits from those years, most strikingly in an 1877 portrait of Chopin at age twenty-seven with four of her young children. Fewer details are known about Chopin's commitments to institutional religion during her later years as a short-story writer and novelist, although soon after Oscar Chopin's untimely death in 1883, she no longer was a practicing Catholic. Still, during her marriage to Oscar Chopin and living in Cloutierville, Louisiana, Chopin was apparently having her children baptized, and the family included among their household possessions a "bedside *prie to*, a prayer stand with velvet knee cushions."[9] Only after Oscar's death would Chopin begin to set her course firmly away from the practice of Catholic religion.

Chopin remains a significant figure in the chapter of American literary history that features the emergence of women writers as modernists, and her career as an artist shows her to be a writer responsive to the creative and social currents of her time. Much has already been written about Chopin's bold assertion of women's agency, especially with regard to her famous story of Edna Pontellier, the affluent but unhappily married Louisiana woman at the center of *The Awakening* (1899). On the weight of that important novel, Chopin's credentials have been well secured as a highly progressive voice sympathetic to women's experiences outside of traditional, patriarchal structures of religion and family life. Departing from the usual view of Chopin as an entirely secular writer, however, the literary historian Jenny Franchot described Roman Catholicism for Chopin and other American non-Catholic writers (Franchot specified as examples Willa Cather, Stowe, Longfellow, and Hawthorne) as "a site not for truth so much as expressivity—an aesthetic and psychological region that enabled their literary production." Roman Catholicism thus provided for Chopin a set of themes, tropes, and conventional moralities whose religious weight was useful for demonstrating the gravity of her propositions of new modes and values for feminine identity.[10]

In considering the place of religion in Chopin's fiction, it is important to emphasize Franchot's crucial distinction between the ways Catholic literary tropes were deployed during the nineteenth century by committed Catholics or converts and the way literary Catholicism was used by Protestants fascinated by a religion whose faith they did not share. Chopin's mature literary work is best described as having the aura of Roman Catholic culture without the strong commitments to church membership and orthodoxy that characterized an earlier generation of American Catholic fiction writers. Kate Chopin therefore appears as a new species of American religious writer: one who stages entirely plausible Catholic scenes but then subtly demonstrates the shortcomings of that religion in the face of modernity's inexorable renovation of social norms. In other words, her fiction is marked by representations of Catholicism handled with a combination of familiarity and ambivalence, attraction and repulsion. According to Franchot's influential analysis of antebellum religious writers, "While [Catholic] converts spoke in polemical or mystical language of the Truth they now possessed, these [Protestant] novelists and poets practiced an ambivalent strategy of partial appropriation and conversion of this Catholic 'Truth' into literary effect. Antebellum Protestant authors, in their investigations of Catholicism as charismatic aesthetic, constructed a language of figurative conversion whose plot often held at its center the mystery of religious conviction." Decades later, well after the most virulent anti-Catholic hysteria had begun to subside in the United States, Chopin began to produce in her fiction representations of Catholicism, which are conveyed without polemic or mysticism, and without the strong anxiety about Roman Catholicism that characterized so many antebellum Protestant writers. In considering the artistic appropriation and conversion of Roman Catholicism into modernist literature by Chopin, a writer who has seldom if ever been characterized as overtly religious, we are faced with a set of literary situations in which "the mystery of religious conviction" circulates through narratives that seem not to be entirely committed to either belief or unbelief.[11]

Although the recent annals of American literary history are filled with revivals of interest in novelists marginalized for reasons of race or gender, few writers have enjoyed the level of admiring critical acclaim directed at Kate Chopin since the publication of her collected writings in the early 1960s.[12] Much of this revivalist enthusiasm has been buoyed by feminist critical energy embracing Chopin's fiction, and especially *The Awakening*, as pivotal literary and political documentation of the history of American women's psychology and sexuality. Ideologically useful though such modern accounts might be for inserting Chopin's fiction into the gender politics of the twentieth century, however, they do not account for the apparatus of Catholic imagery and reference in Chopin's works, or what one critic has described as a deployment of Catholicism that provides her fiction with "a distinguishing texture."[13] Chopin accomplishes this even though the scholarly consensus about her writing has pointed not to religion but to feminist impulses and a broad interrogation of social norms. In fact, she is not simply an example of a writer who uses religion opportunistically, for literary effects desirable within the literary marketplace for local-color fiction, although a reading of her short fiction gives something of that impression. Rather, her work suggests something of what Marcel Gauchet describes as the "residue of religion" at work in the field of modern aesthetics: "the creative after-effects of what used to be religious experience in the order of aesthetic feeling or the order of moral codes."[14] In keeping with Gauchet's view of religious aesthetics in modernity, it is therefore important to stipulate that Chopin's work strongly resists simple categorization as "Catholic fiction" and that Catholicism is used in her narratives in complex ways and for complex reasons.

Colleen McDannell's insight that Kate Chopin's work should be associated with a longer literary tradition of American Catholic women fiction writers is perceptive and correct, but it does not account for the progressive and feminist dimensions of Chopin's proto-modernist narratives. For instance, McDannell observes that most women Catholic novelists in the period 1840–1920 were above all concerned in their fiction with affirming their Catholic faith and with advocating a pious model of virtuous Catholic domesticity. According to this view, feminism and the "woman question" were never the central issues for these mostly Irish American immigrant writers, with the result that "for many Catholic women, the 'woman question' was also a 'Protestant' question."[15] Chopin, of course, was directly invested in questions of women's rights and the politics of gender in ways that most previous American Catholic women novelists were not. Her fiction makes use of her religious knowledge in certain ways, especially in its powerful evocation of Louisiana's Roman Catholic traditions and folkways, but her concerns are much different than those of an earlier generation of American Catholic domestic novelists. Part of Chopin's significance, then, is that she musters themes of Roman Catholicism without using them to evangelize for that religious faith. Instead, she seems to deploy elements of Catholic religion in opposition to her larger aims: in order to set a conservative stage for narratives that stake out a complex but reliably progressive agenda for her women characters.

Chopin's exotic Louisiana bayou country, which to students of American literary history has become as familiar as Sarah Orne Jewett's Maine coast or William Faulkner's Yoknapatawpha County, provides a theater for moral experimentation that is consistently adumbrated by Catholicism. Without taking religion as her primary subject or agenda, Chopin regularly makes use of Catholic references as a marker of her distinctive fictive locale; along with the Cajun, Creole, and African American characters and cultures that enliven her tales, a languid Catholicism suffuses their scenes. In this tendency, Chopin resembles her predecessor George Washington Cable, whose vivid local-color treatments of New Orleans had provided an influential model. The key difference, however, for Chopin's work is that picturesque Louisiana Catholic tradition supplies more than touristic regional interest: it is the Catholic ways of living that provide the very ground for Chopin's interrogation of modern gender identity. Neither bluntly dogmatic about the role of Catholicism in modern America nor content to rehearse the familiar and often blandly narrated local-color patterns of writers like Cable, Chopin's stories appear to draw their radicalism from the pressure of Catholic practices and epistemologies.

Like many other fine writers, Kate Chopin used the quotidian details of her youth and upbringing, including religious details, to create a plausible and compelling fictional world. Among the most direct methods Chopin employed for developing a credible religious aesthetic in her romantic stories was to situate courtship and romance in the context of Roman Catholic churches and clergy. A good example of this technique may be seen in "Love on the Bon-Dieu" (1891–92), a magazine story originally titled "Love and Easter," which was also included in two of her story collections: *Two Tales* (1892) and *Bayou Folk* (1894). This local-color tale of romance between two young Louisiana Creoles, a handsome carpenter named Azenor and a sickly but beautiful girl called Lalie, features a number of important scenes that occur on Easter Sunday in or around the local church under the supervision of the priest, Père Antoine. Lalie, an impoverished girl who has been forced to attend Mass in order to continue receiving financial support from the church, comes to the attention of Azenor, a pious Catholic who has performed carpentry work for the priest. Later recognizing that Lalie's health has been jeopardized from illness and malnutrition, Azenor rescues a feverish and delirious Lalie from her sickbed and brings her to his own home as his "wife," an act that he associates with "the spirit of Christ." By contrast, Lalie's encounter with Catholic religiosity, described vividly in the story, occurs most profoundly when she is absorbing the experience of Easter Mass on a warm spring day.

Well in advance of their "marriage," as Azenor watches intently and mentally plans his courtship with her, Lalie's experience of the church ritual is presented in highly sensuous terms: "It seemed good to her to be there. Sometimes she looked up at the little colored panes through which the Easter sun was streaming; then at the flaming candles, like stars; or at the embowered figures of Joseph and Mary, flanking the central tabernacle which shrouded the risen Christ. Yet she liked just as well to watch the young girls in their spring freshness, or to sensuously inhale the mingled odor of flowers and incense that filled the temple." Whereas for Lalie, whose background is poverty and neglect, the liturgy provides an opportunity to enjoy a sense of ritual sensory stimulation that had been sadly lacking in her own life, for Azenor the Mass offers a welcome social occasion for meeting a young woman whom he increasingly desires. The importance to Lalie of the Catholic aesthetic experience is highlighted even further as the story uncertainly concludes with Azenor literally carrying Lalie away from her bed to his own home for last rites (at the hands of Père Antoine) and medical attention. The only possession that Lalie brings with her to her new bed at Azenor's home is a decorated Easter egg, a gift from Azenor that symbolizes that holiday's traditional theme of fertility as well as her own attraction to the Catholic religion's aesthetic dimension.[16]

Chopin's tactic of placing religion into tension with her broader feminist project can be seen also in the sketch "Madame Célestin's Divorce" (1893), which extends the theme of divorce that had been present in Chopin's work at least since her first novel, *At Fault* (1890), in which the Catholic woman protagonist refuses to continue her relationship with the man she loves because he has been divorced. "Madame Célestin's Divorce," a naturalistic tale, takes the form of a conversation between a lawyer, Judge Paxton, and the unhappily married and financially strapped Madame Célestin, who has been forced to take on a variety of jobs (sewing, teaching music, manual labor) because her absent husband has for months failed to send money for her support and the support of her two children. The irony of the tale begins with Judge Paxton's expressed view that Madame Célestin should seek a divorce and indicates that he will counsel her in those legal proceedings, to which she initially responds with great interest. Steeling her resolve against the disapproval of her family and social circle, who are unified in their opposition to divorce, Madame Célestin is equally adamant about having to defy the local Catholic clergy in seeking to dissolve her marriage: "Maman says it 's a disgrace like it 's neva been in the family. . . . Sher says I mus' go by all means consult with Père Duchéron—it 's my confessor, you undastan'—Well, I 'll go, Judge to please Maman. But all the confessor' in the worl' ent goin' make me put up with that conduc' of Célestin any longa." With the judge's approval, but against her priest's objections, Madame Célestin follows this confident statement with a vow that she will pursue her argument for divorce even further by bringing her case before the bishop.[17]

In a subsequent conversation with the judge, the bracing independence of Madame Célestin is evidenced further as she describes how she had maintained her resolve to end her unhappy marriage even in the face of strong opposition by the bishop: "Ah, he 's a eloquent man. It 's not a mo' eloquent man in Natchitoches parish. I was fo'ced to cry, the way he talked to me about my troubles; how he undastan's them, an' feels for me. . . . How it is the duty of a Catholic to stan' everything till the las' extreme. An that the life of retirement an' self-denial I would have to lead,—he tole me all that." And still, in the face of her bishop's appeal, Madame Célestin remains firm in her wish for a divorce and seems to be willing to defy all religious principle in order to arrange a more happy life for herself. To the judge's astonishment, she goes on in her bold defiance of her priest and bishop, voicing a surprisingly progressive view of her rights: "The bishop don't know w'at it is to be married to a man like Célestin, an' have to endu' that conduc' like I have to endu' it. The Pope himse'f can't make me stan' that any longer, if you say I got the right in the law to sen' Célestin sailing."[18]

The feminist confidence of Madame Célestin turns out to be short lived, however, as the story concludes with an ironic reversal of her attitude toward her own marriage. As though to suggest that defiance of Catholic religious tradition is more readily accomplished than defiance of human nature and sexual desire, the final conversation between Judge Paxton and Madame Célestin concludes with her stunning decision to remain with her husband after all and forget about the divorce entirely, now that he had returned home the night before and had promised "on his word an' honor he's going to turn ova a new leaf." There is humor in this conclusion, but there is also revealed here a fascinating dimension of Chopin's thinking about the place of traditional religion in modern life. Madame Célestin is feminist enough to understand that Roman Catholic dogma about marriage and divorce should no longer stand in the way of her wish for a contented life, happy marriage, and the expression of her personal freedoms. Roman Catholic authority is thus staged as a weakening and less significant force than the deterministic forces that Chopin—like her contemporaries Theodore Dreiser, Jack London, Upton Sinclair, and Stephen Crane—was beginning to understand through her study of Darwin, Spencer, and Huxley. "Madame Célestin's Divorce" uses Roman Catholicism as cultural context and literary aesthetic but ultimately shows Catholic moral force to be in decline, especially for the nominally faithful who live with an awareness of their commitment to a church but also feel a need to make adjustments in light of increasing rights for women.

Tension between Roman Catholic sacramental practice and Chopin's interest in expanding women's erotic expression comes to the surface in a number of her stories, most obviously in works such as "A Sentimental Soul" (1895), in which she traces the secret love of Mamzelle Fleurette, a pious woman shopkeeper, for one of her married customers, a locksmith named Lacodie. Sex and religion are narrated in tandem through this tale, and Fleurette recognizes both the adulterous impropriety of her desire for Lacodie and the way her religiosity interferes with her understanding of sexuality. Chopin's narrator indicates that "she held a vague understanding that men were wickeder in many ways than women; that ungodliness was constitutional with them, like their sex, and inseparable from it." Thus conflicted in her passion for the handsome locksmith, Fleurette regularly confesses her adulterous feelings to her priest, Father Fochelle, who berates her for even considering a relationship with a married man. Soon enough, though, Lacodie dies of a fever, and Fleurette is left with her unrealized passionate attachment to a dead man. After Lacodie dies and Fleurette is in secret, bitter mourning, the Catholic confessional space provides a confidential venue for Chopin to describe the friction created when the stipulations of Catholic morality and sexual desire are put at odds. Sacramental confession, which had previously been a pleasurable experience for Fleurette, becomes a less pleasant but more honest venue for expressing her desires in confidence, albeit to a confessor who is increasingly impatient with her impassioned grieving.[19]

Nevertheless, Fleurette's passion for Lacodie is staged as an integral part of Fleurette's religious activities. She includes him in her confessions, and she gazes longingly at his likeness (which she conceals in her prayer book) as an icon during daily Mass and at her evening devotions at home. Although Lacodie is dead, Fleurette states plainly to the priest: "I cannot help it, father. I try, but I cannot help it. To love him is like breathing; I do not know how to help it. I pray, and pray, and it does no good, for half of my prayers are for the repose of his soul. It surely cannot be a sin, to pray for the repose of his soul?" The movement of the story's plot occurs after Fleurette is stunned to learn that Lacodie's widow had remarried, taking yet another handsome young Creole as her husband. Finally unwilling to conceal her affection for the deceased Lacodie, Fleurette proudly displays his handsomely framed photograph prominently in her shop, "between the crucifix and the portrait of Empress Eugenie—and she did not care if [Lacodie's] wife ever saw it or not." Mamzelle Fleurette's poignant religious adjustment, manifested most obviously by her act of making public her affection for the dead husband of a married woman, extends as well to her practice of confession, in which she continues to participate but declines henceforth to make her erotic desires a subject for conversation with her priest-confessors. Freed of the compulsion to confess her love to religious authority, she nevertheless reserves for herself the privilege of honoring Lacodie's memory in her own way, establishing a place for his beloved photograph and thrilling herself with the privately religious pleasure of finding the ideal memorial wreath to place on his tombstone.[20]

Because Catholicism is somewhat less evident (though still present) in Chopin's firmly canonical *The Awakening* than in a number of her other stories, Chopin's incipient feminism, not her religious views, have provided the primary critical frame for her work. A review of Chopin's short fiction, however, provides a useful reminder of her immersion in Louisiana's Catholic culture, even as her narratives tended to repudiate certain aspects of that religious tradition. But by no means does her ambivalence about the Roman Catholic tradition turn into a polemic against that religion; instead, she narrates some of her most compelling stories in a frame that shows that religion's complex potential for restraining, producing, and sublimating certain kinds of mystical and sensual pleasure. For example, several years before the ambiguous religiosity of *The Awakening*, Chopin had written "Two Portraits (The Nun and the Wanton)," a sketch in which she offers a view of feminine identity underwritten by a Catholic model of spirituality. Alberta, a beautiful and dangerous "wanton" woman, appears as a pleasure-seeker: "She put out her hands to touch things that pleased her, and her lips to kiss them. Her eyes were deep brown wells that were drinking, drinking impressions and treasuring them in her soul." But her transformation comes at the suggestion of a nun, who in turn encourages Alberta to pursue life as a religious, with the result that "when Alberta had reached the age when with other women the languor of love creeps into the veins and dreams begin, at such a period an overpowering impulse toward the purely spiritual possessed itself of her." Apparently, physical pleasure and sexual fulfillment will be sublimated in favor of the more serene meditations of the convent, and yet Alberta's experience of life as a Catholic nun quickly develops into a feast for the sensorium, "a real flood of celestial love deluging her soul" for "when the others are plunged in meditation, Alberta is steeped in an oblivious ecstasy." As the sketch unfolds over its several pages, Alberta shifts her predisposition for physical experience into the transcendent pleasures of Catholic mysticism, pleasures that for her are so profound as to be manifested in deeply sensual and erotic visions:

> Oh, the beautiful visions! The first of them came to her when she was wrapped in suffering, in quivering contemplation of the bleeding and agonizing Christ. Oh the dear God! Who loved her beyond the power of man to describe, to conceive. The God-Man, the Man-God, suffering, bleeding, dying for her. . . .
>
> She pressed her lips upon the bleeding wounds and the Divine Blood transfigured her. The Virgin Mary enfolded her in her mantle. She could not describe in words the ecstasy; that taste of the Divine love which only the souls of the transplanted could endure in its awful and complete intensity.

Chopin's literary feminism follows a path in "The Nun and the Wanton" that illuminates the fraught relationship between religious piety and human erotic impulses. Alberta the novice nun, steeped in mystic Catholic spirituality that makes her eventually capable of healing others, ends not by articulating a model for liberating women from patriarchal hegemony (the most common critical view of Edna Pontellier in *The*

Awakening) but by blending her powers of spiritual access with her unique physical sensibility. Having traced a relationship between Catholic embodiment and feminine ecstasy, Chopin closes the sketch by noting that other believers "have been cured of bodily ailments by the touch of [Alberta's] beautiful hands," thereby embracing a form of women's agency and power that is complexly related to the experience of religious piety and saintliness.[21]

The freedoms that Edna Pontellier so famously sought in *The Awakening*, in which a restless young woman attempts to liberate herself from domestic tyranny, sexual boredom, and intellectual vacancy, hardly suggest the work of a writer who would have an interest in lives of nuns. However, nuns and convent life—an ideal stage for mapping the borders of feminine identity—play an important role in Chopin's fiction, and are in keeping with recent biographical accounts of Chopin that have shown that her early life was profoundly influenced by Catholic education and the choice of some of her close friends to join the Sacred Heart convent in St. Louis. The appeal of the religious life is echoed is Chopin's stories in a number of ways, as with the despair at marriage expressed by the unhappily married young woman in "Athénaïse," whose anguish is made even more bitter by the realization that life as a nun would have been far more pleasant: "Mon Dieu, mon Dieu! Sister Marie Angelique knew w'at she was saying; she knew me better than myse'f w'en she said God had sent me a vocation an' I was turning deaf ears. W'en I think of a blessed life in the convent, at peace! Oh, w'at was I dreaming of!" Here, of course, Chopin appears to be well aware of the centuries-long tradition of women becoming nuns in part because Catholic convent life provided opportunities for education, respect, and safety not always available for women living in conventional family arrangements. Her feminism in this instance, then, is one informed by her knowledge of convent life and its partial (albeit imperfectly realized) advancement toward an expansion of women's rights.[22]

One year before she completed "Two Portraits," Chopin published "Lilacs" (1894), her most detailed consideration of the tension between the pleasures of post-Victorian women's sensuality and the rarified, more strictly controlled sensuality of Catholic convent life. In "Lilacs," the gap between these two worlds seems to grow larger, as a beautiful young actress, Mme. Adrienne Farival, travels annually from Paris to the beloved rural convent where she had spent her youth. For the young woman, who annually spends a summer fortnight basking in the aesthetic pleasures of a richly appointed convent and chapel, those religious spaces fulfill a restorative and therapeutic purpose, its quiet setting and gracefully modest nuns standing as the antithesis of her turbulent public life as an actress. The tension between convent and theater eventually force her into a personal crisis, and the social pressure of her Parisian life and loves affect Mme. Farival to such a degree that her dress and behavior (she invites male callers into the convent) eventually scandalize the nuns, who in turn banish her from further visits to the convent. (Another Farival family, perhaps unrelated, appears prominently in *The Awakening*; there, the Farival twins are described as "girls of fourteen, always clad in the Virgin's colors, blue and white, having been dedicated to the Blessed Virgin at their baptism.")

This literary fascination with nuns' lives would prove a recurring theme in her work, and Chopin would occasionally elaborate on this fascination in her private writings. In a diary entry from 1894, she made one of her most searching analyses of women's religious or contemplative vocations versus a vocation as professional woman:

> I cannot recall what suggested ["Lilacs"]. If the story had been written after my visit of last Sunday to the convent, I would not have to seek the impulse far. Those nuns seem to retain or gain a certain beauty with their advancing years which we women in the world are strangers to. The unchanging form of their garments through the years and years seems to impart a distinct character to their bodily movements. . . . The conditions under which these women live are such as keep them young and fresh in heart and in visage. One day—usually one hey-day of youth they kneel before the altar of a God whom they have learned to worship, and they give themselves wholly—body and spirit into his keeping. They have only to remain faithful through the years, these modern Psyches, to the lover who lavishes all his precious gifts upon them in the darkness—the most precious of which is eternal youth."[23]

This enormously rich and revealing passage brings to light a number of provocative developments in Chopin's thinking. A few years after she wrote this entry, Chopin's more famous contemporary Theodore Dreiser would remark in his novel *Sister Carrie* that "a woman should some day write the complete philosophy of clothes. No matter how young, it is one of the things she wholly comprehends." No such modern pressure exists for the nun that Chopin contemplates, given that the young nun's religious life has truncated any movement into the world of newer fashions.

Important novels by other of Chopin's contemporaries—Henry James's *Portrait of a Lady* (1881) and Edith Wharton's *The House of Mirth* (1905)—would provide their own searing accounts of the high costs paid by independent modern women whose youth and beauty have faded, leaving them poorly equipped to cope with betrayal and death. At this juncture of her career, however, Chopin chooses to speculate about these problems by placing them within the age-old model of Catholic religious life, in which such matters as a "philosophy of clothes," the problem of marriage, and the question of eternal love are provided with solutions in the realm of spiritual devotion. In so doing, Chopin harbors no agenda for evangelism on behalf of the Church, as would have been expected from an earlier generation of American Catholic writers. Nor does she present Roman Catholicism as an object for the kind of feminist critique that would become familiar in the later twentieth century. Rather, her consideration of nuns provides an opportunity to analyze certain core issues related to women's identity and lived experience: fashion, physical appearance, aging, and sexuality.[24]

Occasionally, male characters have the opportunity to negotiate some of these tensions between the discipline of Catholic religious experience and the romantic possibilities of secular life. In Chopin's *A Vocation and a Voice* (1896), a poor, young altar boy becomes infatuated with and is seduced by an exotic female fortune-teller, but he eventually decides against secular life in favor of a vocation as a Catholic monk. Having been infected with the germ of sensuality, however, the day finally comes many years later when the boy, now an adult, hears the alluring song of a woman coming from over the monastery wall and abandons his vocation to follow the temptation of the voice. Once again, as with her diary allusion to the nun's "vocation," Chopin brings into a fine tension the passions inherent within the overlapping realms of the erotic and the religious. And too, the contest of secular and sacred is resolved by a decision to lean gradually but decidedly toward the secular, toward the modern, and away from the traditionalizing influence of Catholic religion.

Having made these observations about the religious texture of her fiction, there is no mistaking that Kate Chopin's work engages substantially with the same issues of psychology, race, gender identity, and sexuality with which some of her contemporaries in modernist fiction were wrestling. It is also true that in creating her own distinctive variety of local-color fiction, Chopin continues the American fictional tradition of placing Catholicism at the geographic and cultural frontiers of the United States but at the same time developing a literary posture marked by deep ambivalence over the question of Roman Catholic ways of experiencing and articulating the modern world. The reasons that Kate Chopin chose to cite Roman Catholicism so frequently in her writing are not comprehensively known, but it appears obvious that this religious motif needs to be considered carefully alongside the more common appraisal of Chopin's representation of women's secular identity. Time and again in her stories, Chopin draws secular and religious pleasures into tension, while emphasizing the aesthetic of Roman Catholicism, even in its attenuated modes as an artifact tied to an exotic region like the bayous of Louisiana, to offer a major context for the incipient promises of liberated sexuality and expanded human potential that her writing anticipates.

By the late nineteenth century, at the peak of Kate Chopin's creative life as a writer, it was no longer possible to take seriously the idea of a purely didactic novel aimed at religious conversions; nor was it possible to write confidently for an audience of the reliably faithful Christian masses. The age of Orestes Brownson's gravest media criticism produced and empowered Catholic writers such as Jedediah Huntington and Anna Hanson Dorsey, along with others who enlisted as literary evangelists to battle the tide of publications flooding from Protestant presses. Toward the end of the century, though, didactic novels appeared in smaller numbers; mass-print culture's religious center of gravity had shifted as well-educated Americans could no longer be presumed to be reliably pious Christian readers who would be responsive to unvarnished religious literature. Indeed, some American readers had abandoned religion altogether. As the historian James Turner has noted, in Western civilization for centuries preceding the nineteenth century, "failing to believe in some sort of deity was not merely rare; it was a bizarre aberration." Suddenly, by the later nineteenth century, millions of Europeans and Americans were turning away from or becoming ambivalent about their religious beliefs. Turner summarizes the scope of this moment in the history of Christianity as a sea change in the compulsory nature of belief: "Before about the middle of the nineteenth century, atheism or agnosticism seemed almost palpably absurd; shortly afterward unbelief emerged as an option fully available within the general contours of Western culture, a plausible alternative to the still dominant theism." All of this is not to suggest that evangelical Christian religion disappeared entirely from American fiction after the Civil War. Instead, the example of Kate Chopin provides strong evidence of a radical displacement and reconstitution of religious modes within the early phases of American literary modernism. What we see in her work is not merely an example of religious "declension" in the literary sphere, even though arguments for such declension have real merit.[25]

More precisely, Chopin's religiously tinged fiction provides support for Marcel Gauchet's assertion in *The Disenchantment of the World* (1985) that "modern society is not a society without religion but one whose major articulations were formed by metabolizing the religious function." In certain respects, Kate Chopin's *The Awakening* and "Lilacs" are narratives located at the furthest remove from traditional Catholic dogma, sermons, apologetics, or didacticism. Yet our grasp of her fiction will be incomplete if we understand Chopin only as a "lapsed" Catholic who turns to feminism and becomes a proto-modern voice for sexual freedom. Her engagement and critique of Catholicism shows her as well to be a writer whose fiction would be substantially less powerful without the religious modes that it employs in what Gauchet describes as "metabolized" form. Acknowledging her engagement with Catholic tradition, we come closer to seeing the extent of Chopin's complex advances in fiction, in which her embrace of progressive ideas for women and her critique of marriage occurred at the same time a Catholic religious aesthetic was infusing her literary art.[26] This ambivalent posture toward Roman Catholic religion was a distinctive aspect of Chopin's writing and would continue to provide a useful technique in the hands of other writers who enlisted Catholic ideas and themes but stopped well short of evangelism or commitment to a Church.

6

"A Kind Woman in Heaven"

Willa Cather's Religious Aesthetic

> Miss Cather is not a Catholic, yet certainly no Catholic American writer that I know of has ever written so many pages so steeped in spiritual knowledge of Catholic motives and so sympathetically illustrative of the wonder and beauty of Catholic mysteries, as she has done in [her book].
>
> Michael Williams, review of *Death Comes for the Archbishop* (1927)

> How was [Willa Cather] able to write two of the most Catholic novels in American literature?
>
> Ralph McInerny, "Willa Cather" (2005)

At the turn of the twentieth century, the era of the didactic religious pamphlet camouflaged as a novel had clearly ended. Sophisticated American readers, apparently no longer so susceptible to tendentious literary evangelism, continued to peruse local-color fiction and novels that featured important strains of Catholicism, but the best Catholically influenced writers of the early twentieth century tended to avoid propaganda or even clear statements of religious faith. American Catholic publishing had fallen on rather hard times, a problem summarized in a scathing 1909 essay by the Reverend John Talbot Smith, a New York priest and literary critic who wrote frequently for Catholic periodicals. Fifty years after the vigorous efforts of nineteenth-century Catholic literary men like Orestes Brownson and Jedediah Huntington to establish a solid American Catholic literary culture and commercial publishing enterprise, the picture appeared very bleak to Smith as surveyed Roman Catholic publishing on the American scene: "Numerous Catholic publications of little consequence; a few eminent magazines; small demand for contributed articles; little or no pay for the same; publishers not many, trying to get books for next to nothing, oftenest for nothing . . . and among the Catholic millions, high and low, clergy and laity, intellectual and simple, a grand indifference to the Catholic press at home and abroad."[1] And several decades after Father Hecker founded the *Catholic World* with high hopes for its influence among the swelling population of American Catholic readers, Smith's comments suggest that the enterprise of evangelical Catholic publishing had largely become a commercial and intellectual failure. In a remarkable transition, though, some of the most powerful American Catholic writing of the early twentieth century would be produced by writers who were not themselves Catholics, and who published their books with prominent secular publishers.

American writers such as Kate Chopin frequently drew upon the resources provided them by Roman Catholic tradition but did so most often by deploying religion as exotic ambiance and aesthetic stimulation. The blunt instrument of nineteenth-century Catholic dogmatism, wielded most expertly in the field of literature not just by Catholic novelists who frequently targeted the immigrant masses but also by sophisticated thinkers like Orestes Brownson, had by the turn of the century undergone a transformation in which Catholicism could appear as one of a number of artistic effects in the hands of modernist writers, even some of those who have rarely been understood as explicitly religious writers.

Roman Catholicism continued to hold appeal for American writers and their readers after the turn of the century, but sometimes for different reasons and with altered rhetorical modes. To be sure, some early twentieth-century writers continued to follow the nineteenth-century tradition of locating Catholicism, as did Kate Chopin, at exotic extremes of geography, history, and culture. And when the Catholic convert Charles Warren Stoddard published *The Lepers of Molokai* (1885), his sentimental hagiography of Father Damien, a Belgian missionary to the Hawaiian lepers, he became one of the best-known exponents of the

Catholic travelogue.[2] Also notable in this respect was the Italian-born American writer Francis Marion Crawford (1854–1909), a prolific novelist and one of the best-selling fiction writers of his generation, who authored a highly regarded narrative history of ancient Rome, *Ave Roma Immortalis* (1898). After converting to Catholicism in 1880, at the age of twenty-six, Crawford wrote dozens of books in which Catholic religion is prominent but not evangelically presented, frequently using his native Italy as the setting for his stories. Although Crawford made extensive use of Catholic themes and scenes, and developed a wide readership that enjoyed the religious ambiance that he created in his works, he was not disposed to think of his writing as having an evangelical or didactic purpose. At the height of his fame, in a remarkable theoretical pamphlet titled *The Novel: What It Is* (1893), Crawford took the time to be very clear about his literary purposes: "The novel [is] a marketable commodity" and an "intellectual artistic luxury [that] must amuse, indeed, but should amuse reasonably, from an intellectual point of view. . . . Its intention is to amuse and please, and certainly not to teach and preach; but in order to amuse well it must be a finely-balanced creation."[3] Roman Catholicism served as Crawford's private faith and as one of the ingredients of a successful body of fiction, but he stopped well short of attempting to use his writing as a means for advancing dogma or gaining Catholic converts. Indeed, the *Catholic Encyclopedia* for 1911 includes Crawford as a notable writer, but mentions serious reservations about the sincerity of his faith: "While Marion Crawford in his public life always professed himself a Catholic, he can scarcely be called a Catholic novelist, and his treatment of Catholic subjects in several of his works does not recommend itself to his coreligionists."[4]

Writers like Crawford—and he is a significant and influential figure because of his commercial success and high visibility in the print marketplace—invested their fiction with the religious dimensions of what has variously been called a regionalist aesthetic or "local color" and in effect anticipated some of the literary techniques that characterize twentieth-century "Catholic realism" more generally: by "invest[ing] the mundane world itself with spiritual significance."[5] A corollary of this strategy is that while these early twentieth-century writers produced literary works that were infused with spiritual significance, the religious discourse in these works on the whole forfeits the evangelism and theological controversy of earlier American authors of religious fiction.

This retreat from evangelism during the late nineteenth and early twentieth century marks one of the most significant shifts in the way that Roman Catholicism is represented in American fiction. For even the most sophisticated mid-nineteenth-century Catholics who wrote evangelical novels, the typical objective of their fiction was to portray Roman Catholicism as a religion not just to admire but also to adopt wholeheartedly and to defend against other religions. Theirs was a literary imagination in the service of larger evangelical purposes. By the early decades of the twentieth century, however, the urgency of Catholic (and anti-Catholic) controversial writing had greatly subsided, a development that was undoubtedly connected with the rapid assimilation of immigrant Catholics into United States culture, commerce, and politics during the latter half of the nineteenth century.

Why would it be, then, that the Nebraska-bred writer Willa Cather (1873–1947) would elect to present Roman Catholic themes in so many of her writings, and especially her novels of the late 1920s to the early 1930s? And why would Cather, a learned woman with a keen understanding of the secular literary scene, elect to use strongly Catholic motifs in her work when in fact she was an adult convert to the Episcopal Church? One possibility is that she had absorbed the lesson presented by the tremendous publishing success of Francis Marion Crawford, whom she met during her years in Pittsburgh, where the twenty-two-year-old Cather had taken her first job as a magazine writer. Cather disliked Crawford personally because she found him to be a snob and had scant regard for him artistically. His commercial success was enviable but his "prolific rapidity" (publishing a novel every few months) signified to her an interest mostly in commerce rather than art. But Crawford was undoubtedly a striking literary figure whose work was noted by Cather in her early book reviews, in which she showed her awareness of his many Catholic-themed novels and their popularity with American readers.[6]

Cather may also have taken to heart some of Crawford's statements about literary craft in his *The Novel: What It Is*. *The Novel* sets out an agenda comprised of equal parts realism and romance, but Crawford also offers therein a kind of apologia for the professional mass-market writer: it is Crawford's theory of the novel as a text meant for pleasurable consumption, rather than as a vehicle for moralizing of any sort. He states: "What we call a novel may educate the taste and cultivate the intelligence; under the hand of genius it may purify the heart and fortify the mind." The novel at its best, according to Crawford's theory, can accomplish these lofty goals without serving as a blunt instrument of theological orthodoxy. He argues that novels are wrenched away from their finer qualities when they are presented in the form of the "purpose-novel," a category in which many American Catholic novels of the nineteenth century could be included. Crawford's objection to such works is that their evangelism is both unseemly and presumptuous: "The purpose-novel is an odious attempt to lecture people who hate lectures, to preach at people who prefer their own church, and to teach people who think they know enough already. It is an ambush, a lying-in-wait for the unsuspecting public, a violation of the social contract—and as such it ought to be either mercilessly crushed or forced by law to bind itself in black and label itself 'Purpose' in very big letters."[7] Crawford's moralism on this subject is striking by comparison with the preceding generations of Catholic novelists and bespeaks a new tolerance for religious difference and even an accommodation of those who lack any religious belief. Crawford's new Catholic intellectual style thus matched very well the temper of his generation, for as the historian James Turner has observed, "a key to Victorian unbelief was precisely the newly rigorous moral principle that only knowledge provided truth and that believing in what one could not know was immoral."[8] Like a long succession of nineteenth-century predecessors, Crawford was an intellectual who converted to Roman Catholicism on the way to a distinguished literary career, but unlike Orestes Brownson, Isaac Hecker, Jedediah Huntington, or Anna Dorsey, Crawford was a new kind of post-Victorian Catholic writer: one for whom religion was an integral part of his literary aesthetic but also one who preferred to eschew the burdens of evangelism or special pleading.

Although, unlike Crawford, Cather consistently declined to identify herself as a Catholic writer, she nevertheless managed to construct a substantial body of work—including her most highly regarded novels—in which explicitly Catholic themes and scenes are pivotal. But Cather's decision to embrace Roman Catholic cultures and make them an important dimension of her mature fiction is curious, given her religious background. Raised as a Baptist, Willa Cather was confirmed in 1922 in the Episcopal Church in Red Cloud, Nebraska, and for years attended regular Episcopal services in her adopted home of New York City. For her literary purposes, however, it was Roman Catholicism (as she imagined it) that fostered some of her most notable fiction. Roman Catholic scenes are increasingly important dimensions in her major novels beginning with *One of Ours* (1922) and continuing through *A Lost Lady* (1923),

The Professor's House (1925), *My Mortal Enemy* (1926), *Death Comes for the Archbishop* (1927), and *Shadows on the Rock* (1931). These last two novels are entirely Roman Catholic historical tales; they are based, respectively, on the lives of nineteenth-century missionaries in the American Southwest and a twelve-year-old girl in seventeenth-century Canada who grows up among the Ursuline nuns and Jesuit priests of Quebec. Other Cather novels provide Catholic flavor without entirely focusing on that religion, as in *The Professor's House*, the story of Godfrey St. Peter, who is a scholar writing a history called *Spanish Adventurers in North America*. We learn from Cather not only the Catholic dimensions of his name and scholarship but that his "sewing woman" is not just a "reliable, methodical spinster" but a "German Catholic and very devout." From such hints, the fading traces of Roman Catholicism are in some ways the vital center of Cather's religious aesthetic, for in *The Professor's House* it is a religious culture placed at a distance but never out of sight, as when the professor is described as a person who is not religious but who nevertheless is noted to be the son of "a strong-willed Methodist mother" and a "gentle-weaned away Catholic father."[9]

It is impossible to read Cather's mature period without coming to the conclusion that Roman Catholic themes and traditions were foundational to her broader artistic project, even though her many Catholic references are sometimes made obliquely. Before turning to *Death Comes for the Archbishop*, one can observe the growing religious intensity of Cather's writing in a story she wrote the year before that novel appeared in print. In the curious novella *My Mortal Enemy*, Cather uses one of her favored techniques: an adolescent who narrates a tale about adults whom she observes. In this case, a fifteen-year-old girl named Nellie Birdseye, who lives in the fictional town of Parthia, Illinois, relates the story of Myra Hanshawe (née Driscoll), a beautiful adult woman from Parthia who marries Oswald Hanshawe against her wealthy guardian uncle's wishes. Because he opposed their romance and marriage—but especially her indifference to Catholic faith—when her uncle John Driscoll dies he leaves his property mainly to the Catholic Church and provides his mansion for use as a convent. Only six years old when she attends John Driscoll's funeral, Nellie Birdseye recalls the overwhelming aesthetic and spiritual impression made by that event:

> The high altar blazed with hundreds of candles, the choir was completely filled by the masses of flowers. The bishop was there, and a flock

> of priests in gorgeous vestments. . . . I thought of John Driscoll as having escaped the end of all flesh; it was as if he had been translated with no dark conclusion to the pageant, no "night of the grave" about which our Protestant preachers talked. From the freshness of the roses and lilies, from the glory of the high altar, he had gone straight to the greater glory, through smoking censers and candles and stars.[10]

These pleasurable impressions of the Catholic sensorium comprise only one of several ways that Nellie encounters Catholicism as she narrates the life of Myra Hanshawe. On a visit to Myra in California many years later, Nellie recounts Myra's unhappy adult life as a shabbily bohemian woman who is neglected by her husband, frustrated in her romantic hopes, and bedridden with terminal cancer. Thus stymied by the difficulties of her life, an aging and unwell Myra takes the opportunity to explain herself to her young friend Nellie, who is now in her twenties. Having recognized the errors and tragedy of her own life, Myra in her illness has returned to a version of Catholic faith and a rejuvenated relationship with the Church, admitting: "I broke with the Church when I broke with everything else and ran away with a German free-thinker; but I believe in holy words and holy rites all the same." Cather reinforces Myra's confession of errors by introducing a young priest who visits her during her terminal illness and describes the aura of holiness surrounding the suffering woman: "I wonder whether some of the saints of the early Church weren't a good deal like her. She's not at all modern in her make-up, is she?"[11]

For a writer whose career has seldom been sufficiently described in terms of its religious commitments, it is striking to observe the extent to which Roman Catholicism infuses the concluding pages of *My Mortal Enemy*. Most impressive of all in this novella, there is a concluding statement of spiritual longing that is arresting both in its of disavowal of the free-thinking trajectory of Myra Hanshawe's life and its subtle theorization of religion's deeper attractions. Here, as in Kate Chopin's fiction, Cather uses Roman Catholicism as a useful (but problematic) framework for working through issues of concern to women. To the young priest who attends her at bedside, Myra articulates a mature epistemology of religion, which is rather precisely framed by Cather's free indirect narration: "'Religion is different from everything else; *because in religion seeking is finding*'". . . . [Myra] accented the world 'seeking' very strongly, very deeply. She seemed to say that in other searchings it might be the object of the quest that brought satisfaction, or it could be something incidental that one got on the way; but in religion, desire was fulfillment, it was the seeking itself that rewarded" (116). The Cather scholar Susan J. Rosowski has pointed out the irony of this statement and setting in *My Mortal Enemy*, noting: "It is not unusual for a priest to attend the dying, but here it is the priest who is instructed by his parishioner, rather than the reverse."[12] From the evidence of this scene, too, we can see that Cather presents Myra as dying in an ambivalent or unsettled relation to her own religious background, even as her religion provides a framework for articulating her inchoate desires. Myra's husband, Oswald, from whom she had become increasingly alienated, claims after her death that "the Church has been on her mind for a long while. . . . It is one of her delusions that I separated her from the Church. I never meant to." In any case, the conclusion of this peculiar story points neither to an unambiguous religious commitment nor to an agnostic resistance to belief; instead, Myrna's statement that "in religion seeking is finding" points to view of religion as a structure that adds gravity to an individual's personal quest.[13]

Having set the stage for the subsequent movement of her artistic project, published as *Death Comes for the Archbishop* in 1927, Cather in *My Mortal Enemy* demonstrates at once her commitment to the expression of Catholic religious principles as a bulwark against modernity as well as her reluctance to pursue denominational membership with propaganda or evangelism. It is thus no surprise that she would discover the importance of frontier Catholicism in the American Southwest—the subject of *Death Comes for the Archbishop*—to reside not in its ability to enlist membership but in its emotional content and uncanny moral reach. The Catholic missions in that remote country, which Cather thought comprised "the most interesting of all its stories," came to her through study of its church histories but also by reading the ruins of its sacred architecture. "The old mission churches," she insisted, "even those which were abandoned and in ruins, had a moving reality about them."[14]

While Catholicism is present in a great many of her writings, Cather's deployment of a Roman Catholic literary aesthetic reached its most significant expression in *Death Comes for the Archbishop*. However, Cather's preoccupation with themes and scenes of Catholicism has gone largely unexamined by her critics, although it is well known to all biographers that the events recounted in *Death Comes for the Archbishop* are based directly on her biographical research into the lives of the French priests Jean

Baptiste Lamy and Joseph P. Machebeuf, the latter of whom she encountered in W. J. Howlett's *Life of the Right Reverend Joseph P. Machebeuf, D.D.* (1908). Although Cather did not mention Howlett's work in the novel, she later acknowledged her debt to that book.[15] Sharon O'Brien's feminist biography of Cather avoids the issue of Cather's religious novels and goes so far as to argue that her decision to join the Episcopal Church in 1922 was among the "deeply conservative" aspects of Cather's personality. O'Brien's *Willa Cather: An Emerging Voice* (1987) goes to considerable lengths to describe the feminist and lesbian currents at work in Cather's fiction but overlooks almost entirely the question of how Cather used various aspects of Catholicism in her novels. Preferring to de-emphasize Cather's seeming fascination with Catholic history, the Cather biographer Hermione Lee has advanced the idea that "Cather's attraction to Catholicism (*which understandably led many readers to suppose that she was a practitioner*) is mainly explained by her pleasure in . . . Christianized paganism."[16] Despite such views, it is abundantly clear that Catholicism plays pivotal roles in a number of Cather's books. Along with *Death Comes for the Archbishop*, her earlier novels *O Pioneers!* (1913) and *My Ántonia* (1918) also feature ethnic characters drawn from a European Catholic background, while her subsequent *Shadows on the Rock* (1931) turns to a historical treatment of seventeenth-century Quebec, with Catholic bishops, priests, and nuns serving as significant characters.

There are times when literary criticism does not benefit as much as it should from historical perspective and the advantages of hindsight. This is especially true with respect to Cather scholarship of recent decades, which, as the critic Joan Acocella has argued quite persuasively, has frequently put political concerns ahead of literary analysis.[17] The extent to which Willa Cather's fiction made substantial use of Roman Catholic tropes and themes was considerably more obvious to her contemporaries than it has been to critics and biographers in more recent years, who have devoted their attention above all to the gender politics of her writings. Of her several recent biographers, James Woodress has addressed most completely the matter of Catholic readers finding in Cather a kindred spirit and a presumed Catholic herself. For instance, Woodress documents the admiring 1927 review of Willa Cather's work by Michael Williams in the Catholic intellectual journal *Commonweal*. Woodress notes that scholars and students of the 1920s and 1930s frequently presumed, on the basis of her fiction, that Willa Cather was herself a Catholic, and many wrote letters to her in which they inquired about the details of her conversion to their faith.[18] By 1931, in its review of Cather's popular *Shadows on the Rock*, a reviewer in the *Catholic World* found her writing to be not just suitably Catholic in its views but also a welcome rejoinder to the "crude realism, Freudism [*sic*], inchoate prose, shallow philosophy," and other irreligious tendencies in modern literature.[19] In any event, contemporary readers recognized that Cather was writing with an acute consciousness of Roman Catholic tradition, although her larger purpose in doing so was never made entirely clear to those readers.

As with Kate Chopin's conventional local-color technique, which in her fiction emphasized the regional and cultural peculiarities of postbellum Louisiana (including its religious flavor) but did not promote Roman Catholic faith, Cather's novels also lack the evangelical ardor and dogmatism of nineteenth-century Catholic fiction.[20] Or, as suggested by the situation of the fictional Claude Wheeler, the protagonist of her novel *One of Ours*, it is possible in Cather's fiction to appreciate the essence of religion without subscribing to every aspect of its dogma. About the religious anxieties of the teenaged Wheeler, Cather wrote that "Claude had gone through a painful time of doubt and fear when he thought a great deal about religion. For several years, from fourteen to eighteen, he believed that he would be lost if he did not repent and undergo that mysterious change called conversion. But there was something in him that would not let him avail himself of the pardon offered. He felt condemned, but he did not want to renounce a world he as yet knew nothing of." Eventually Claude arrives at a kind of equilibrium in his religious attitudes after rejecting the discursiveness and abstractions of theology as "something too full of evasions and sophistries to be reasoned about" and then concludes: "Though he wanted little to do with theology and theologians, [he] would have said he was a Christian."[21]

The ambivalent religious attitude of the fictional Claude Wheeler makes its way into most of the novels Cather wrote after she joined the Episcopal Church in 1922, which is to say that her fiction of this period is saturated in the discourse of Catholic Christianity without being framed in terms of compulsory piety, even though her contemporary reviewers in Catholic magazines (such as the *Catholic World*, *America*, and *Commonweal*) "slapped on her novels pious readings completely out of line with the text."[22] It would be much more accurate to say that the particulars of theology and the pressures of evangelism are largely subdued in her fiction in favor of narratives in which religion serves more to promote a mood of moral seriousness and historical gravity instead of a blunt discourse promoting specific beliefs.

Roman Catholic religion and culture are thus presented by Cather as a kind of moral theater in which human problems can be addressed as her characters face the distinctively modern problems of materialism, alienation, and crumbling tradition. For instance, in *Death Comes for the Archbishop*, as the literary critic David H. Porter has asserted, Cather is working out what might be described as a profound tension between the limits of human life and the broader context of deep time in which individual lives are experienced: "Contributing to this sense that human lives, and everything that happens in them, are all *sub specie aeternitatis* is the Catholic faith that suffuses the book."[23] Alfred Kazin, in a memorable passage from *On Native Grounds* (1942), his classic study of early twentieth-century American fiction, argued that the most salient aspect of Cather's fiction was what he called its traditionalism or what was sometimes mistaken for simple nostalgia:

> It was a candid and philosophical nostalgia, a conviction and a standard possible only to a writer whose remembrance of the world of her childhood and the people in it was so overwhelming that everything after it seemed drab and more than a little cheap. Her distinction was not merely one of cultivation and sensibility; it was a kind of spiritual clarity possible only to those who suffer their loneliness as an act of the imagination and the will. . . . [The] very intensity of her nostalgia had from the first led her beyond nostalgia; it had given her the conviction that the values of the world she had lost were the primary values, and everything else merely their degradation. (251)

Kazin concluded that the evidence of her writing was sufficient to describe Willa Cather as not only a "spiritual aristocrat with democratic manners" but also "a Catholic by instinct" whose tendencies in the direction of that religious tradition were part of her wholesale rejection of "modern industrial culture." In this way, Kazin adroitly skirts the issue of Cather's religious beliefs and her relationship to Roman Catholic theology by showing her religious "instinct" to be conditioning and sensitizing her artistry in order to address more robustly the larger crisis of morals in the face of industrial modernity.[24]

The development of neo-Catholic aesthetic techniques in the hands of writers like Cather and Chopin may be understood as an outcome produced by an earlier generation of Roman Catholic efforts to evangelize the American people by means of print media. This possibility would be especially intriguing if evidence existed that either of these women had been an admiring reader of the earlier generation of Catholic evangelical fiction. But, because this evidence does not exist and because both women were steeped in modern secular writing to a large extent, their turn to Catholic literary tropes of a less dogmatic sort likely reflects the fin-de-siècle anti-modernist impulse traced by the cultural historian T. J. Jackson Lears, who has observed a broad turn to various forms of "primitivism" during the "crumbling Protestant culture of the late nineteenth century." According to Lears, this period featured a precipitous cultural shift, during which religious tropes were (haltingly and ambivalently) "adjusted" to serve not the historical "Protestant ethos of salvation through self-denial" but rather "a therapeutic ideal of self-fulfillment in *this* world through exuberant health and intense experience." So powerful was this shift in mentality among well-educated Americans of the period that "Even Catholic mysticism, art, and ritual were adjusted to secular purposes."[25]

The choice by a sophisticated writer like the non-Catholic Willa Cather to use the traditions and tropes of Roman Catholicism as a kind of grammar for describing the moral dimensions of a secular world thus becomes understandable within a broader cultural movement toward modern identity that found anti-modernisms (especially that of Roman Catholic culture) useful in its transformations. Taking up Lears's model of anti-modern religious primitivism (which he associated with numerous Americans who turned to Catholicism in the late Victorian period) sheds a useful light on Cather's literary adaptations of Roman Catholic culture. Whereas nineteenth-century American writers of religious novels tended almost exclusively to be endorsing (or attacking) some aspect of denominational religion in order to persuade or dissuade readers with respect to a particular faith, Cather wrote Catholic religion into her fiction for purposes that seem closer to the model of "self-fulfillment" that Lears identifies rather than any deep concern with specific religious affiliations.

While the inclusion of a modernist icon like Willa Cather in a study of the American Catholic literary tradition may seem unlikely to some, it is clear that her narrative strategies participate in the representational modes developed within both Catholic didactic fiction and "secular" modernism. Just as clearly, though, her writing avoids both the argumentative strains of nineteenth-century religious fiction just as it avoids the kind of modernist secularism that characterized much literary work by her contemporaries. Although her fiction draws some of its greatest energy from representations of the Catholic tradition, Willa Cather—like Kate Chopin—has more typically been described as an avatar of the modern feminist tradition and, lately, of the kinds of gender instability promulgated within recent exchanges in queer theory.[26] Along with the cultural work that her fiction undoubtedly performs in the area of gender representation, Willa Cather has produced a body of work whose infatuation with American landscape and regional difference uncannily orients the local-color tradition toward the complexities of modernism, using religious themes to develop forms of resistance to the modern (a deeply ethical resistance that is misread, according to Kazin, as mere nostalgia). Most uncanny of all, though, is the coexistence in Cather's writing of representations of Catholicism alongside a characterization of women that appears as both mythic and radically subversive. Or, as Lears has suggested, her religious fiction corresponds with and advances the broader cause of anti-modernism during this period, with the result that "the fascination with Catholic forms had both social and personal significance; it eased adjustment to a streamlined modern culture even as it sustained protest against that culture."[27]

This thematic duality—apparently meant to arrest both the corrosions of modernity and to advance new views of the feminine—holds true even in *Death Comes for the Archbishop*, a novel that Cather herself described as "a story with no woman in it but the Virgin Mary."[28] In order to accomplish these objectives, *Death Comes for the Archbishop* returns historically to the antebellum period to conceive of the narrative possibilities of Catholic missions in the provincial American Southwest. The narrative, which opens in 1848, features celibate male priests: Catholic missionaries attempting to revive and consolidate mission territory precisely at the moment the Southwestern territories had been acquired for the United States but well before the arrival of statehood for New Mexico in 1912. Drawing on actual events experienced by French missionaries, *Death Comes for the Archbishop* returns to the scene of colonial expansion in the desert Southwest by employing the methods of historical romance. Cather's depiction of Catholic proselytization thus places the tale outside the usual narrative of American colonial history, occluding the actual process by which the vast New Mexico territory was acquired and highlighting instead the exoticism of the land itself and of the men whose efforts promoted Catholicism among the local Indian and Spanish residents. As one overly enthusiastic Church official indicates early in the novel, the historical resonances and religious gravity of New Mexican colonialism were immense: "You can scarcely understand what it means that the United States has annexed that enormous territory which was the cradle of the Faith in the New World. The Vicarate of New Mexico will be in a few years raised to an Episcopal See, with jurisdiction over a country larger than Central and Western Europe, barring Russia."[29] Roman Catholic missionary work thereby frames and conditions the U.S. imperial narrative of manifest destiny, whose theme and rhetorical function is modern political conquest rather than religious or moral insight.

The languorously narrated novel features the exploits of two French missionaries, one (Jean Latour) a sophisticated and cosmopolitan bishop of considerable erudition and the other (Joseph Vaillant) a zealous priest and baker's son. Over the course of three decades, the French priests are depicted as gentle and loving missionaries to the people of New Mexico, who had been practicing their own form of Catholicism inherited from the Spanish explorers. In all of Cather's descriptions, the missionaries are distinguished not so much for their religious zeal but for their ability to blend comfortably with the provincial communities they inhabit. Their goal of building a monumental cathedral in the desert is finally realized with the financial assistance of local citizens, but at all times Bishop Latour maintains a deep respect and tolerance toward indigenous beliefs and avoids any trace of the dogmatism or authoritarianism so prevalent in anti-Catholic novels of the nineteenth century. In Cather's telling of the provincial history, the celibate Catholic priests become key figures advancing her own idiosyncratic, modernist version of American local-color narrative, blending their aesthetic appreciation for the rustic desert Southwest with religious sincerity. As with earlier novelists such as Huntington, Dorsey, and Chopin, Cather adroitly writes Catholicism into the continent's provinces, locating idealized Catholic characters across the space of mythic geographic scenes—familiar in American narrative from Cooper through Hemingway—that develop a good part of their intrigue from their exotic positioning at national borders and frontiers.

Quite apart from the largely unresolved biographical question of Cather's precise religious disposition, her extensive use of frontier Catholicism in the local-color mode knits together a successful kind of literary resolution to tensions between traditional religion and women's concerns, a resolution that had eluded earlier Catholic writers such as Brownson and Hecker. The troublesome and corrosive "femininity" that Brownson located in popular fiction and saw as a threat to orthodox Catholicism is turned back on itself in *Death Comes for the Archbishop*. Here the priests themselves are feminized in sensibility and affect, and they exemplify what one critic has observed as a persistent theme in Cather's fiction: a "flagrant lack of interest in the drama of heterosexual desire." At the same time, *Death Comes for the Archbishop* manifests what Marilee Lindemann, in a study guided by queer theory, has called Cather's "insistent tenderness, . . . utopian aims, and . . . quietly lavish displays of male bodies and male intimacies."[30] Not only is the New Mexican Catholic Church a place where troubled young women, for example, can "bloom again in the house of God," but its sophisticated priests are themselves equipped with the finest religio-aesthetic sensibilities: it is they who are in fact the ideal "feminized readers" of Cather's local-color narrative.

Bishop Latour, in particular, makes direct assertions in this novel about the usefulness of Catholicism for refining the aesthetic sense: "The Miracles of the Church seem to me to rest not so much upon faces or voices or healing power coming suddenly near to us from afar off, but upon our perceptions being made finer, so that for a moment our eyes can see and our ears can see what is there about us always."[31] Along with this call to aesthetic refinement, which appears to be directed at both religious feeling and at reading practices (i.e., Catholicism and modernist forms of local-color writing, respectively), comes the recognition on the part of the priests themselves that the essential features of Catholic faith can be understood as analogous to unspoiled, unmodernized native life. Bishop Latour finds in the New Mexican indigenous natives—unsophisticated as they are—an instinctive, though joltingly literal religious outlook: "The Bishop . . . observed in Indian life a strange literalness, often shocking and disconcerting. The Acomas, who must share the universal yearning for something permanent, enduring, without shadow of change,—they had their idea in substance. They actually lived upon their Rock; were born upon it and died upon it."[32]

Although *Death Comes for the Archbishop* is far from being a dogmatically religious novel, the presence of Catholicism in the novel remains inescapable, and vexing for interpretations of Cather that have identified her as a standard-bearer for feminist consciousness in the twentieth and twenty-first century. How, then, is it possible for Cather the feminist to resolve patterns of misogyny in the Catholic literary tradition, voiced most clearly in the antebellum rhetoric of Brownson but also of course in the long-standing patriarchal traditions of the Catholic church itself? If we are to understand Cather as a modern feminist, how can we account for her recourse to Catholicism at all in her work? These are difficult questions to answer comprehensively, but in terms of *Death Comes for the Archbishop* it would be well to begin with the recognition that despite Cather's claims to the contrary, there are indeed significant woman-centered scenes in the novel, and not all of them make reference to the Virgin Mary. For instance, one of this novel's recurrent themes is the plight of hapless New Mexican women victimized by frontiersmen, who place them into a kind of domestic servitude, forcing the women to bear their children and care for their households. One of these frontier scoundrels, who is described as "the degenerate murderer, Buck Scales," is finally brought to justice for his crimes, which included killing the infant children of his wife Magdalena by "ways so horrible she could not relate it." Childless and abandoned after her husband is finally executed by hanging, Magdalena's rescue comes at the hands of Bishop Latour, who by that time had brought to the New Mexico territory "five courageous nuns . . . to found a school for girls in letterless Santa Fé." Whereas Anna Dorsey, a half century earlier in her novel *Coaina*, developed a rustic Native American into an exemplary and pious Madonna figure, one whose boundless devotion turned her away from all human relationships in favor of the purely religious life, Cather's humble Mexican girl becomes the ideal recipient of Catholic benevolence, safely harbored in feminine shelter. Once she is taken in by the convent, "she became housekeeper and manager of the Sisters' kitchen. She was devoted to the nuns and so happy in the service of the Church that when the Bishop visited the school he used to enter by the kitchen-garden to see her serene and handsome face. For she became beautiful, as . . . she had been as a girl. After the blight of her horrible youth was over, she seemed to bloom again in the household of God."[33]

For Cather, as for the elder generation of print evangelists that included Isaac Hecker and James Gibbons, there is something deeply appealing about the notion of a profoundly maternal and sheltering Catholicism, and she writes this aspect of the faith tradition into the masterpiece of her late fiction. Her protagonists in *Death Comes for the Archbishop* are male, but the social problems their work alleviates are experienced primarily by the women in provincial New Mexico, for whom

Catholicism is figured as a comfortably pious route to a life of social tranquility. In another instance of beset native women, a young Mexican girl is abducted by Indians and yet clings bravely to her Catholic faith as her only resort during captivity. As Latour's aide Father Joseph relates the story, the girl's virginity is dangerously at risk while in the hands of the Indians. Later, she is victimized by the corrupt Mexican priest Father Martinez, in an indication that Catholic power—so critical for the physical and spiritual safety of women—can be used for evil works as well as good:

> Only a few weeks ago [Father Joseph] was told a pitiful story of a Mexican girl carried off in one of the Indian raids on the Costella valley. She was a child of eight when she was carried away, and was fifteen when she was found and ransomed. During all that time the pious girl had preserved her virginity by a succession of miracles. She had a medal from the shrine of Our Lady of Guadeloupe tied round her neck, and she said such prayers as she had been taught. Her chastity was threatened many times. . . . After she was found . . . she was so devout that she wished to become a religious. She was debauched by this [Father] Martinez, and he married her to one of his peons. She is now living on one of his farms.[34]

The scenery and adventure of local-color and captivity narratives, set on the dramatic landscaped of the Southwest American frontier, thus accompany a set of events that present Catholicism in a highly favorable way, but without the dogmatic tenor so typical of nineteenth-century American Catholic fiction writers. This sort of literary Catholicism, much like that presented in Kate Chopin's Louisiana stories, continues to draw the concerns of women into sharp focus. However, absent Chopin's deterministic attitudes toward her characters, Cather's female myth-making allows for an imagined and historical Catholicism to be one of the rare settings for women's safety, respect, and contentment.

This fiction created by Willa Cather is almost entirely unlike Anna Dorsey's *Coaina*, a Catholic novel from the mid-nineteenth century that had presented an engagement between Roman Catholic culture and indigenous North American people. Whereas *Coiana* offered the exemplary figure of a Roman Catholic Indian Madonna, Cather's writing here suggests a more democratic, and perhaps less saintly, array of spiritual possibilities. More than a simple call to unerring chastity or steadfast piety, *Death Comes for the Archbishop* forgoes the strict theological concerns that bound earlier, self-consciously Catholic novelists to rehearsals of Church authority and orthodoxy. Instead, the most profound religiosity of the novel can be felt in those scenes that express the nurturing and sheltering dimensions of Catholic experience. This is apparent from the ways Cather describes the torments of the young provincial girls, but even more so from her rewriting of American provincial Catholicism as a haven for both the virginal and maternal instincts. It is equally clear that Cather produces not only representations of the Virgin but also a distinct sense of female divinity written into the Roman Catholic tradition and narrated across some of the emerging nation's most dramatic landscapes.

In the *Archbishop* chapter "The Great Diocese," Bishop Latour himself recognizes this paradoxical return of the feminine by means of Catholic culture in an exchange with an elderly Mexican slave woman who had toiled for decades in the household of "low-caste Protestants." Praying together as she neared her death, "[Latour] seemed able to feel all it meant to her to know that there was a Kind Woman in Heaven, though there were such cruel ones on earth. Old people, who have felt blows and toil and known the world's hard hand, need, even more than children do, a woman's tenderness. Only a Woman, divine, could know all that a woman can suffer."[35] Having associated Woman with the Divine, Cather avoids evangelism at every turn but nevertheless makes a powerful argument for the ethical potential of Catholic religion while sustaining for her readers a productive and creatively powerful tension between faith, gender, and belonging.

Conclusion

In reviewing the literary terrain surveyed by this study, it should be apparent that during the period from 1844 to 1931 favorable representations of Roman Catholicism, although often deployed for evangelical purposes, were consequential in many different ways and for many different reasons. Anti-Catholic fiction and nonfiction had been a staple of commercial print during much of the nineteenth century, and thus faithful Catholic writers did their part to create novels, essays, reviews, and other works that portrayed their religious beliefs in a favorable light. These efforts to some degree countered the nativist political rhetoric of that period, when Catholic migration to the United States had dramatically adjusted the nation's religious profile. However, to allow merely that Roman Catholicism became a significant aspect of American writing during these years, or to assert that their literary efforts were frequently defensive, does not entirely explain the complex engagements that various writers made with the commercial publishing scene during these years. Some of that complexity suggests that our understanding of the way Catholicism figures in American literature might indeed be deeper to the extent that we venture beyond simply identifying writers according to their membership in a church.

It is necessary to see past the categories of "Catholic writer" or "Catholic novelist" in order to grasp what that religious tradition actually meant in the hands of individual writers. Religious affiliations are not genetic traits but instead are complex human decisions about faith and belonging: choices that are sometimes impermanent and that signify affiliations that vary between persons (and over time) in degree of intensity and commitment. Although their dominant concerns are often deeply religious, it would be unthinkable to reduce canonical literary figures like Stowe, Douglass, Hawthorne, Dickinson, and Melville to identities as merely "Protestant" or "Christian" writers, although for each of those writers religion is extremely important. Like their better-known literary contemporaries, many nineteenth- and early twentieth-century Catholics took seriously their work as writers and shouldered significant commercial, artistic, and personal challenges as they created a diverse body of literature in which religious issues were of primary concern.

In the cases of Orestes Brownson and Isaac Hecker, converts who defined themselves as public intellectuals, to be a Catholic writer meant tirelessly affirming Roman Catholicism as a national religion while looking always to the commercial print media in order efficiently to spread the faith as they understood it. It meant other things as well to these sometime transcendentalists: it meant high-mindedly guarding the nation's literature from the dangers of private and public immorality, while directing the Catholic faithful to buttress their piety with a more virtuous program of reading. For Brownson, in particular, it meant serving as the kind of reactionary critic who would always be opposed to what he judged to be a dangerous feminine influence in American letters, even as women were coming more fully into their own as accomplished professional writers and successful literary evangelists for Christian principles. Both men had ambitions of large-scale Catholic evangelism and hoped to influence ordinary Americans through their religious advocacy, but their philosophical habits of mind and the recondite style of their works—many of which are fascinating and absorbing in their own right—meant that their influence was quite modest on the national publishing scene. They performed the challenging work of clearing a space for Roman Catholic intellectual discourse in the United States, and thus are notable for their unique place in American literary history, but they never harnessed the power of mass-print culture in ways that would realize their goal of developing a pious Catholic nation.

Anna Hanson Dorsey and Jedediah Vincent Huntington, both talented novelists who converted to Roman Catholicism during their young adulthood, shared with Brownson and Hecker a firm commitment to the Roman Church but demonstrated in their fiction a more flexible and less doctrinaire presentation of religious faith. They exemplify the more successful literary approach taken by Catholic fiction writers in the mid-nineteenth century, whereby religious dogma and rigid orthodoxy were moderated by the kinds of characterization and narrative techniques that would appeal to large numbers of American readers across the religious spectrum. Their decision to write for popular audiences, rather than for the much smaller cohort of Catholic clergy and intellectuals whose attention was sought by Brownson and Hecker, conditioned their works in ways that made accommodations to the print marketplace. As professional fiction writers and faithful evangelical Catholics, they combined religious conviction with a practical understanding of the literary market and contemporary tastes in reading. Their books thus combined a favorable view of Catholic religious life with the kinds of romantic and adventurous stories that had broad appeal, especially among the growing audience for fiction that centered on women's concerns.

By contrast, the rather unconventional literary career of Bishop James Gibbons demonstrates how a perceptive student of nineteenth-century culture was able draw on a variety of resources in American and European literature in order to construct an appealing Roman Catholic catechism, which would appeal to a popular readership and yet still advance a highly orthodox view of the faith. To enlist the attention of his American readers, Gibbons chose to deploy in *Faith of Our Fathers* select tropes from popular sentimental fiction and to emphasize at numerous points the admirable feminine qualities of the historic Church and its contemporary members. For the literary historian, an important lesson to take from Gibbon's success with *Faith of Our Fathers* is that by the later nineteenth century, American readers of popular books, including Roman Catholics, were presented with an unprecedented variety of possible reading experiences. We know from the extraordinary enlargement of the commercial print industry in the nineteenth century that just like other cohorts of American readers, many faithful Catholics who had the ability and means to do so read widely across a variety of genres: novels, stories, newspapers, magazines, tracts, and even catechisms. As often as not, the reader of Saturday's sentimental novel and Sunday's Catholic catechism were one and the same person, and a cosmopolitan writer-priest like James Gibbons would surely have been attuned to this truth of the modern print marketplace. Consequently, Gibbons wrote his catechism in ways he thought best suited to a generation of Catholic readers educated simultaneously by church precept and popular culture. There is a secondary lesson to be learned from the wide distribution and steady sales of *Faith of Our Fathers*, which would have been purchased or otherwise distributed among Catholic readers at revival meetings or in classrooms, settings where it quite likely would have been an object of careful instruction and study. Literary history has tended not to look very deeply into genres like the religious catechism, but surely any book that is so widely distributed should to be recognized for potential influence among its readers, many of whom were in the process of coming to terms with some combination of textual experiences: some religious, some secular, and some—like *Faith of Our Fathers*—an uncanny blend of the two.

Literary choices about Catholic religion and the secular framed the discussion of fiction by Kate Chopin and Willa Cather. In the development of their careers, we can see new options emerging for American writers who discovered in Catholic traditions an aesthetic repertoire and an ambivalent legacy, rather than a faith to accept. As writers who were at various points aloof from or disaffected with Roman Catholic orthodoxy, they cannot be described as standard-bearers or evangelists for Catholic authority or the advancement of religious faith. Yet their fiction shows an unmistakable (if ironic) debt to the moral traditions, literature, iconography, and emotional structures of Roman Catholicism. Their work also extends an earlier set of American literary conversations about religion by addressing some of the many ways that women's experiences can be understood in light of actual or imagined Catholic cultures. Perhaps most importantly, Chopin and Cather remind us of how vastly different styles and themes were able to find useful expression through the adaptation of Roman Catholic cultures for literary ends. They were at work in the vanguard of an emerging generation of American fiction writers in subsequent decades, many of whose religious beliefs were uncertain or nonexistent but whose writing was profoundly shaped by the lived—or observed—experience of Catholicism.

It is important to note that the evolving presence of Roman Catholicism in American writing—from the now-obscure scholarly sermons of European-born missionaries like Anthony Kohlmann in the 1820s to Willa Cather's popular novels of the 1920s and 1930s—signifies more than a mere rise or decline in Roman Catholic writing. As the nineteenth century gave way to the twentieth, large numbers of Catholic Americans gained socioeconomic status and political power, and they began to play a more visible role in the cultural life of the United States. The insularity of nineteenth-century Catholic theological writing, the conservatism of antebellum Catholic literary activists, and the stubborn evangelical rhetoric of the early phase of Catholic fiction were all part of an effort, made urgent by tides of immigration and leveraged by the expansion of commercial publishing, to consolidate American Catholics into a more unified nation of the faithful. However, as realist and modernist literary styles became more prevalent in the early decades of the twentieth century, writers who cited Roman Catholicism in their writing did what other American writers were doing during those years: they changed with the times and adapted their work in response to contemporary literary trends, and many of them left church membership behind or avoided it altogether. And yet they adapted their representations of Catholic religion to pressing concerns, such as women's increasing social autonomy and empowerment, relevant for their moment in American history.

American Catholic criticism and literary culture persists, of course, into the postmodern era, as do its critics. Catholic literary culture in the United States has resisted the kinds of intellectual and critical leadership that Brownson and Hecker were driving to implement in an imagined Catholic America. To be certain, some contemporary elite periodicals, successors of *Brownson's Quarterly Review* such as *Commonweal* and *First Things*, have reviewed and critiqued a range of practical and intellectual issues (such as theology, human rights, the politics of abortion and birth control, the economics of the Third World) for a small number of intellectuals within the American Catholic tradition. Since Brownson, though, staunchly Catholic criticism, by which is meant a critical discourse produced by writers who have clearly stated loyalties to the Roman Catholic Church, appears to have had only the most limited influence on contemporary American civilization. More often, the persistent energies and intractable problems of Catholicism have found their way more obliquely into American literary culture, resisting the old-fashioned didacticism and evangelism of the nineteenth century and instead following the subtler discursive and moral paths blazed by Kate Chopin and Willa Cather.

Theodore Dreiser, Eugene O'Neill, F. Scott Fitzgerald, Ernest Hemingway, Flannery O'Connor, James T. Farrell, Jack Kerouac, Robert Lowell, Charles Olson, Anne Sexton, William Kennedy, Louise Erdrich, Anne Rice, and Ron Hansen, to name only a few notable American writers active since the 1930s, have all attempted to address Roman Catholic culture in their work. With the exception of Flannery O'Connor, though, these are writers whose relationships with the organized Roman Catholicism were ambiguous and whose beliefs are difficult to summarize.[1] This fact makes them fit heirs to the American tradition of writing about Catholic life, which suggests that over the course of a century, writers both faithful and ambivalent participated in the "dream-work" of religious literary culture. There the changing desires of the print marketplace register, select, and distribute those elements of Roman Catholicism that have the most narrative leverage, the broadest popular appeal, and the most compelling relationship to American readers confronting modernity under the changing lights of religious tradition. By revisiting their attempts to articulate ideas about the proper relationship between religion and its readers, we can see more clearly how they participated in a crucial period of national and cultural development, and how they prepared the way for contemporary writers to explore and critique with greater freedom the role of Catholic religion in American life.

Notes

Introduction

1. Howe, *What Hath God Wrought*, 3.

2. Tweed, *Retelling U.S. Religious History*, 12. For a compelling new theory of religions as cultural mapping phenomena, see also Tweed, *Crossing and Dwelling*.

3. Loughran, *The Republic in Print*, 24. For a compact but highly detailed survey of US development by 1815, see Howe, *What Hath God Wrought*, especially the chapter "The Continental Setting" (19–62), which describes the significant shortcomings in transportation and communications infrastructure during the early nineteenth century.

4. Cavanaugh, "Catholic Book Publishing in the United States, 1784–1850," 126.

5. An important study of the relationship between Roman Catholicism and key American Protestant writers of the nineteenth century is Franchot, *Roads to Rome*. Noteworthy examples of social history investigating American Catholic life include McDannell, *Material Christianity*, especially the discussion of Lourdes water and Catholic devotional practices (132–62), and Taves, *The Household of Faith*, which surveys early American Catholic devotional practices.

6. Richard Hofstadter includes nineteenth-century anti-Catholicism in the United States, along with anti-Masonic fears, as part of the "paranoid style" in American politics ("The Paranoid Style in American Politics," 19–23). Anti-Catholicism found its way into the popular press and became a staple of political agitation during the nineteenth century and drew energy from such documents as the "bogus encyclical attributed to Leo XIII instructing American Catholics on a certain date in 1893 to exterminate all heretics," with the result that "a great many anti-Catholics . . . expected a nation-wide uprising" (ibid., 23).

7. For a comprehensive discussion of antebellum evangelicals and their use of mass print media, see Nord, *The Evangelical Origins of Mass Media in America, 1815–1835*.

8. Cary, "Plan of Mathew Cary for the Institution for Printing Roman Catholic Books, 1791," 135.

9. Zboray, *A Fictive People*, 16. On the extremely unreliable and sometimes dysfunctional communication networks in pre-nineteenth-century America, and their effect on the transmission of letters, periodicals, and other printed materials, see Loughran, *The Republic in Print*, in which the author argues that "there was no 'nationalized' print public sphere in the years just before and just after the Revolution, but rather a proliferating variety of local and regional reading publics scattered across a vast and diverse geographical space" (xix). For an excellent survey of nineteenth-century religious publishing, see Gutjahr, "Diversification in American Religious Publishing," which extends David Paul Nord's important observation that nineteenth-century religious publishers took early advantage of the burgeoning print marketplace. Gutjahr notes that Protestant religious publishers by the 1830s were "years ahead" of trade publishers in "taking full advantage of changes in papermaking technology, stereotyping, centralized mass production, and power presses" ("Diversification in American Religious Publishing,"195).

10. For a useful survey of early nineteenth-century Catholic literary culture in New York City, see Meehan, "Catholic Literary New York, 1800–1840," 399–414.

11. Anthony Kohlmann became a novitiate soon after Pope Pius VII permitted the Society of Jesus in Russia to accept new members. Kohlmann worked first as a missionary in Germany, Holland, and England before being dispatched to the United States in 1807, there to embark on a series of missions to German congregations in Pennsylvania. In addition to founding the Old St. Patrick's Cathedral, he also helped to administer a short-lived school in New York called the "New York Literary Institute," which closed after several years of mixed success, 1808–13 (see Meehan, "Catholic Literary New York," 405). His work on Unitarianism is described as a "reply to the Rev. Jared Sparks, which has always been regarded as of the highest authority" (Shea, "Memorial of the First Centenary," 56–57; for a more complete Kohlmann biography, see Nevils, *Miniatures of Georgetown*, 126–27).

12. Meehan, "Catholic Literary New York," 402. For a thorough account of Irish Catholicism's eventual rise to power in Boston, see Kane, *Separatism and Subculture*.

13. Halttunen, *Confidence Men and Painted Women*, 194–95.

14. Thorp, *Catholic Novelists in Defense of their Faith, 1829–1865*, 54–55.

15. Gauchet, *Disenchantment of the World*, 163.

16. Patricia Dunlavy Valenti provides an excellent account of Rose Hawthorne in *To Myself a Stranger*. For discussion of the controversy surrounding the Catholic conversion of Rose and her husband George Parsons Lathrop, see Valenti, *To Myself a Stranger*, 99–131.

Chapter 1. Orestes Brownson in Young America

1. Melville, *Pierre; or, the Ambiguities*, esp. 244–64. On the Young America literary and political movement in New York, see Miller, *The Raven and the Whale*, and especially Bender, *New York Intellect*, 120–68. Bender places the interest generated by "Young America" within the context of New York economics, pointing out that from 1840 to 1860 publishing was the fastest growing industry in the city, and by 1860 publishing was New York's leading industry (Bender, *New York Intellect*, 156). Building on the work of Miller, Edward Widmer's *Young America: The Flowering of Democracy in New York* is an excellent accounting of political ramifications and evolving literary agendas of Young American ideologies.

2. Several years before his conversion to Roman Catholicism, Brownson had caused a political firestorm with the publication of his remarkable essay "The Laboring Classes" in the July 1840 issue of the *Boston Quarterly Review*. Shocked by the Great Depression of 1837 and writing with an eye toward the impending Democratic versus Whig presidential election of 1840, Brownson's proto-Marxian essay predicted violent insurrection by the working classes. As partial remedies to the crisis among wage laborers, he advocated that the current banking system—which represented the interests of employers and merchants—be dismantled and that the hereditary descent of property be abolished. Although, once converted to Catholicism, Brownson turned away from the problem of wage labor, his early commitment to the laboring classes corresponds closely to ideas of social and economic justice that have been consistently favored by Roman Catholic teaching.

3. A more detailed accounting of the activities of the American Tract Society is included in Nord, *The Evangelical Origins of Mass Media in America, 1815–1835*.

4. T. Ryan, *Orestes A. Brownson: A Definitive Biography*, 154. Ryan's 1976 biography is now the standard account of Brownson's life. Also useful, especially for Brownson's pre-conversion years, is Schlesinger Jr., *Orestes Brownson: A Pilgrim's Progress*. Charles C. Hollis's dissertation, "The Literary Criticism of Orestes Brownson," provides a thorough discussion of Brownson's career as a literary reviewer.

5. Brownson, "The Scarlet Letter: A Romance," 528.

6. The use of the terms "feminine," "sentiment," and "sentimentality" in this essay follows Brownson's usage and definition of those terms, and is not intended to ignore the substantial research that has set out to understand with more precision the meaning of those terms in constructing literary value and in evaluating or representing the experiences of women. For Brownson, these terms were a shorthand way of designating women's feelings, and a way of indicating certain failures to adopt true Catholic principles, which he understood to have a "masculine" and "rational" character.

7. Brownson, "Sick Calls: 'From the Diary of a Missionary Priest, by Rev. Edward Price,'" 115.

8. Brownson, "The Woman Question I," 391.

9. Brownson, "The Woman Question II," 415. Despite his harsh criticism of women, Brownson's views about the role of women in developing the moral qualities of their children correspond in many ways to nineteenth-century feminist opinions about women's parental function. The opinions of the women's rights advocate Sarah M. Grimké are illustrative of liberal perspectives that nevertheless place the burden of children's training squarely on women: "The influence of women over the minds and character of children of both sexes, is allowed to be far greater than that of men. This being the case by the very ordering of nature, women should be prepared by education for the performance of their sacred duties as mothers and as sisters" (Grimké, Selections from *Letters on the Equality of the Sexes, and the Condition of Woman*, 229). Catharine Beecher's *A Treatise on Domestic Economy* similarly called upon women to serve as the shapers of children's character in the young republic. Unlike Brownson, though, Beecher championed the successes "enacted by American women, in this great moral enterprise," rather than dwelling on a litany of their failures: "the formation of the moral and intellectual character of the young is committed mainly to the female hand. . . . Let the women of a country be made virtuous and intelligent, and the men will certainly be the same. . . . educate a woman, and the interests of a whole family are secured" (Beecher, *Treatise on Domestic Economy*, 27–28). On nineteenth-century domesticity and women's moral sphere, see also Cott, *Bonds of Womanhood*; Sklar, *Catharine Beecher*; and Douglas, *The Feminization of American Culture*.

10. Brownson, "Women's Novels," 371.

11. Brownson, "Longfellow's *Evangeline* and *Kavanaugh*," 59.

12. Ibid., 86 (emphasis in original).

13. Ibid., 57.

14. Brownson, "The Sea Lions: or the Lost Sealers, by James Fenimore Cooper," 399, 400.

15. In his sharp critique of Stowe and Beecherism, and in his deep anxiety about certain forms of feminine cultural power, Brownson anticipates Ann Douglas's *Feminization of American Culture*, in which Douglas admires the power of Stowe's fiction but laments the ways that "Harriet triumphantly displayed the scene of man abject under feminine rule" (244).

16. Brownson, "Literary Policy of the Church of Rome," 4.

17. Brownson's concerns about the role of popular literature—and especially fiction—in the moral lives of young women are in keeping with those of other nineteenth-century critics of such books. To take a prominent example from a far different ideological position, the abolitionist Sarah M. Grimké placed novel-reading at the center of her well-known critique of American

gender roles, noting that young women "seldom think that men will be allured by intellectual acquirements, because they find, that where any mental superiority exists, a woman is generally shunned and regarded as stepping out of her 'appropriate sphere,' which, in their view, is to dress, to dance, to set out to the best possible advantage her person, to read the novels which inundate the press, and which do more to destroy her character as a rational creature, than any thing else" (Grimké, Selections from *Letters*, 228).

18. Brownson, "'The Vision of Sir Launfal.' By J[ames] R[ussell] Lowell," 270, 271.

19. Brownson, "Mission of America," 567.

20. Brownson, "Modern Idolatry," 101.

21. Ibid., 102.

22. Brownson, "American Literature," pt. 3, 19:215.

23. Ibid., 213–14.

24. Ibid., 216–17.

25. Brownson, "The Catholic Press," 277.

26. For a detailed and fully documented account of the circumstances surrounding the publication of Maria Monk's *Awful Disclosures of Maria Monk* and other convent exposés, see Billington, *The Protestant Crusade*, 53–117. Billington also points to the great popularity of anti-Catholic literature, beginning at least as early as the Reformation and continuing with much fervor during the mid-nineteenth century in the United States; Monk's *Awful Disclosures of Maria Monk*, for example, sold 300,000 copies or more before the Civil War. Other useful studies of American nativist movements include Higham, *Strangers in the Land*, and Davis, "Some Themes of Countersubversion." The sensational aspects of convent exposés and their relation to the achievements of canonical writers are discussed in Reynolds, *Beneath the American Renaissance*. Jenny Franchot's treatment of these same lurid works in *Roads to Rome* extends her thesis that for antebellum American Protestant culture, Roman Catholicism served as an enormously fascinating category of the "other" against which to define, repress, and imagine itself.

27. Brownson, "The Catholic Press," 218. Brownson's disenchantment with Jacksonian politics led him toward a deep skepticism about pure democracy in the United States, and even before his conversion his essays consistently demonstrate his aversion to unalloyed democracy as an invitation to demagoguery and an erosion of necessary moral leadership. Indeed much of the friction between Brownson and John O'Sullivan, his editor at the *Democratic Review* (which had hired Brownson in 1842 after the demise of the *Boston Quarterly Review*), stemmed from political disagreements about the role of populism in American government. Brownson's turbulent and short-lived relationship with O'Sullivan is detailed in T. Ryan, *Orestes Brownson*, 230–44.

28. Brownson, "Thornberry Abbey," 134.

29. Ibid., 136.

30. All of Brownson's fictional writing and memoirs are marked by a strong religious didacticism. His fictional efforts included *Charles Elwood; or, The Infidel Converted* (1840), a semi-autobiographical account of his many early religious conversions; and *The Spirit-Rapper* (1854), a romance that satirizes the spiritualist movement in the United States. The autobiographical *The Convert; or, Leaves from My Experience* (1857) documents his conversion to Catholicism.

31. Brownson, "Archbishop Hughes and the Catholic Press," 51

32. Ibid., 59.

33. Brownson, "American Literature," pt. 1, 19:13.

34. Brownson, "Catholicity Necessary to Democracy," 517.

35. Brownson, "American Literature," pt. 1, 19:15, 14.

36. Channing, "Remarks on National Literature," 168.

37. Ibid., 171.

38. Ibid., 188.

39. Brownson, "The Vision of Sir Launfal. By J[ames] R[ussell] Lowell," 272.

40. Hollis quoted in T. Ryan, *Orestes A. Brownson*, 74.

41. Emerson, "The American Scholar," 58.

42. Brownson, "An Oration," 29.

43. Brownson, "The Scholar's Mission," 67.

44. Ibid., 67–68.

45. Brownson, "Thornberry Abbey," 131.

46. Brownson's full-scale theological treatment of literal idolatry, or the veneration of sacred objects, appeared in *Brownson's Quarterly Review* as "Guevara on the Veneration of Images." In that review, Brownson defended Catholics against charges that such practices have historically been threatening to true Christianity.

47. Brownson, "The Blithedale Romance, by Nathaniel Hawthorne," 563.

48. Quoted in Billington, *The Protestant Crusade*, 185. On American anti-Catholicism as expressed by nativist groups, see especially Billington, *Protestant Crusade*, and Higham, *Strangers in the Land.* Davis, "Some Themes of Countersubversion," shows patterns of nativist rhetoric deployed in the nineteenth century against Mormons and Freemasons as well as Catholics. Barbara Welter's "From Maria Monk to Paul Blanshard" contains a more comprehensive bibliography of critical analyses focused on the history of American nativism from the founding to the twentieth century.

49. Brownson, "Archbishop Hughes on the Catholic Press," 59.

50. Brownson, "The Blakes and the Flanagans," 24, 25. Brownson's reluctance to support ethnically oriented religious practices and his firm belief that differing versions of Catholicism served to undermine the larger midcentury project of Catholic unity situate him directly in opposition to most historiog-

raphy of nineteenth-century Catholicism, which has pointed to the strength and durability of ethnic traditions as the key to Catholic culture. Even Will Herbert's *Protestant, Catholic, Jew*, a study that purported to find a softening of ethnic religion in the twentieth century, has not held sway over recent religious historians' interest in the specificity of American religions understood according to ethnic legacies. Typical of the numerous histories of American Catholicism that focus on the ethnic basis of American Catholicism are Orsi, *Madonna of 115th Street*; Liptak, *Immigrants and Their Church*; Gleason, *The Conservative Reformers*; and Tweed, *Our Lady of the Exile*. Charles Lippy's survey of popular religiosity in the United States, *Being Religious, American Style*, and Paul Messbarger's study of American Catholic fiction, *Fiction with a Parochial Purpose*, emphasize the link between Catholic immigrant cultures in the nineteenth century and the development of fictional themes involving popular piety and devotionalism tailored to ethnicities (Lippy, *Being Religious, American Style*, 73–166; Messbarger, *Fiction with a Parochial Purpose*, 140, passim). See Franchot, *Roads to Rome*, 337–49, for a discussion of Brownson's role in antebellum religious culture. The two sustained commentaries on the matter of idolatry in the Catholic Church Brownson takes up are in "The Two Brothers" (1847–48) and "Professor Park Against Catholicity" (1845). The former is a lengthy essay featuring a response to Protestant accusations and their subsequent catechistic answers. The latter includes the most detailed and formal response to this question in his response to Edwards A. Park of Andover Theological Seminary, who had attacked Catholicism in a lecture at Harvard, titled "Intellectual and Moral Influence of Romanism" and subsequently published in the *Andover Theological Review* of August 1845. From "Two Brothers" it is clear that Brownson was well aware of the objections to Catholic iconography, what one of the two rhetorical brothers identifies as the Catholic church's "peculiar worship,—her saint worship, her veneration of relics, her beads and crucifixes, her fasts and feasts, her empty forms and idle ceremonies" (344).

51. On male understandings of women's sexuality during this period, see Barker-Benfield, *The Horrors of the Half-Known Life*. On the relation between spiritualism and conceptions of masculinity during the nineteenth century, see Carroll, "The Religious Construction of Masculinity in Victorian America."

52. Brownson, "Miss Fuller and Reformers," 225.

53. Ibid., 225.

54. Welter, "From Maria Monk to Paul Blanshard," 51–52 (Brownson quote taken from "Spiritism and Spiritists," *Works*, 9:346).

55. Brownson, "Literature, Love, and Marriage," 326.

56. Even more directly than Orestes Brownson himself, his daughter Sarah Nicolena Brownson Tenney participated in the culture of midcentury women's novels by writing two of her own, *Marian Elwood; or, How Girls Live* (1859) and *At Anchor: A Story of Our Civil War* (1865). Each of these novels features Catholic

themes, although neither book assumes the extreme didactic posture of the elder Brownson's efforts in fiction. In *Marian Elwood*, the eponymous protagonist of Sarah Brownson's novel is portrayed as a young Catholic woman of apparently independent means who moves confidently and virtuously through the hostile Protestant waters of the fictional Westonville, Massachusetts. A highly conventional work of pious exemplary writing, *Marian Elwood* ends with young Marian succeeding in leading her intended to a successful conversion and a happy Catholic life together. *At Anchor*, which also concerns young women and romance, plays less on Catholic themes except for the presence of the exemplary friends of the heroine, who are Catholic Sisters of Charity.

57. Brownson, "Literature, Love, and Marriage," 511.
58. Brownson, "Use and Abuse of Reading," 519.
59. Brownson, "The Yankee in Ireland," 92.
60. Brownson, "Religious Novels," 145.
61. McGee, "On Catholic Libraries," 708.
62. Brownson, "Use and Abuse of Reading," 531, 519.
63. Brownson, "Religious Novels," 146.
64. Brownson, "Women's Novels," 597.

Chapter 2. Print Evangelism

1. Later in his life, Hecker used his review of Octavius Brooks Frothingham's *Transcendentalism in New England* (1876) to critique the transcendentalist movement as well as Frothingham's condescending view that "the religion of New England was Protestant and of the most intellectual type. Romanism had no hold on the thinking people of Boston. None besides the Irish laboring and menial classes were Catholics, and their religion was regarded as the lowest form of ceremonial superstition" (qtd. in Hecker, "Transcendentalist Movement in New England," 536).

2. Farina, *American Experience of God*, 95. Walter Elliott's biography of Hecker reports that Hecker had difficulties with his studies at seminary, was rather poorly educated overall, and was at the time rather weak in English-language skills (Elliott, *Life of Father Hecker*, 221). Much of the biographical information about Isaac Hecker is drawn from David J. O'Brien's excellent biography, *Isaac Hecker*.

3. Hecker's participation in the Vatican Council is notable for his work behind the scenes to oppose (unsuccessfully) bringing the question of papal infallibility before the council. For a superb summary of Hecker's activities at the council, based on materials made available in recent decades from the Paulist archives, see Portier, *On the Divide*, 206–27. Portier explains, on the basis of Hecker's private writings during the Vatican Council, that while serving as a delegate to Rome "his Americanism underwent significant development as he

made explicit the providential role that he envisioned for America with regard to Europe" (*On the Divide*, 207).

4. Shuster, *Catholic Spirit in Modern English Literature*, 303.

5. R. M. Kelly, "Journey to Faith," 207. Charles Grandison Finney (1792–1875), an American Christian evangelist and abolitionist, was one of the most famous preachers in the great Protestant revivals of 1825–35. He served as president of Oberlin College from 1851 to 1866.

6. In an address (probably in 1853) to the Conference of St. Vincent de Paul Society, Huntington seemed to have in mind those poorly funded writers like Orestes Brownson as he was describing the financial plight of Protestant ministers who had converted to Catholicism: "They might edit papers or write books, and some of them are quite competent, but, to our shame be it spoken, we have not a sufficient Catholic reading public; I have never heard of a Catholic editor receiving a salary large enough to support a married man, except in one solitary case and that was myself when I was at Saint Louis, and I think the exception proves the rule" (Walsh, "Doctor Jedediah Vincent Huntington and the Oxford Movement in America," 249).

7. Brownson's biographer Patrick W. Carey provides evidence that lecture fees were necessary to support his publishing efforts: "The lecture tours provided a substantial amount of income and supplemented the paltry sum [Brownson] earned from publishing his *Quarterly*. . . . Lay Catholic Institutes, or discussion clubs, had been established in many of the larger cities across the country by the time Brownson began to lecture to Catholic audiences. He was enticed to the lecture tour because he hoped to promote and defend the Catholic cause, but also to supplement his income and to increase subscriptions to the *Quarterly*" (P. W. Carey, *Orestes Brownson*, 206–7).

8. Ibid., 207.

9. Schaff, *America*, 234, 224–25.

10. Finke and Stark, *Churching of America, 1776–1990*, 141.

11. Hecker's plans for these pamphlets and tracts are outlined in a brief article for the *Catholic World*, "The Catholic Publication Society" (1867).

12. O'Brien documents Hecker's lecture career in detail, indicating that Hecker spoke to large audiences across the country, and in doing so raised considerable money for his publishing ventures (*Isaac Hecker*, 197). For additional biographical reflections on Hecker by Paulist priests, see Elliott, *Life of Father Hecker*, and McSorley, *Isaac Hecker and His Friends*.

13. R. M. Kelly, "Journey to Faith," 208.

14. French Catholic progressives were especially attracted to Hecker's Americanist version of religious doctrine, which had been expressed most vividly in Walter Elliott's posthumous biography of Hecker, and this led to the so-called Americanism controversy in Europe, which in 1899 led Pope Leo XII to exert pressure on James Gibbons, by this time cardinal of Baltimore, to reaffirm

American Catholic adherence to traditional church authority. Publishing figures and other information about the Paulist Press are taken from their website, http://www.paulistpress.com/about_us.shtml (accessed Mar. 10, 2010). Additionally, demonstrating the depth of Hecker's commitment to American forms of Roman Catholic thought, Portier has shown that Hecker's notebooks from the 1869–70 Vatican Council reveal his growing confidence that US Catholicism would become a model for the world. As Hecker wrote in an early 1870 journal entry, "Who knows, Europe may find not only her political regeneration in the civilization on the other side of the Atlantic, but also the renewal of Catholicity" (Portier, "Isaac Hecker and the First Vatican Council," 216).

15. The historian Peter D'Agostino has made a compelling case for the enduring influence of ultramontane Catholic authority on American Catholic life and culture. See especially his discussion of the "Roman question" for the linkages between Catholic Italy and Catholic America (D'Agostino, *Rome in America*, 19–83).

16. Brownson qtd. in Murray, *A Popular History of the Catholic Church in the United States*, 533. On Brownson's visits to the Paulists in New York City, see Elliott, "Personal Reminiscences," 54. According to James A. Rooney ("Reminiscences of Early Days," 89), at the time the *Catholic World* was established there were only 119 Catholic priests active in New York City; Elliott ("Personal Reminiscences," 55) notes that only 5 of these priests were Paulists.

17. Murray, *A Popular History*, 553. Una M. Cadegan points out the centrality of newspapers to nineteenth-century discourse Catholicism but also traces their steady decline in popularity through the early twentieth century, when diocesan control over Catholic newspapers was greatly increased. As a result, "newspapers thus evolved from being perhaps the most unfettered of Catholic print media to the one most religiously partisan, charged primarily with protection and communication of orthodoxy" (Cadegan, "Running the Ancient Ark," 395). Many Catholic papers and magazines were ephemeral. For example, in its entry on "Periodicals," the 1911 edition of the *Catholic Encyclopedia* states: "From 1809 to 1911 some 550 Catholic periodicals were started in the United States, but only five of those published during the first half of the nineteenth century survive" (11:692).

18. Concern about the limited commercial success of American Catholic writers was a regular topic in the *Catholic World* in the early twentieth century as well. Notable opinions on this topic are "On Catholic Writers and their Handicaps" (1909) by the poet Louise Imogen Guiney, and "Catholicism and Authorship" (1909) by the essayist Agnes Repplier, both of whom advocated that Catholic writers begin reaching out to larger audiences while remaining true to their religious commitments.

19. On the success of nineteenth-century American Catholic revivalism,

see Dolan, *Catholic Revivalism*, 186; and Finke and Starke, *Churching of America*, 117–23.

20. Strong connections may be made between the parish missions (revivals) of the mid-nineteenth century and the commercial book trade. Hecker would have been aware of these events as host to what historian Jay Dolan has described as a "super bowl of Catholic piety." Revival events such as the missions at which Hecker preached were "a primary occasion for the sale of large numbers of prayer books and devotional guides as well as rosaries, pictures, and other religious articles" (Dolan, *American Catholic Experience*, 213; Dolan, *Catholic Revivalism*, 178).

21. Hecker qtd. in O'Brien, *Isaac Hecker*, 104. Hecker's historical essay "The Catholic Church in the United States" (1879) similarly proposes the enormous religious potential of the United States as a Catholic nation and cites Columbus mission, at the behest of Queen Isabella of Spain, which expressed "the burning desire to carry the blessings of the Christian faith to the inhabitants of a new continent" (433).

22. Hecker, letter to Father Rouquette, July 24, 1859, in Ellis, *Documents in American Catholic History*, 1:341. For a brief discussion of Rouquette's career, including his attempts to found a utopian Catholic religious community among rural Louisiana Choctaws, see Chris Michaelidis, "The Tree of the Choctaws."

23. The most significant religious publishers during the nineteenth century were Protestant: important early presses were the Methodist Book Concern (1789), the American Bible Society (1816), the American Sunday-School Union (1824), and the American Tract Society (1825). The literary historian Paul Gutjahr notes: "By the 1840s these societies reported publishing several million pages per year: gargantuan press runs of Bibles, tracts, Sunday school lesson books, religious biographies, sermons, and devotional classics. By 1855 the output of the [latter] three societies accounted for approximately 16 percent of all books produced in the United States" ("Diversification in American Religious Publishing," 195).

24. Hecker, *Questions of the Soul*, 184–85.

25. Repplier, "Catholicism and Authorship," 170.

26. Catholic periodicals in the nineteenth century proliferated in cities with significant Catholic populations, but even most of these had very modest circulation figures. For instance, the *Ave Maria* magazine, a well-known periodical based at Notre Dame University, seems to have had a peak circulation of only about 7,000 in the late nineteenth century (Murray, *A Popular History*, 547). Writing in 1915, James A. Rooney cites somewhat larger circulation figures of 10,000 per issue by the first decade of the *Catholic World*'s publication (Rooney, "Reminiscences of Early Days," 98).

27. Publication figures for the *Catholic World* are from O'Brien, *Isaac Hecker*,

203–18. For Kehoe's remark about the *Catholic World*, see his letter from Lawrence Kehoe to Father Daniel E. Hudson, May 18, 1882, University of Notre Dame archives.

28. For a discussion of the *Tablet*, one of the more influential Irish-leaning Catholic newspapers of the day, see Szabo, "My Heart Bleeds to Tell It."

29. Cadegan, "Running the Ancient Ark," 395.

30. Farina, *American Experience of God*, 95.

31. Elliott, *Life of Father Hecker*, 348.

32. Ibid., 359.

33. Ibid., 349, 359.

34. Hassard,"Catholic Literature and the Catholic Public," 402–7.

35. In addition to Brownson and the Paulist Fathers, notable contributors to the *Catholic World* during its first fifty years (1865–1915) included John Gilmary Shea, Dr. Henry A. Brann, Bishop Patrick Lynch of South Carolina, Bishop Martin Spalding of Baltimore, John R. G. Hassard, James Meline, Miles Gerald Keon, Eliza Starr, Christian Reid (Frances Fisher Tiernan), Katherine Tynan, Agnes Repplier, William Seton, and Maurice Francis Egan (Rooney, "Reminiscences of Early Days," 92).

36. B. M. Kelly, "John Rose Green Hassard," 25.

37. For perspectives on Emerson's view of Anna Barker Ward's conversion, see Birdsall, "Emerson and the Church of Rome," 273–81. Glenn Johnson examines Emerson's unpublished draft of an essay on Catholicism and surveys the relationship between the two men, which was damaged by Hecker's role in converting Anna Ward, who was the sister of Sam Ward, an old friend of Emerson and Margaret Fuller ("Ralph Waldo Emerson on Isaac Hecker," 54–60).

38. Emerson journal manuscript in Johnson, "Ralph Waldo Emerson on Isaac Hecker," 55.

39. Farina, *American Experience of God*, 107.

40. Letter to Hecker, in ibid., 107.

41. Melville, "Hawthorne and His Mosses," 248.

42. Brownson, *Works*, 14:538.

43. Hecker, *Questions of the Soul*, 34.

44. Ibid., 35

45. Ibid., 36.

46. Ibid., 35, 36.

47. Ibid., 36.

48. Una M. Cadegan has compared the *Catholic World* (and similar Catholic periodicals such as *Ave Maria* and the *Messenger of the Sacred Heart*) to prominent American magazines such as *Harper's* or the *Atlantic Monthly*, which "targeted . . . middle-class audience with leisure and money to spare" and advanced themes of domesticity and religious piety (Cadegan, "Running the Ancient," 395). Catholic magazines, however, lacked the substantial circulation numbers of the

major national periodicals aimed at prosperous middle-class readers. In spite of these weak circulation figures, Jay Dolan has asserted that the rise in Catholic magazines and newspapers during the later nineteenth century assisted the rise in Catholic devotionalism during that period, and that while some Catholic periodicals carried secular news, "the primary focus of the Catholic press was religious" and thus featured "stories of the deeds of the saints, accounts of miraculous healings, reports of religious festivals or parish missions, or news about the latest papal encyclical promoting a particular devotion" (Dolan, *American Catholic Experience*, 214).

49. Hecker, *Questions of the Soul*, 186.

50. Ibid., 186–87.

51. Ibid., 187.

52. Ibid. The biography to which Hecker refers was written jointly by Emerson, William Henry Channing, and James Freeman Clarke. Titled *Memoirs*, it appeared in 1852 and, despite Hecker's consternation, was in fact a substantially censored account of Margaret Fuller's life and activities, as subsequent biographers have discovered.

53. Hecker, *Questions of the Soul*, 188, 189.

54. Letter, Hecker to family, Sep. 14, 1846, in O'Brien, *Isaac Hecker*, 87–88.

55. Hecker, *Questions of the Soul*, 132–33.

56. Ibid., 174–75.

57. Ibid., 143.

58. Ibid., 37.

59. Hecker, *Aspirations*, 54–55.

60. Ibid., 125.

61. For a broad overview of the literary interest in American destiny during the antebellum period, with special emphasis on New York writers, see Miller, *The Raven and the Whale*, esp. 69–118. The nuances of the antebellum Young America movement and the various iterations of "manifest destiny" are described in Widmer, *Young America*.

62. Hecker's enthusiasm for a boundless American geography suitable for the ideal expression of Catholicism resembles the structure and dynamics of American myth that R. W. B. Lewis has previously outlined in *American Adam*, 90–109.

63. Hecker, *Aspirations*, 57.

64. Ibid., 7.

65. Brownson reviewed *Aspirations of Nature* soon after its publication in 1857 (*Works*, 14:548–77). Brownson proceeded with the review despite resistance from Hecker's colleagues who had heard about negative parts of the review (which would be published in Brownson's own *Brownson's Quarterly Review*) and had asked Brownson to temper his attack on *Aspirations of Nature*. Although Brownson claimed to have softened his rhetoric in response to suggestions from

Hecker's supporters, the review as published nevertheless was a great disappointment to Hecker (see T. Ryan, *Orestes Brownson*, 543ff., for a complete discussion of the episode).

66. Hecker, *Aspirations of Nature*, 360.
67. Elliott, *Life of Father Hecker*, 291.
68. Hecker, *Aspirations of Nature*, 275.
69. Ibid., 185, 2.
70. Ibid., 26–27.
71. Elliott, *Life of Father Hecker*, xi.
72. Hecker, *Aspirations of Nature*, 27.
73. Ibid., 12.
74. Ibid., 269.

Chapter 3. Entering the Mainstream

1. Brownson's incendiary, proto-Marxist essay *The Laboring Classes* (1840), written several years before his conversion to Catholicism, is the single work that brought him the broadest public attention.

2. P. Fisher, *Hard Facts*, 91. Definitions of sentimental writing must remain flexible in order to encompass the thematic range found in both the classic seduction plot found in early British and American novels (a plot popular until about 1818) and the domestic melodramas that followed; see Davidson, *Revolution and the Word*, 135. Fisher's summary of the sentimental sphere is one in which there are "extended central scenes of dying and deathbeds, mourning and loss, the rhetorical treatment of the central theme of suffering, the creation of the prisoner as the central character, the themes of imprisonment, the violation of selfhood, power relations in the intimate and familiar territory, freedom, the centrality of the family, and the definition of the power of literary representation in terms of tears" (P. Fisher, *Hard Facts*, 93). Nina Baym differentiates American women's fiction of the period from the seduction novels of Samuel Richardson, which she describes as advancing "trivializing and contemptuous views of women" and ties the American genre to the eighteenth-century novel of manners as exemplified by Maria Edgeworth and Fanny Burney (Baym, *Woman's Fiction*, 29).

3. The American novelistic tendency toward a "Sentimental Love Religion," developing primarily from the decay of Calvinist religion but with roots in important English precursors such as Samuel Richardson's *Clarissa Harlowe* (1747–48), forms the basis of Fiedler's argument in *Love and Death in the American Novel* (1960) that American novels have achieved true artistic success only to the extent that they have avoided the trap of sentimentality. Ann Douglas, in *The Feminization of American Culture* (1977), argues that the relationship between middle-class women and Christian clergy was an important factor in

the production of sentimental writing during this period. Significant responses to critiques of American sentimental literature by Fiedler and Douglas include Tompkins, *Sensational Designs* (1985), and Davidson, *Revolution and the Word* (1986).

4. Reynolds, *Beneath the American Renaissance*, 338.

5. Sánchez-Eppler, "Bodily Bonds," 28–59. Her analysis focuses on the relationship between bodily identity and discourses of sentimentality, particularly the troubled dialectic between sentimental abolitionism and sentimental feminism. Sentimental texts, according to Sánchez-Eppler, have inescapable ties to the body, since the success or failure of the sentimental text may be measured by its ability to make the heart race or to produce tears in the eyes of the reader; it is a literary genre that depends on, and strives for, a visceral reaction on the part of the reader.

6. Samuels, introduction to *The Culture of Sentiment*, 5.

7. Willard Thorp (1968) argues that early American Catholic novelists, by and large, were intellectually defensive: reacting to anti-Catholic attacks with "affirmative" rhetoric intended to mend damaged relations between Catholics and others, and that these novelists also tended toward characterization that was "exemplary, written to show how good Catholics lived and practiced their faith" (*Catholic Novelists in Defense of their Faith*, 27). Paul Messbarger (1971), documenting primarily the later nineteenth and early twentieth century rather than the midcentury novelists, places the Americanism crisis at the center of Catholic literary concerns (Messbarger, *Fiction with a Parochial Purpose*). Echoing the view that American Catholic novelists were focused on supporting the authority of the Catholic Church, Jay Dolan (1985) has asserted that the primary role of nineteenth-century Catholic novelists was to "[stress] the authoritative position of Roman Catholicism, endorsing its claims to absolute and infallible authority in matters of faith and morals" (Dolan, *American Catholic Experience*, 223). David S. Reynolds (1981) maintains that antebellum Catholic novelists were essentially didactic in their writing, using "theoretical and polemical" modes in order to counter what they perceived as distortions of their beliefs in the anti-Catholic writing of the period (see Reynolds, *Faith in Fiction*, 145–68).

8. Jenny Franchot has listed Harriet Beecher Stowe among a large cohort of antebellum American writers who used Catholic themes in their work; Franchot points to *Agnes of Sorrento* (1862) as the Stowe novel that most thoroughly engages with Roman Catholicism (Franchot, *Roads to Rome*, 246–55).

9. Tompkins, *Sensational Designs*, 157, 123.

10. Reynolds, *Faith in Fiction*, 148–49.

11. Ibid., 150.

12. Liz Szabo has written an excellent survey of the D. & J. Sadlier & Co., and she shows that Mary Anne Sadlier, wife of publishing executive James Sadlier of the Montreal office of that firm, was its leading novelist for many years. A number of Mary Anne Sadlier's novels were serialized in the *New York Tablet*, a

weekly Catholic paper published in Brooklyn by the Sadliers, before appearing in book form. Szabo also presents evidence that she served as the de facto editor of the *Tablet*: "Mary Anne Sadlier contributed heavily to the *Tablet*, writing and editing a large proportion of its articles and recruiting Catholic writers from around the country." In addition, Sister Mary Stephana Cavanaugh's 1954 master's thesis, "Catholic Book Publishing in the United States, 1784–1850," remains the most thorough treatment of American Catholic publishing during those years.

13. The Robert Appleton Company, headed by the son of D. Appleton's founder, Daniel Appleton, was formed in 1905 for the express purpose of publishing the sixteen-volume *Catholic Encyclopedia* (1907–14).

14. Dolan rightly emphasizes the extent to which, during the nineteenth century, the increasingly popular devotional style of Catholic spirituality was a function of an immigrant church whose parishes and other ecclesiastical structures had not yet been fully established: "[devotional] spirituality, which de-emphasized the mediating role of priests and sacraments, blended in well with the social situation of the Catholic community, in which there was a scarcity of both clergy and churches" (Dolan, *American Catholic Experience*, 210–11).

15. Shuster, *Catholic Spirit in Modern English Literature*, 312.

16. Howe, *What Hath God Wrought*, 3. On oratory in the early national and antebellum United States, see Gustafson, *Eloquence Is Power*, and Waldstreicher, *In the Midst of Perpetual Fetes*. On the development and use of industrial print media by nineteenth-century evangelical publishers, see Nord, *Evangelical Origins of Mass Media in America, 1815–1835*.

17. In a recent study of nineteenth-century anti-Catholic fiction, Sandra Frink notes the connection between anti-Catholic writing and prevailing discourses about gender identity and family life in the United States. Frink urges that more attention be paid to the ways that the emphasis on sexual scandal in anti-Catholic writing "operated on along the same continuum as other discourses on the family, specifically on the role of mothers in shielding daughters and providing moral guidance, found in prostitution reform literature and in advice, health, and sexuality manuals" (Frink, "Women, the Family, and the Fate of the Nation in American Anti-Catholic Narratives, 1830–1860," 238–39). For a general survey of novels opposed to Roman Catholicism, see Griffin, *Anti-Catholicism and Nineteenth-Century American Fiction*.

18. Forming a "canon" of American Catholic writers is an elusive project, in part because of the vexing identity problems that arise because of Catholic writers' being categorized variously as "cradle-Catholics," "converts," "lapsed Catholics," or—more stridently—"bogus Catholics" (on the putative difficulties tied to "bogus Catholics," see Messbarger, *Fiction with a Parochial Purpose*, 165–66). David Reynolds, in detailing what he sees as the doctrinal quality of writing produced by the major Catholic fiction writers of the antebellum

period, lists the following authors as important figures: Charles Constantine Pise, John Boyce, John T. Roddan, Hugh Quigley, Charles James Cannon, George Henry Miles, Jedediah Vincent Huntington, Anna Hanson Dorsey, Mrs. James Sadlier (formerly Mary Anne Madden), and Orestes Brownson (Reynolds, *Faith in Fiction*, 148). Ross Labrie's *The Catholic Imagination in American Literature*, which details mainly twentieth-century writers, includes a chapter on Orestes Brownson before turning to a roster of writers including Caroline Gordon, Allen Tate, Paul Horgan, Walker Percy, Thomas Merton, Robert Lowell, Flannery O'Connor, and others. See also Thorp, *Catholic Novelists in Defense of their Faith*, for detailed readings of antebellum Catholic fiction. The essays collected in Thomas J. Ferraro's *Catholic Lives / Contemporary America* offer usefully flexible models of religious identity; see especially James T. Fisher's synthetic view of the ways that late-twentieth century "lapsed Catholicism" makes a return in American popular music and film ("Clearing the Streets of the Catholic Lost Generation," 76–103).

19. Daniel Huntington (1816–1906) was a distinguished landscape and portrait painter whose subjects included Abraham Lincoln, Martin Van Buren, Louis Agassiz, William Cullen Bryant, and Jefferson Davis. Students of American Catholic fiction are indebted to the scrupulous research of the literary historian Willard Thorp, whose readings and summaries of works by many nineteenth-century Catholic writers, including Mary Anne Sadlier, Jedediah V. Huntington, and Anna Hanson Dorsey, provide the foundation for my discussion of their novels. See Thorp, *Catholic Novelists in Defense of their Faith*.

20. On international copyright debates of the antebellum period, see McGill, *American Literature and the Culture of Reprinting, 1834–1853*.

21. For the most complete biographical information on Jedediah V. Huntington, see Walsh, "Doctor Jedediah Vincent Huntington and the Oxford Movement in America," pt. 1.

22. Thorp, *Catholic Novelists in Defense of their Faith*, 71.

23. *North American Review*, review of *Lady Alice*, 233.

24. *Southern Literary Messenger* review qtd. in Walsh, "Doctor Jedediah Vincent Huntington," pt. 1, 257.

25. Huntington's success in England also led him to become a proponent of international copyright protection for professional authors. For a discussion of Huntington's copyright advocacy, see Walsh, "Doctor Jedediah Vincent Huntington," pt. 1, 259–67.

26. Sadlier moved to Montreal, Canada, from Ireland and married the Canadian Catholic publishing executive James Sadlier of D. and J. Sadlier and Company. On Hecker's encouragement of Mary Anne Sadlier's writing about Irish servant women, see White, *Era of Good Intentions*, 20. Sadlier had been a significant force in Catholic fiction since 1845, when she published her first collection of stories. Most of her novels dealt with the Irish experience in both

Ireland and America, and by midcentury she was best known for *The Blakes and the Flanagans: A Tale Illustrative of Irish Life in the United States* (1850), which was first serialized and later appeared in multiple English and German editions.

27. Qtd. in Lacombe, "Frying-Pans and Deadlier Weapons," 96.

28. Huntington letter to Brownson, Aug. 19, 1855.

29. Walsh, "Doctor Jedediah Vincent Huntington," pt. 2, 418.

30. Ibid., 425. Although his representations of erotic situations are extremely mild by today's standards, Huntington and his contemporaries in the book trades were active during a period when evolving views of sexuality were bringing new scrutiny to the American publishing industry, even though federal statutes regulating "obscene" published materials were not enacted until after the Civil War. In her study of American debates over sexual knowledge in the nineteenth century, Helen Lefkowitz Horowitz describes the tensions created in literary culture by reform physiologists, whose scientific concept of sexuality was beginning to show the relationship between the mind and sexual habits: "In turning to health and disease, [reform physiologists] focused concern on the nervous system. As they added new notions of romantic love that put feeling and its expression at the center, some found reasons to separate sexual intercourse from conception. Locating sex in mind at a time when poems and centered on heightened emotion emphasized the potential power of imaginative literature and thus its danger" (*Rereading Sex*, 6).

31. Huntington, *Alban*, viii.

32. Huntington, *Lady Alice*, 4.

33. Brownson, "*The Forest*, by J[edediah] V[incent] Huntington," 135–36.

34. *North American Review*, review of *Lady Alice*, 235–36.

35. Ibid., 235.

36. Huntington, *The Forest*, 6; Huntington, *Alban*, 43.

37. Huntington, *Alban*, 13, 54–55.

38. Ibid., 53 (emphasis added).

39. Ibid., 71.

40. Ibid., 95.

41. Ibid., 190.

42. *Southern Literary Messenger*, review of *Alban*, 702.

43. On the politics of banning and censoring sexually explicit print in nineteenth-century America, see Horowitz, *Rereading Sex*, and Dennis, *Licentious Gotham*. The classic study of British Victorian-era pornographic literature is Marcus, *The Other Victorians*.

44. Brownson, "Rosemary; or Life and Death," 527–28. Before it was published in book form, *Rosemary* was first serialized in the Sadliers' *New York Tablet*.

45. Huntington, *Rosemary*, 162.

46. Thorp, *Catholic Novelists in Defense of their Faith*, 83–85.

47. Ibid., 83.

48. Unpublished manuscript by Huntington qtd. in Walsh, "Doctor Jedediah Vincent Huntington," pt. 2, 435–36.

49. David Jerome Callon's doctoral dissertation, "Converting Catholism," contains the most complete biographical information about Anna Dorsey, who was born into a prominent Baltimore family and was a descendant of John Hanson (1715–83), a signer of the Declaration of Independence and a leader of the Continental Congress. Beginning in 1781, John Hanson served as the first president of Congress under the Articles of Confederation. Dorsey's father, William McKenney, was a prominent member of the American Colonization Society. Anna Dorsey's daughter, Ella Lorraine Dorsey, was also a Catholic writer of some distinction. Ella's short fiction and poetry appeared in the *Catholic World* as well as in *Harper's* and *Cosmopolitan*, and she became well known for her popular juvenile fiction.

50. Dorsey publication information for the *Boston Pilot* is from Callon, "Converting Catholicism," 188.

51. As editor of the *Ave Maria*, Father Daniel E. Hudson, who also served as an English faculty member at the University of Notre Dame, was an influential figure in American Catholic letters and for many years was a chief rival of Isaac Hecker for preeminence among Catholic magazine editors. He was a member of the Congregation of Holy Cross (CSC). In addition to his support of Anna Dorsey, Hudson also made it possible for the poet and travel writer Charles Warren Stoddard, a convert to Roman Catholicism who published with numerous presses including the Ave Maria Press, to spend a year on the English faculty at Notre Dame. Stoddard's conversion memoir, *A Troubled Heart and How It Was Comforted at Last* (1885), was published anonymously by the Ave Maria Press the year he began teaching at Notre Dame, and his best-known work, *The Lepers of Molokai* (1885), was also published by Ave Maria to great acclaim among Catholic readers.

52. Qtd. in White, *Era of Good Intentions*, 13.

53. Dolan, "Social Catholicism," 192.

54. Ella Lorraine Dorsey for many years contributed articles to newspapers in Washington, DC, and served as a correspondent for the *Chicago Tribune* and other newspapers in Massachusetts and Ohio. Her stories for Catholic children appeared most often in *Ave Maria* and the *Catholic World*, but also in secular periodicals like *Harper's*. As Kathleen Sprow Cummings's study of Catholic women in the progressive era has shown, Dorsey made important contributions to Catholic women's education in her role as promoter and board member of Trinity College in Washington, DC, which opened in 1900 (Cummings, *New Women of the Old Faith*, 84–88).

55. White, *Era of Good Intentions*, 19–20.

56. Letters from Anna Dorsey to Daniel Hudson, 1879 and 1883, www.archives.nd.edu (accessed Apr. 10, 2011).

57. Callon, "Converting Catholicism," 16. In a brief review of Hanson's *Father Felix: A Tale*, Orestes Brownson found Dorsey's novels to "feed a sickly sentimentalism [rather] than to nourish a robust piety" (Brownson, "Father Felix: A Tale," 402).

58. Callon, "Converting Catholicism," 204.

59. Anna Dorsey's letter to Archbishop Gibbons, on December 30, 1879, was discovered by David Jerome Callon in the archives of the Archdiocese of Baltimore, St. Mary's Seminary and University. Callon also has determined that the papal medals Dorsey received came as a result of her request to Archbishop Gibbons that she receive commendations in order to promote her own book sales and thereby better support her growing family (Callon, "Converting Catholicism," 141, 228–29).

60. For a useful survey of the nineteenth-century fictional encounter between whites and Native Americans, with a special emphasis on the possibilities of cross-racial sympathy, see Mielke, *Moving Encounters*.

61. See Franchot, *Roads to Rome*, 35–82, for a detailed analysis of Parkman's view of Roman Catholicism.

62. Armand François-Marie, Comte de Charbonnel (1802–91), was born into a distinguished aristocratic family in Monistrol sur-Loire, France. Although he is noted primarily for his career as bishop of Toronto, a position that he accepted after working with Irish immigrants in Montreal from 1840 to 1847, Charbonnel spent considerable time in Baltimore, where he learned English and made the acquaintance of noted Catholics like Anna Dorsey and her circle (Nicolson, "Bishop Charbonnel," 51).

63. Dorsey, *Coaina*, v.

64. Ibid., 6.

65. Ibid., 8.

66. Ibid., 12–13.

67. Ibid., 26–27.

68. Ibid., 91.

69. For a more complete discussion of Hawthorne's characterization of female heroines in his fiction, see Reynolds, *Beneath the American Renaissance*, 368–86.

70. Dorsey, *Coaina*, 107. For a discussion of the Roman Catholic elements in Hawthorne's *The Scarlet Letter*, see Franchot, *Roads to Rome*, 260–69. Scenes of public punishment had long been a staple in the popular literature of the nineteenth century; for a complete discussion of this phenomenon, with direct reference to the ways Hawthorne adapted such scenes for *The Scarlet Letter*, see Reynolds, *Beneath the American Renaissance*, 118–32, 259–68.

71. Dorsey, *Coaina*, 135, 138.

72. Major studies that examine—with wide-ranging and sometimes contradictory conclusions—the complex literary manifestations of women's iden-

tity and place in nineteenth-century society include Welter, "The Cult of True Womanhood"; Douglas, *The Feminization of American Culture*; Kelley, *Private Woman, Public Stage*; Tompkins, *Sensational Designs*; Davidson, *Revolution and the Word*; Brown, *Domestic Individualism*; and Coultrap-McQuin, *Doing Literary Business*. Broader perspectives in the history of American reading practices, including research on literacy and the role of gender in the history of the book, may be found in Hall, *Cultures of Print*, especially his essays "The Uses of Literacy in New England, 1600–1850" (36–78) and "Readers and Reading in America: Historical and Critical Perspectives" (169–88).

73. Key studies that include descriptions of women's reading in the antebellum period include Davidson, *Revolution and the Word*; Gilmore, *Reading Becomes a Necessity of Life*; and Zboray, *A Fictive People*.

74. Dolan, *American Catholic Experience*, 233.

75. A number of publishers provided support and marketing force for key Catholic writers in the nineteenth century. Well-known Catholic publishers (many of them of Irish descent) such as P. O'Shea, James Sadlier, P. J. Kenedy, and John Murphy published many of the most important and widely disseminated Catholic novels. The D. Appleton publishing house also seems to have been friendly to the Catholic cause in fiction, having published a great number of Anna Dorsey's and Christian Reid's late nineteenth-century novels.

76. Ferraro, *Catholic Lives / Contemporary America*, 8.

Chapter 4. Sentimental Catechism

1. Taves, *The Household of Faith*.

2. See, for example, Bynum, *Jesus as Mother*, and Bynum, *Fragmentation and Redemption*. In her study of American nuns of New Orleans during the antebellum period, the historian Emily Clark summarizes important aspects of female Catholic devotionalism, noting: "In the Middle Ages, women used the unique biological attributes of their sex and their role as mothers to fashion a symbolic rationale for feminine sanctity, and authority in religious terms. They created a spirituality in which their own bodies became powerful symbols that recapitulated and reenacted the sacrifice of Christ, opening a new, often dynamic avenue for enacting religious belief" (Clark, *Masterless Mistresses*, 85).

3. Ellis, *Life of James Cardinal Gibbons*, 1:75.

4. Gibbons was appointed Apostolic Vicar of North Carolina (bishop) in March 1868. The census of 1870 lists a total of 1,071,361 inhabitants in North Carolina, an area of 49,412 square miles. Ninety-six percent of the population lived in rural areas at that time (Ellis, *Life of James Cardinal Gibbons*, 1:77). Gibbons's precursor in supervising the North Carolina region, Father Henry P. Northrop of the Diocese of Charleston, South Carolina, wrote to Gibbons that he had counted only about 700 Catholics in the entire state. Two years after

his arrival, Gibbons was able to document 1,200 Catholics, very few of whom were attributable to immigration. See Ellis, *Life of James Cardinal Gibbons*, 1:104.

5. Gibbons was assigned to Wilmington, North Carolina, as bishop for the entire state. As the youngest Catholic bishop in the world at that time (Ellis, *Life of James Cardinal Gibbons*, 1:17), Gibbons was responsible for supervising three other priests and four churches in the Wilmington area and in Raleigh, Edenton, and New Bern. He also oversaw missions in about fifteen other towns around the state that had Catholic residents. See Ellis, *Life of James Cardinal Gibbons*, 1:71.

6. O'Connell, *Catholicity in the Carolinas and Georgia*, 398–99.

7. Ellis, *Life of James Cardinal Gibbons*, 1:85. During the consecration of Gibbons as bishop of North Carolina, Rev. Thomas Foley, a priest at the Baltimore Cathedral, mixed esteem for the young Gibbons with caution about the desperate situation for Catholicism in late nineteenth-century North Carolina: "I cannot congratulate you on going to North Carolina, but I do rejoice for the honor which the Church of God has conferred upon you, and I congratulate your flock, few and scattered, upon the advantage they are to derive from the apostolic mission you are to establish in that state, which, in a religious sense, may be called a desert" (*Catholic Mirror*, Aug. 22, 1868; qtd. in Garaventa, "Bishop James Gibbons and the Growth of the Roman Catholic Church in North Carolina," 21); Hassard, "Catholic Literature and the Catholic Public," 407.

8. Interestingly, Ellis writes in his biography of Gibbons that the future cardinal had been inspired, in part, toward his Catholic vocation by reading religious tracts by the former-transcendentalist and late convert to Catholicism, Orestes Brownson. As a nineteen-year-old youth living in New Orleans with his parents, Gibbons heard Father Hecker and others preach during a mission held there in 1853. That same year, he had been deeply impressed by Brownson, the mercurial New England convert. According to Gibbons's brother John: "[James] had Brownson in his mind and on his lips for a long time, and the impression that eminent man made on him must have been very great. . . . Brownson lectured here in the armory hall on Camp Street, within a few doors of the building in which my brother was employed, and of course, he went to hear him and was charmed with his independent American way of speaking and the way he put forth his sledge-hammer arguments in defense of the Church. If the Brownson smile left his face at any time, it was only when he read of what some few Catholic writers of the day had to say in criticism of his idol" (A. E. Smith and V. de P. Fitzpatrick, *Cardinal Gibbons*, 30–31).

9. Douglas, *Feminization of American Culture*, 6.

10. Fiedler, *Love and Death in the American Novel*, 10–11. Fiedler observes the deeper structure and themes of sentimental texts, marking the contiguity of mass-market popularity and the idiom of spirituality, and proposing that the immensely popular books from the sentimental genre "pretend to be novels,

but are in fact secret scriptures" and that "best-sellers are by and large holy books" (ibid., 11). Although Jane Tompkins places a much higher literary value on antebellum sentimental writing than did Fiedler, she agrees with his view of sentimental writers as having strongly didactic aims, noting that their novels were written to "win the belief and influence the behavior of the widest possible audience. These novelists have designs on their audiences, in the sense of wanting to make people think and act in a particular way" (Tompkins, *Sensational Designs*, xi).

11. Baym, *Women's Fiction*, 21.

12. Ellis, *Life of James Cardinal Gibbons*, 1:118.

13. Douglas, *Feminization of American Culture*, 347. Douglas remarked acerbically on the changing status of the Protestant minister in the late nineteenth century that the primary identifying characteristic of the postbellum minister was his moral effeminacy: "The minister between 1820 and 1875 was beginning to experience the enforced self-simplification women had long known. In 1820 the statement 'I am a minister' had a series of possible precise connotations, theological and political. By 1875, the statement meant roughly what it does today: it connotes vague church-bound efforts at 'goodness'" (ibid., 347).

14. Ellis, *Life of James Cardinal Gibbons*, 1:119.

15. Gibbons, *Faith of Our Fathers*, 19 (emphasis added). While Ann Taves does not take up the question of Catholic catechisms, she has shown convincingly the extent to which Catholic devotional literature (prayer books) in the nineteenth century used the figure of the family to coordinate devotional worship. In *The Household of Faith*, she deploys the image of the faithful household to "to describe the network of affective, familial relationships between believers and supernatural "relatives," such as Jesus and Mary, presupposed by the devotions" (viii). The bourgeois family or household in which the mother played such a prominent role was frequently used [in devotional books] as a metaphor for the relationships between Catholics and the inhabitants of the other supernatural world (47). Taves also maintains that by the mid-nineteenth century, the devotional practices that the prayerbooks describe and prescribe had, for many American Catholics, taken precedence over the actual reception of the sacraments. This devotional revolution meant that sacramentalism had been substantially replaced by prayers to Mary, Jesus, the Sacred Heart, and the Blessed Sacrament.

16. Baym, *Women's Fiction*, 27.

17. Warner, *Wide, Wide World*, 531.

18. Ibid., 531–32.

19. See Taves, *The Household of Faith*, 48ff., for a detailed discussion of home devotions among mid-nineteenth-century American Catholics.

20. Ibid., 71.

21. Ibid., 71–74.

22. Faber, *All for Jesus; or, the Easy Ways of Divine Love*, 128–29; quoted in Taves, *The Household of Faith*, 48.

23. Devotional texts by Frederick W. Faber were published and reprinted many times in Baltimore by Gibbons's eventual publisher, John Murphy. In *The Household of Faith*, Taves notes several of these in addition to Faber's *All for Jesus* (1854): *Devotion to the Pope* (1860); *The Foot of the Cross; or, The Sorrows of Mary* (n.d.); *Growth in Holiness; or, The Progress of the Spiritual Life* (n.d.); and *The Precious Blood; or The Price of our Salvation* (1860). Faber's hymns became standards not only in Catholic churches but also in Protestant churches: the most widely known are "Faith of our fathers" and "There's a wideness in God's mercy." Gibbons and his biographers make no mention of his books, but it appears likely that he knew of them and perhaps drew directly on them when writing *Faith of Our Fathers*.

24. Gibbons, "Relative Condition," 665. In Caroline Walker Bynum's *Fragmentation and Redemption* (a study of the body in medieval art), she examines such maternal metaphors in great detail. Her analysis shows the complex gendering of the medieval Church: "Medieval texts and medieval art saw the Church as the body of Christ. And *ecclesia* was, of course, feminine, as a noun and as an allegorical personification. Thus, the Church was depicted in medieval art as a woman—sometimes as Christ's bride, sometimes a nursing mother" (*Fragmentation and Redemption*, 93). For a discussion of traditions of devotional theory and discourse among Catholic nuns, which emphasized the feminine dimensions of Roman Catholic piety, see Clark, *Masterless Mistresses*, esp. 83–122.

25. B. G. Smith, *Changing Lives*, 184. See B. G. Smith, *Changing Lives*, 181–221, for a detailed discussion of Victorian domesticity and the changing conceptions of female virtue in Europe, including the rise of the Catholic convent as a prototype for women's domestic education. According to Smith's earlier study, *Ladies of the Leisure Class*, middle-class women in nineteenth-century France buttressed domestic ideology with conservative adherence to Christianity. Profoundly conservative during a century of increasing rationalism and progressive dismantling of mythical and religious systems of belief, women "not only maintained their relationship with the Christian God, but invented a new cult of the virtuous heroine [in the domestic novel] who ruled a domestically constructed universe" (*Ladies of the Leisure Class*, 12). At the same time, retrograde female religiosity (especially Catholicism) during this period stems largely from female bodily experience and continuing exposure to the dangers of pregnancy and sanguinous childbirth. Smith's most basic formulation of this notion holds that "reproduction predisposed them to a religious world view" (107) and that "the mathematical explanation of life proposed by modern science appeared as patent fatuity to the visibly bleeding, swelling, pained women of the nineteenth century" (95).

26. B. G. Smith, *Changing Lives*, 178.

27. The first edition of *Faith of Our Fathers* was published in late 1876; four editions sold out in six months; 50,000 copies were in print by 1879, sold at $1.00 in cloth and $.0.50 in paper binding; 250,000 copies, in forty-seven editions, were in print by 1895; translations eventually appeared in French, German, Spanish, Italian, Norwegian, Swedish, Japanese, Bohemian, and Braille; 1.5 to 2 million copies were in print by 1917; during a single six-month period in the year before Gibbons's death in 1921, the book sold more than 22,000 copies (Will, *Life of Cardinal Gibbons*, 1:151).

28. Dolan, *Catholic Revivalism*, 86.

29. Gibbons, *Faith of Our Fathers*, vii (emphasis in original). Not all of those who converted to Catholicism as a result of the popular catechism were immigrants, nor were they all unschooled. Among the more notable of the converts to Catholicism who attributed their new faith to Gibbons's *Faith of Our Fathers* was George Parsons Lathrop, the essayist, novelist, and associate editor of the *Atlantic Monthly*. Following his marriage to Rose Hawthorne, younger daughter of Nathaniel Hawthorne, both George and Rose converted to Catholicism in 1891. According to a letter written from Lathrop to Gibbons in May 1891, Gibbons's catechism figured significantly in their decision to become Roman Catholics, attesting that they were both "largely converted by your cogent, simple, sincere & winning presentation of the truth." After founding the Servants for the Relief of Incurable Cancer, a charitable religious sisterhood, Rose Hawthorne (now known in the Catholic Church as Mother Alphonsa Lathrop) reiterated what she felt personally to be the enduring influence of *Faith of Our Fathers*. Writing to Gibbons in 1906, she told the cardinal that her reading of the book had immediately alleviated her anxieties about the difficulties of becoming a Catholic, devotedly allowing that the book had "kept me observant of the beautiful influence of your holy power during many years" (Ellis, *Life of James Cardinal Gibbons*, 2:585.

30. Dwight L. Moody (1837–99) was an evangelist, preacher, publisher, and founder of the (now) Northfield Mount Hermon school in Massachusetts and the Moody Bible Institute in Chicago.

31. Gibbons, *Faith of Our Fathers*, xi (emphasis added).

32. The use of the term "habitus" in this context draws upon the sociological analysis of culture and lifestyle in Bourdieu, *Distinction*. Here habitus refers to those cultural tastes and preferences (e.g., music, literature, clothing, decor, leisure activities, and so forth) that become naturalized and standardized within social classes, classes defined by a matrix of economic capital and "cultural capital." For a complete theoretical discussion of this concept in terms of domestic space, see Bourdieu, *Distinction*, 170–225.

33. This is not to say, however, that Gibbons's theology itself conformed to mainstream Protestant teachings. Edward J. Stearns, examining chaplain for the Anglican diocese of Easton, Maryland, wrote a refutation of Gibbons's

catechism titled *Faith of Our Forefathers* (1879), and in 1880 published a response to a two-part review of his book and Gibbons's in the *American Catholic Quarterly Journal* of January 1880, in which *Faith of Our Fathers* was highly praised by that leading Catholic journal of Philadelphia. See Stearns, *The American Catholic Quarterly Review and "Faith of Our Forefathers."* In the same *ACQJ* review Stearns, on the other hand, had been harshly criticized for his attack on Gibbons and was accused there of being a Freemason, and thus an enemy of Catholicism (a charge Stearns denied). Stearns also notes, unhappily, the addition of Gibbons's chapter on the "Blessed Virgin Mary" for the tenth edition (1879) of *Faith of Our Fathers.*

34. Gibbons, *Faith of Our Fathers*, vii.

35. Will, *Life of Cardinal Gibbons*, 1:133, 92–93. A typical record of Gibbons's periodic trips through rural North Carolina reads as follows: "Arrived in Wilmington tonight after an absence of four weeks. The following is a brief summary of our travel and its results: Number of miles travelled by rail, stage, and steamboat, 925; number of towns and stations visited, 16; number of Catholics in various places, 400; converts confirmed, 16; total number, 64; converts baptized, 10; total number, 16" (ibid., 1:101).

36. Ibid., 1:145.

37. Gibbons, *Faith of Our Fathers*, xv.

38. Ibid., xi–xii.

39. Ibid., 65.

40. Ibid., 4, 63.

41. Ibid., 4.

42. Ibid., 25.

43. Ibid., 24.

44. Ibid., 51.

45. Ibid., 56.

46. Ibid., 59.

47. Fisher, *Hard Facts*, 109.

48. Demonstrating once more his ability to reach large audiences, Gibbons published a bluntly antifeminist essay, "Restless Woman," in a 1902 issue of the widely circulated *Ladies Home Journal* in which he asserted his view of Catholic womanhood: "I regard 'women's rights' women, and the leaders of the new school of female progress as the worst enemies of the female sex. They teach that which robs a woman of all that is amiable and gentle, tender and attractive, and which gives her nothing in return but masculine boldness and brazen effrontery. . . . They withdraw her from those sacred obligations which properly belong to her sex, and fill her with ambition to usurp a position for which neither God nor Nature ever intended her" (Gibbons, "Restless Woman," 6).

49. Gibbons, *Faith of Our Fathers*, 73.

50. Ibid., 88.
51. Ibid., 75.
52. Ibid., 75–76.
53. Ibid., 96. For broader consideration of the tension between matriarchal and patriarchal models of nineteenth-century Protestantism and Catholicism in America, see McDannell, *The Christian Home in Victorian America, 1840–1900*. McDannell charts the development of Catholic attitudes toward domesticity and shows the centrality of Irish immigrants as both producers and consumers of domestic ideology, arguing that "as English speakers and heirs of British colonial rule they could better understand and respond to the Anglo-Saxon sentiments of Victorian American Protestants" (xvi). McDannell marks the 1880s (when more immigrant Catholics could afford to live in middle-class homes) as the period when an identifiable American Catholic domestic/sentimental ideology finally appeared consistently in the popular press in such periodicals as the *Sacred Heart Review* or the *Catholic World*, which often printed articles on the subject by European authors. An early example from this genre, though, came in 1876 with the publication of "Father O'Reilly's" *Mirror of True Womanhood*, which stayed in print through seventeen editions by 1892 (McDannell, *The Christian Home in Victorian America*, 53). Additional European influence on the subject of domestic/sentimental ideology came from the French advice books (often written by upper-class women or by priests) that were steadily translated and published by American Catholic presses in the late nineteenth century (ibid., 52–76).
54. Gibbons, *Faith of Our Fathers*, 168.
55. Ibid., 173–74.
56. On the Protestant use of the Virgin Mary as mythical Madonna, by writers as diverse as Nathaniel Hawthorne, Margaret Fuller, Harriet Beecher Stowe, Harold Frederic, Henry Adams, and T. S. Eliot, see Gatta, *American Madonna*. Gibbons wrote in other publications about the importance of Marian devotions, as in an 1886 essay for the *American Catholic Quarterly Review* in which he asserted Mary's importance as both aesthetic and spiritual: "Hers is exquisite beauty, but a beauty more of the soul than of the body; it delights without intoxicating. . . . She is the mother of fair love devoid of sickly sentimentality or sensuality" (Gibbons, "Relative Condition," 656).
57. Gibbons, *Faith of Our Fathers*, 178–79.
58. Ibid., 179 (emphasis in Gibbons's citation). The Holmes poem that Gibbons excerpts (without naming it) is "L'Inconnue" (Holmes, *Complete Poetical Works*, 421), and the remainder of the poem, which is written to a secret love, illustrates Gibbons's willingness to overlook Holmes's more general characterization of nonfamilial eros in order to "discover" veneration of Mary within secular discourse. The remaining lines of "L'Inconnue" continue:

I hear thy voice, I see thy smile,
I look upon thy folded hair;
Ah! while we dream not they beguile,
Our hearts are in the snare;
And she who chains a wild bird's wing
Must start not if her captive sing.

So, lady, take the leaf that falls,
To all but thee unseen, unknown:
When evening shades thy silent walls,
Then read it all alone;
In stillness read, in darkness seal,
Forget, despise, but not reveal.

59. Other non-Catholics quoted within the catechism, in addition to the ones in the chapter on the "Blessed Virgin Mary," include Byron, Tennyson, Macauley, Orestes Brownson (in his Protestant incarnation), and Shakespeare.

60. Gibbons, *Faith of Our Fathers*, 180.

"SONNET TO THE VIRGIN"
Mother! whose virgin bosom was uncrossed
With the least shade of thought to sin allied;
Woman! above all women glorified,
Our tainted nature's solitary boast;
Purer than foam on central ocean tost,
Brighter than eastern skies at daybreak strewn
With fancied roses, than the unblemished moon
Before her wane begins on heaven's blue coast,
Thy image falls to earth. Yet some, I ween,
Not unforgiven, the suppliant knee might bend
As to a visible power, in which blend
All that was mixed and reconciled in thee
Of mother's love with maiden purity,
Of high with low, celestial with serene.

61. Ibid., 183.
62. Ibid., 181.
63. Ibid., 188.
64. Ibid., 190.

65. The correspondence between Longfellow's view of womanhood and Gibbons's teaching about Mary may be seen in Gibbons's chosen quotes from the *Golden Legend*. One reads in part:

And if our faith had given us nothing more
Than this example of all womanhood,
So mild, so merciful, so strong, so good,
So patient, peaceful, loyal, loving, pure,
This were enough to prove it higher and truer
Than all the creed the world had known before. (193)

66. Gibbons, *Faith of Our Fathers*, 193.
67. Ibid., 190 (emphasis added).
68. Ibid., 191.

At morn—at noon—at twilight dim—
Maria! thou hast heard my hymn;
In joy and woe—in good and ill—
Mother of God, be with me still!
When the hours flew brightly by,
And not a cloud obscured the sky,
My soul, lest it should truant be,
Thy grace did guide to thine and thee;
Now, when storms of fate o'ercast
Darkly my present and my past,
Let my future radiant shine,
With sweet hopes of thee and thine.

69. Ibid., 194.
70. Douglas, *Feminization of American Culture*, 200–226.
71. Ibid., 201.
72. Gibbons, *Faith of Our Fathers*, 224.
73. Ibid., 418.
74. Ibid., 410.
75. Ibid., 415.
76. Gibbons, *A Retrospective of Fifty Years*, 1:146.
77. On the role of John Foxe's *Acts and Monuments* in the modern development of "the anti-Catholic public sphere," see Barrington, "Studies in the Anticatholic Origins," 25–84.
78. Gibbons, *Faith of Our Fathers*, 20.
79. Ibid., xi.
80. Gibbons, *Faith of Our Fathers*, xi. Monk's *Awful Disclosures of Maria Monk* (1836), a virulently anti-Catholic, quasi-pornographic novel focusing on alleged corruptions of domesticity and sexuality in a convent, sold 300,000 copies by the time of the Civil War; only Stowe's *Uncle Tom's Cabin* sold more copies during that period. Like *Faith of Our Fathers*, Monk's *Awful Disclosures* was in circulation

for many years; even after the exposure of Monk as a fraud and former prostitute, it managed in the late 1880s to interest the "aged Walt Whitman, who reread it while under Horace Traubel's care in Camden" (Reynolds, *Beneath the American Renaissance*, 65). It is intriguing to observe the sometimes-concealed support for virulent Catholicism among major American publishers. Jody M. Roy, in her study of American anti-Catholic literature, observes that Herman Melville's future publishers—the redoubtable Harper and Brothers—were Maria Monk's original publishers for *Awful Disclosures*. J. Henry Harper, who inherited the Harper fortune, made his own disclosure in 1912 that the "Howe and Bates" firm credited with the 1836 edition of that book was actually an alias for "Harper and Brothers" (Roy, "Nineteenth-Century American Catholicism," 36).

81. Gibbons, *Faith of Our Fathers*, xi–xii.

82. Ibid., 370.

83. Ibid., xii.

84. Ibid., xiv.

85. Ibid., xiv.

86. Ibid., 21–22.

87. Ibid., 22–23.

88. Ibid., 23.

89. By 1855 Baltimore already had a population of 188,251 persons, of whom approximately 25 percent were foreign born, and with a large number of these being Catholics from Ireland and Germany. See Ellis, *Life of James Cardinal Gibbons*, 1:32. Nonetheless, the political climate in Baltimore in the antebellum years was anything but hospitable for immigrant Catholics. Seminarians in Baltimore during the years of Gibbons's training at St. Charles College (opened 1848 as a preparatory school for seminarians) and St. Mary's seminary were sometimes singled out for attack on the streets of the city, due to the nativist antagonism that led to the dominance of the Know-Nothing Party in Baltimore during the years leading up to the Civil War. Politically, the Know-Nothings controlled the city and thirteen of twenty-one Maryland counties until 1860, when they were voted out of the Baltimore city government (Ellis, *Life of James Cardinal Gibbons*, 1:32–33).

90. Will, *Life of Cardinal Gibbons*, 1:105.

91. O'Connell, *Catholicity in the Carolinas and Georgia*, 443.

92. See, for example, Christian Reid's *Morton House* (1871), *Nina's Atonement* (1873), and *Valerie Aylmer* (1870). For a complete bibliography of Christian Reid, see Becker, *Biography of Christian Reid*, 178–83. Dorothea Davenport Burkhart's study "Catholicism, Confederacy, and Colonialism" provides close readings of several of Reid's novels, arguing on behalf of the literary value of Reid's work.

93. The baptism and confirmation of the Fisher family are noted in Becker,

Biography of Christian Reid, 15; and in A. E. Smith and V. de P. Fitzpatrick, *Cardinal Gibbons*, 68–69.

94. Will, *Life of Cardinal Gibbons*, 1:85.

95. Ibid., 1:91.

96. Becker's biographical sketch of Christian Reid maintains that Reid looked upon the young bishop, who was twelve years her senior (she was twenty-two years old when Gibbons first arrived in North Carolina; her first novel was published anonymously in 1870, when she was only twenty-four), as her "spiritual guide" (*Biography of Christian Reid*, 22). In this role, he wrote to her expressing his disapproval of her career as a sentimental novelist, a disapproval that is ironic in light of his later appropriations of the conventions of sentimental fiction in his own writings. Her rapid success in the field of fiction led him shortly thereafter to offer his support for her career as a novelist in a letter to her in late 1871 congratulating her on the success of her second novel, *Morton House*, a southern plantation novel that her biographer has called "a tale of patient suffering and unscrupulous intrigue" (ibid., 25–27).

97. Franchot, *Roads to Rome*, xxiii.

98. Occasionally, the sensationalism of the convent exposé genre exceeded the limits of American nationality in order to heighten its exotic cultural flavors. See, for example, S. B. Smith, *Rosamond: or, a Narrative or the Captivity and Sufferings of an American Female Under the Popish Priests, in the Island of Cuba* (1848).

99. Gibbons, *Faith of Our Fathers*, xvi.

100. Ibid., xvii.

101. Ibid., xv.

102. Reynolds, *Faith in Fiction*, 6.

103. Ibid., 6.

104. Thorp, *Catholic Novelists in Defense of their Faith*, 27.

105. Reynolds, *Faith in Fiction*, 145.

106. Ibid., 147.

107. Ibid., 148.

Chapter 5. Trading Religion for Feminism

1. The publication of *The Complete Works of Kate Chopin* under the editorship of Per Seyersted and Seyersted's *Kate Chopin: A Critical Biography* inaugurated the modern revival of critical interest in her writing. For updated biographical information based on recently discovered Chopin papers, see Toth, *Unveiling Kate Chopin*.

2. Gilbert, "Introduction: The Second Coming of Aphrodite," 33. In his introductory comments for the *Complete Works of Kate Chopin*, Per Seyersted points to Chopin's close friend and physician in St. Louis, Frederick Kolbenheyer, as

an influential figure in her decision to end her practice of Catholicism. Seyersted concludes, moreover, that Chopin's study of Darwin eventually brought her to new and naturalistic views of human morality: "That she drifted away from Catholicism did not mean that she became an atheist, however, but only that she sought God in nature rather than through the Church" (*Complete Works of Kate Chopin*, 1:22–23).

3. Baker, "Delineation of Life and Character," 848.

4. Brodhead, *Cultures of Letters*, 116–17.

5. Chopin was also familiar with the religious references in fiction by Joel Chandler Harris, an influential local-color writer and an adult convert to Catholicism whose work Chopin had admired and reviewed. In his article "Joel Chandler Harris, Catholic," Bryan A. Giemza stresses the importance of Chandler's Roman Catholic faith in stories such as "A Belle of St. Velerien" (1892) and other works.

6. The critical debates concerning local-color writing versus naturalism/realism emerged after the publication of Sarah Orne Jewett's *The Country of the Pointed Firs* (1896), a work often said to mark the highest achievement in the local-color genre. After Jewett's novel was published, essays criticizing local-color writing as artistically weak and inherently feminine (and thus undesirable) appeared in *Harper's* and the *Atlantic*, two of the genre's leading outlets. Michael Davitt Bell's *The Problem of American Realism* asserts that tensions about gender identity had much to do with the concern about these seemingly opposed genres, noting that "a prominent function of claiming to be a realist or naturalist during this period was to provide assurance to one's society and oneself that one was a 'real' man rather than an effeminate 'artist'" (10). Well-theorized perspectives on New England regionalism are included in Buell, *New England Literary Culture*, esp. 283–370; and Brodhead, *Cultures of Letters*. Ann Douglas's *The Feminization of American Culture* remains an important negative assessment of local colorists as producers of a "literature of impoverishment." Much-needed subtlety applied to mapping the relation between interpretation and genre categorizations like "local color" may be found in June Howard's helpful discussions in "Unraveling Regions, Unsettling Periods."

7. Emily Toth provides valuable new information about Chopin's years at Sacred Heart Academy and her relationships with Mary O'Meara and Kitty Garesché in *Unveiling Kate Chopin*, 22–29.

8. Chopin, *Private Papers*, 14–15, 131.

9. Toth, *Unveiling Kate Chopin*, 84.

10. Franchot, *Roads to Rome*, 197.

11. Ibid., 197.

12. See n. 1.

13. Bonner, "Christianity and Catholicism in the Fiction of Kate Chopin," 118.

14. Gauchet, *Disenchantment of the World*, 201.
15. McDannell, "Catholic Women Fiction Writers," 401.
16. Chopin, *Complete Works*, 1:157.
17. Ibid., 1:277. Emily Toth describes in some detail the events in Chopin's life around the time in about 1891 when she stopped attending the Catholic Church: "Kate Chopin had many reasons to stop going to mass. There were not traditional people in her family to push her to go, and she and Oscar, even on their honeymoon, had been lax about churchgoing. Her years in Cloutierville turned her against the Church's position on divorce—and she very much disliked having priests poke about in her business" (Toth, *Unveiling Kate Chopin*, 135).
18. Chopin, *Complete Works*, 1:278.
19. Ibid., 1:389.
20. Ibid., 1:394, 397. Empress Eugenie Montijo was a fashionable and well-educated French Catholic woman, whose romantic relationship with her husband, Napoleon III, was ridiculed at the time because she was not considered to be of sufficiently high aristocratic rank for her marriage to him in 1853.
21. Chopin, "Two Portraits," 45–51.
22. Chopin, *Complete Works*, 1:431.
23. Chopin, *Awakening*, 68–69; Chopin, *Private Papers*, 181–82.
24. Among the few critics to have made connections between Chopin's Catholic scenes and a progressive view of women's erotic experience, Kathleen Wheeler has noted that Chopin's style "lacks the harsh pessimism and bleakness of other local colourists, such as Sarah Orne Jewett, Mary Wilkins Freeman, and McEnery Stewart" and that her writing is "enriched . . . with intense and varied symbolism, eroticism, and sensuality (as she explored, for example, the sexual sublimation evident in Catholic rituals)" (qtd. in Bloom and Bloom, *Willa Cather's Gift*, 120).
25. Turner, *Without God*, xi–xii.
26. Gauchet, *Disenchantment of the World*, 163.

Chapter 6. "A Kind Woman in Heaven"

1. John Talbot Smith, "Young Catholic Writer" (published in New York City in the *St. John's Quarterly*, July 1909); qtd. in Guiney, "On Catholic Writers and their Handicaps," 205.
2. Charles Warren Stoddard was already well known as a journalist and travel writer when he became a member of the English faculty at the University of Notre Dame in 1885. *The Lepers of Molokai* was published by the Ave Maria Press, under the leadership of Rev. Daniel E. Hudson, the same editor who had worked extensively to publish fiction by Catholic writers such as Anna Hanson Dorsey and Christian Reid.

3. Crawford, *The Novel*, 8, 9, 82.

4. *Catholic Encyclopedia*, 30

5. Giles, *American Catholic Arts and Fictions*, 168. For a broader discussion of twentieth-century representations of Roman Catholicism in popular culture, see A. B. Smith, *The Look of Catholics*.

6. On Cather's meeting with Crawford, see Woodress, *Willa Cather: A Literary Life*, 125. In an 1896 article about Crawford, Cather expressed her dismay at Crawford's literary productivity: "The *Chicago Chronicle* remarks with great veneration that Mr. Crawford wrote the whole . . . 150,000 words of [*Adam Johnston's Son* (1895)] in twenty-five days, and how is that for America? Good heavens, yes. Of course he did! But why noise the fact abroad? Just as though Mr. Crawford's prolific rapidity were not his bane and curse" (Cather, *World and the Parish*, 1:262).

7. Crawford, *The Novel*, 17–18.

8. Turner, *Without God*, 215.

9. Lee, *Willa Cather: Double Lives*, 177; Cather, *Professor's House*, 16, 30.

10. Cather, *Mortal Enemy*, 26–27.

11. Ibid., 102, 111.

12. Rosowski, *Voyage Perilous*, 151.

13. Cather, *My Mortal Enemy*, 116.

14. Cather, *Willa Cather on Writing*, 5.

15. For a full accounting of Cather's extensive reliance on Howlett's life of Machebeuf in the composition of *Death in the Afternoon*, see Bloom and Bloom, *Willa Cather's Gift*, 197–236.

16. Lee, *Willa Cather: Double Lives*, 285 (emphasis added).

17. See Acocella, *Willa Cather and the Politics of Criticism*, for her critique of the various politicized modes of recent Cather scholarship.

18. Woodress, *Willa Cather: A Literary Life*, 410–11.

19. McCole, "New Books," 752.

20. Shared interest in Catholic culture was not enough to persuade Willa Cather of the value of Kate Chopin's fiction. Acocella rightly explains that Cather generally took a dim view of other women as writers. Cather wrote in a negative review that Chopin's novel *The Awakening* was disappointing in that Chopin had used her talents as a writer on "so trite and sordid a theme" as adultery (qtd. in Acocella, *Willa Cather and the Politics of Criticism*, 40).

21. Cather, *One of Ours*, 49–50.

22. Acocella, *Willa Cather and the Politics of Criticism*, 26.

23. Porter, *On the Divide*, 255. In following Cather's approach to using Roman Catholicism in her novels of the late 1920s, my argument corresponds with that of Anthony Burke Smith's study of Catholic representations in mid-twentieth-century America. Cather's work anticipates the profound shift in the status of Roman Catholicism during that period of the mid-twentieth century

when, as Smith argues, "Catholics in mass culture challenged the long history of Protestant nationalism and anti-Catholicism in the United States—one thoroughly textualized and semiotic—to deploy Catholic difference for new understandings of the nation" (A. B. Smith, *Look of Catholics*, 14).

24. Kazin, *On Native Grounds*, 184–88.

25. Lears, *No Place of Grace*, xiii–xiv. The concept of the "therapeutic society" that Lears uses is drawn from the influential work of Philip Reiff, especially his *Triumph of the Therapeutic*.

26. For further analysis of Cather as a queer writer, see Lindemann, *Willa Cather: Queering America*. For an important countervailing argument that strongly criticizes feminist interpretations and the politicization of Cather's career in fiction, see Acocella, *Willa Cather and the Politics of Criticism*, esp. 37–66.

27. Lears, *No Place of Grace*, 185.

28. Qtd. in Woodress, *Willa Cather: A Literary Life*, 396. Cather's comment is drawn from a letter to Fanny Butcher.

29. *Death Comes for the Archbishop*, 4. The 1845 annexation of Texas encouraged U.S. expansionists to demand the annexation of all the Southwest and California, and the United States declared war on Mexico in 1846. The Mexican War ended in 1848 with the Treaty of Guadalupe Hidalgo, which formally ceded New Mexico to the United States. In 1850 the area east of California was divided into the territories of New Mexico (now New Mexico and Arizona) and Utah. In 1853 the United States purchased more territory from Mexico, which added land south of the Gila River to New Mexico. During the American Civil War (1861–65) the New Mexico territory was temporarily controlled by the Confederacy. After the Confederate withdrawal the U.S. government organized the Arizona Territory in 1863 in the western portion of the Territory of New Mexico, reducing New Mexico to its present boundaries.

30. Lindemann, *Willa Cather: Queering America*, 5, 121.

31. *Death Comes for the Archbishop*, 79, 50–51.

32. Ibid., 99.

33. Ibid., 83–89.

34. Ibid., 181–82.

35. Ibid., 252–53.

Conclusion

1. For extended considerations of Roman Catholicism's influence on twentieth-century art and culture, see Giles, *American Catholic Arts and Fictions*, and Ferraro, *Catholic Lives / Contemporary America*.

Works Cited

Acocella, Joan. *Willa Cather and the Politics of Criticism.* Lincoln: University of Nebraska Press, 2000.

Astore, William J. "Gentle Skeptics? American Catholic Encounters with Polygenism, Geology, and Evolutionary Theories from 1845 to 1875." *Catholic Historical Review* 82 (1996): 40–76.

Baker, Carlos. "Delineation of Life and Character." In *Literary History of the United States*, 3rd rev. ed., edited by Robert E. Spiller, Willard Thorp, Thomas H. Johnson, Henry Seidel Canby, and Richard M. Ludwig, 843–61. New York: Macmillan, 1963.

Barker-Benfield, G. J. *The Horrors of the Half-Known Life: Male Attitudes Toward Women and Sex in Nineteenth-Century America.* New York: Harper & Row, 1976.

Barrington, John Patrick. "Studies in the Anticatholic Origins of the Anglo-American Self." PhD diss., College of William and Mary, 1997.

Baym, Nina. *Woman's Fiction: A Guide to Novels by and About Women in America, 1820–1870.* 1978. 2nd ed. Urbana: University of Illinois Press, 1993.

Becker, Kate Harbes. *Biography of Christian Reid.* Belmont, NC: Privately printed, 1941.

Beecher, Catharine E. *A Treatise on Domestic Economy, for the Use of Young Ladies at Home, at School.* Rev. ed. New York: Harper and Bros., 1846.

Bell, Michael Davitt. *The Problem of American Realism: Studies in the Cultural History of a Literary Idea.* Chicago: University of Chicago Press, 1993.

Bender, Thomas. *New York Intellect: A History of Intellectual Life in New York City, from 1750 to the Beginnings of Our Own Time.* Baltimore: Johns Hopkins University Press, 1987.

Billington, Ray Allen. *The Protestant Crusade, 1800–1860: A Study of the Origins of American Nativism.* Gloucester, MA: Peter Smith, 1963.

Birdsall, Richard D. "Emerson and the Church of Rome." *Catholic Historical Review* 31 (1959): 273–81.

Bloom, Edward A., and Lillian D. Bloom. *Willa Cather's Gift of Sympathy.* Carbondale: Southern Illinois University Press, 1962.

Bonner, Thomas, Jr. "Christianity and Catholicism in the fiction of Kate Chopin." *Southern Quarterly* 20 (1982): 118–25.

Bourdieu, Pierre. *Distinction: A Social Critique of the Judgement of Taste.* Cambridge, MA: Harvard University Press, 1984.

Brodhead, Richard. *Cultures of Letters: Scenes of Reading and Writing in Nineteenth-Century America.* Chicago: University of Chicago Press, 1993.

Brown, Gillian. *Domestic Individualism: Imagining Self in Nineteenth-Century America.* Berkeley: University of California Press, 1990.

Brownson, Orestes A., and Isaac Thomas Hecker. *The Brownson-Hecker Correspondence.* Edited by Joseph F. Gower and Richard M. Leliaert. Notre Dame, IN: University of Notre Dame Press, 1979.

Brownson, Orestes A. "American Literature (pts. 1–3)." 1839. Reprinted in *The Works of Orestes Brownson* (hereafter *Works*), 19:1–21 (pt. 1), 19:22–39 (pt. 2), 19:203–446 (pt. 3).

———. "Archbishop Hughes on the Catholic Press." *Brownson's Quarterly Review* (Jan. 1857). Reprinted in *Works*, 20:50–73.

———. "Bacon's Poems." *Boston Quarterly Review* 1 (Jan. 1838): 74–83.

———. "Beecherism and Its Tendencies." *Catholic World* (Jan. 1871). Reprinted in *Works*, 3:460–84.

———. "The Blakes and the Flanagans." *Brownson's Quarterly Review* (Apr. 1856). Reprinted in *Works*, 20:23–39.

———. "The Blithedale Romance, by Nathaniel Hawthorne." *Brownson's Quarterly Review* (Oct. 1852): 561–64.

———. "The Castle of Rossilon, by Madame Le Rochere [translated by Mrs. J. Sadlier]." *Brownson's Quarterly Review* (Apr. 1851): 266–71.

———. "The Catholic Press." *Brownson's Quarterly Review* (Jan. 1849). Reprinted in *Works*, 19:269–93.

———. "Catholic Secular Literature." *Brownson's Quarterly Review* (July 1849). Reprinted in *Works*, 19: 293–308.

———. "Catholicity Necessary to Democracy." *Brownson's Quarterly Review* (Oct. 1845): 514–29.

———. *Charles Elwood; or, The Infidel Converted.* Boston: Charles C. Little and James Brown, 1840.

———. "The Church and the Republic." *Brownson's Quarterly Review* (Oct. 1856). Reprinted in *Works*, 12:1–32.

———. *The Convert; or Leaves From My Experience.* New York: Edward Dunigan and Brother, 1857.

———. "Democracy." *Boston Quarterly Review* (Jan. 1838). Reprinted in *Works*, 15:1–33.

———. "Emerson's Prose Works." *Catholic World* (May 1870). Reprinted in *Works*, 3:424–38.

———. "The Everlasting Yes" (excerpted from *The Convert: or, Leaves from My Ex-*

perience, 2nd ed., 1877). In *The Transcendentalists: An Anthology*, edited by Perry Miller, 45–47. Cambridge, MA: Harvard University Press, 1950.

———. "Explanations to Catholics." *Brownson's Quarterly Review* (Oct. 1854). Reprinted in *Works*, 20:361–81.

———. "Faith and Reason, Revelation and Science." *Brownson's Quarterly Review* (Apr. 1863). Reprinted in *Works*, 3:565–95.

———. "Faith and the Sciences." *Catholic World* (Dec. 1867). Reprinted in *Works*, 9:268–91.

———. "Father Felix: A Tale." *Brownson's Quarterly Review* (July 1846): 402–3.

———. "The Forest, by J[edediah]. V[incent]. Huntington." *Brownson's Quarterly Review* (Jan. 1853): 135–36.

———. "Grantley Manor, or Popular Literature." *Brownson's Quarterly Review* (Oct. 1848). Reprinted in *Works*, 19:244–68.

———. "Guevara on the Veneration of Images." *Brownson's Quarterly Review* (Jan. 1850): 39–60.

———. "Hereditary Genius." *Catholic World* (Sep. 1870). Reprinted in *Works*, 9:401–17.

———. "Literary Notices and Criticism." *Brownson's Quarterly Review* (July 1846): 402–3.

———. "The Literary Policy of the Church of Rome." *Brownson's Quarterly Review* (Jan. 1845): 1–28.

———. "Literature, Love, and Marriage." *Brownson's Quarterly Review* (July 1864). Reprinted in *Works*, 19:493–516.

———. "Longfellow's *Evangeline* and *Kavanaugh*." *Brownson's Quarterly Review* (Jan. 1850): 56–87.

———. *The Mediatorial Life of Jesus*. Boston: Charles C. Little and James Brown, 1842. Reprinted in *Works*, 4:140–72.

———. "Miss Fuller and Reformers." *Brownson's Quarterly Review* (Apr. 1845). Reprinted in *Works*, 6:220–29.

———. "The Mission of America." *Brownson's Quarterly Review* (Oct. 1856). Reprinted in *Works*, 11:551–84.

———. "Modern French Literature." *Boston Quarterly Review* (Apr. 1842). Reprinted in *Works*, 19:48–65.

———. "Modern Idolatry." *Brownson's Quarterly Review* (July 1845). Reprinted in *Works*, 19:100–118.

———. "Native Americanism." *Brownson's Quarterly Review* (Jan. 1845): 76–98.

———. "An Oration, Delivered before the United Brothers Society of Brown University, at Providence, R.I., September 3, 1839." *Boston Quarterly Review* 3 (1839): 57–79.

———. "Philosophy of the Supernatural." *American Catholic Quarterly Review* (Jan. 1876). Reprinted in *Works*, 2:271–83.

———. "Professor Park Against Catholicity." *Brownson's Quarterly Review* (Oct. 1845). Reprinted in *Works*, 6:353–426.

———. "Protestant Revivals and Catholic Retreats." *Brownson's Quarterly Review* (July 1858): 289–322.

———. "Religious Novels." *Brownson's Quarterly Review* (Jan. 1847). Reprinted in *Works*, 19: 123–54.

———. "Revivals and Retreats." *Brownson's Quarterly Review* (July 1858): 289–322.

———. "Rosemary; or, Life and Death. A Tale of Our Own Times. By Jedediah Huntington." *Brownson's Quarterly Review* (Oct. 1860): 526–28.

———. "R. W. Emerson's Poems." *Brownson's Quarterly Review* (Apr. 1847). Reprinted in *Works*, 19:189–202.

———. "The Scarlet Letter: A Romance, by Nathaniel Hawthorne." *Brownson's Quarterly Review* (Oct. 1850): 528–32.

——— "The Scholar's Mission: An Address Pronounced before the Gamma Sigma Society of Dartmouth College, N.H., July 26, 1843." Reprinted in *Works*, 19:65–87.

———. "Schiller's Aesthetic Theory." *Brownson's Quarterly Review* (Apr. 1846). Reprinted in *Works*, 19:118–29.

———. "Science and the Sciences." *Brownson's Quarterly Review* (July 1863). Reprinted in *Works*, 9:254–68.

———. "The Sea Lions: or the Lost Sealers, by James Fenimore Cooper." *Brownson's Quarterly Review* (July 1849): 397–408.

———. "Shandy McGuire: or Irish Liberty." *Brownson's Quarterly Review* (Jan. 1849): 58.

———. "Sick Calls: from the Diary of a Missionary Priest, by Rev. Edward Price." *Brownson's Quarterly Review* (Jan. 1852): 115–20.

———. *The Spirit-Rapper: An Autobiography*. New York: Little, Brown, 1854.

———. "Thornberry Abbey." *Brownson's Quarterly Review* (Oct. 1846). Reprinted in *Works*, 19:130–42.

———. "The Two Brothers; Or, Why Are You A Protestant?" *Brownson's Quarterly Review* (1847–48). Reprinted in *Works*, 6: 244–352.

———. "Use and Abuse of Reading." *Catholic World* (July 1866). Reprinted in *Works*, 19:517–32.

———. "The Vision of Sir Launfal, by J[ames] R[ussell] Lowell." *Brownson's Quarterly Review* (Apr. 1849): 265–74.

———. "Whittier's Poems." *Boston Quarterly Review* 1 (Jan. 1838): 21–53.

———. "The Woman Question I." *Catholic World* (May 1869). Reprinted in *Works*, 18:381–97.

———. "The Woman Question II." *Brownson's Quarterly Review* (Oct. 1873). Reprinted in *Works*, 18:398–417.

———. "Women's Novels." *Brownson's Quarterly Review* (July 1875). Reprinted in *Works*, 19:595–605.

———. *The Works of Orestes Brownson*. 20 vols. Detroit: Thorndike Nourse, 1882–1907.

———. "The Yankee in Ireland." *Brownson's Quarterly Review* (Jan. 1860). Reprinted in *Works* 20:83–93.

Buell, Lawrence. *New England Literary Culture: From Revolution through Renaissance*. Cambridge, MA: Harvard University Press, 1986.

Burkhart, Dorothea Davenport. "Catholicism, Confederacy, and Colonialism: A Study of Frances Christine Fisher Tiernan." PhD diss., University of North Carolina–Greensboro, 2001.

Bynum, Caroline Walker. *Fragmentation and Redemption: Essays on Gender and the Human Body in Medieval Religion*. New York: Zone Books, 1991.

———. *Jesus as Mother: Studies in the Spirituality of the High Middle Ages*. Berkeley: University of California Press, 1982.

Cadegan, Una M. "Running the Ancient Ark by Steam: Catholic Publishing." In *A History of the Book in America*, 4:392–410. Chapel Hill: American Antiquarian Society/UNC Press, 2009.

Callon, David Jerome. "Converting Catholicism: Orestes A. Brownson, Anna H. Dorsey, and Irish America, 1840–1896." PhD diss., Washington University–St. Louis, 2008.

Carey, Mathew. "Plan of Mathew Cary for the Institution for Printing Roman Catholic Books, 1791." *American Catholic Historical Researches* 16, no. 1 (Jan. 1899): 134–36.

Carey, Patrick W. *Orestes Brownson: American Religious Weathervane*. Grand Rapids: Wm. Eerdman's, 2004.

Carroll, Bret E. "The Religious Construction of Masculinity in Victorian America: The Male Mediumship of John Shoebridge Williams." *Religion and American Culture* 7 (Winter 1997): 27–60.

Cather, Willa. *Death Comes for the Archbishop*. New York: Alfred A. Knopf, 1927.

———. *A Lost Lady*. New York: Alfred A. Knopf, 1923.

———. *My Mortal Enemy*. New York: Alfred A. Knopf, 1926.

———. *One of Ours*. New York: Alfred A. Knopf, 1922.

———. *The Professor's House*. New York: Alfred A. Knopf, 1925.

———. *Shadows on the Rock*. New York: Alfred A. Knopf, 1931.

———. *Willa Cather on Writing: Critical Studies on Writing as Art*. Lincoln: University of Nebraska, 1988

———. *The World and the Parish: Willa Cather's Articles and Reviews*. Edited by William M. Curtin. 2 vols. Lincoln: University of Nebraska Press, 1970.

Catholic Encyclopedia: An International Work of Reference on the Constitution, Doctrine, Discipline, and History of the Catholic Church. 15 vols. Edited by Charles George Herberman et al. New York: The Encyclopedia Press, 1911.

Catholic World 28. "The American Novel: With Samples." Catholic World 28 (1878): 326–36.

Cavanaugh, Mary Stephana. "Catholic Book Publishing in the United States, 1784–1850." Master's thesis, University of Illinois, 1954.

Channing, William Ellery. "Remarks on National Literature." In *William Ellery Channing: Selected Writings*, edited by David Robinson, 166–93. New York: Paulist Press, 1985.

Chopin, Kate. *The Awakening and Selected Stories*. Edited by Sandra M. Gilbert. New York: Penguin Classics, 1986.

———. *The Complete Works of Kate Chopin*. Edited by Per Seyersted. Baton Rouge: Louisiana State University Press, 1969.

———. *Kate Chopin's Private Papers*. Edited by Emily Toth and Per Seyersted. Bloomington: Indiana University Press, 1998.

———. "Two Portraits (The Nun and the Wanton)." In *A Vocation and a Voice*, edited by Emily Toth, 45–51. New York: Penguin, 1991.

———. *A Vocation and a Voice: Stories by Kate Chopin*. Edited by Emily Toth. New York: Penguin, 1991.

Clark, Emily. *Masterless Mistresses: The New Orleans Ursulines and the Development of a New World Society, 1727–1834*. Chapel Hill: Omohundro Institute/UNC Press, 2007.

Cott, Nancy. *Bonds of Womanhood: "Woman's Sphere" in New England, 1780–1835*. New Haven, CT: Yale University Press, 1977.

Coultrap-McQuin, Susan. *Doing Literary Business: American Women Writers in the Nineteenth Century*. Chapel Hill: University of North Carolina Press, 1990.

Crawford, F. Marion. *Ave Roma Immortalis: Studies from the Chronicles of Rome*. 1898. Rev. ed. New York: Macmillan, 1902.

———. *The Novel: What It Is*. New York: Macmillan, 1893.

Cummings, Kathleen Sprows. *New Women of the Old Faith: Gender and American Catholicism in the Progressive Era*. Chapel Hill: University of North Carolina Press, 2009.

D'Agostino, Peter R. *Rome in America: Transnational Catholic Ideology from the Risorgimento to Fascism*. Chapel Hill: University of North Carolina Press, 2004.

Davidson, Cathy N. *Revolution and the Word: The Rise of the Novel in America*. New York: Oxford University Press, 1986.

Davis, David Brion. "Some Themes of Countersubversion: An Analysis of Anti-Masonic, Anti Catholic, and Anti-Mormon Literature." *Mississippi Valley Historical Review* 47 (1960): 205–24.

Delano, Sterling F. *Brook Farm: The Dark Side of Utopia*. Cambridge, MA: Belknap Press of Harvard University Press, 2004.

Dennis, Donna. *Licentious Gotham: Erotic Publishing and Its Prosecution in Nineteenth-Century New York*. Cambridge, MA: Harvard University Press, 2009.

Dolan, Jay P. *The American Catholic Experience: A History from Colonial Times to the Present*. New York: Doubleday, 1985.

———. *Catholic Revivalism: the American Experience, 1830–1900.* Notre Dame: University of Notre Dame Press, 1978.

———. "Social Catholicism." In *Making the Nonprofit Sector in the United States: A Reader*, edited by David C. Hammack, 188–202. Bloomington: Indiana University Press, 2000.

Dorsey, Anna H. *Coaina, The Rose of the Algonquins.* New York: P. O'Shea, 1857.

———. Letter from Anna Dorsey to Daniel Hudson, 1879. Online: www.archives.nd.edu (accessed Apr. 10, 2011).

———. *The Oriental Pearl; or the Catholic Immigrants.* Baltimore: John Murphy, 1848.

———. *Nora Brady's Vow.* Boston: Donahoe, 1869.

———. *The Student of Blenheim Forest.* Baltimore: John Murphy, 1867.

Douglas, Ann. *The Feminization of American Culture.* New York: Alfred A. Knopf, 1977.

Durkheim, Emile. *The Elementary Forms of Religious Life.* 1912. Translated by Karen E. Fields. Reprint, New York: Free Press, 1995.

Elliott, Rev. Walter. *The Life of Father Hecker.* 1891. Reprint, New York: Arno Press, 1972.

———. "Personal Reminiscences." *Catholic World* 101 (1915): 51–55.

Ellis, John Tracy, ed. *Documents of American Catholic History.* 3 vols. Wilmington, DE: Michael Glazier, 1987.

———. *The Life of James Cardinal Gibbons, Archbishop of Baltimore, 1834–1921.* 2 vols. Milwaukee: Bruce Publishing Company, 1952.

Emerson, Ralph Waldo. "The American Scholar." 1837. Reprinted in *The Essential Writings of Ralph Waldo Emerson*, edited by Brooks Atkinson, 43–62. New York: Modern Library, 2000.

———. "Literary Ethics: An Oration Delivered Before the Literary Societies of Dartmouth College, July 24, 1838." Reprinted in *Emerson's Complete Works*, vol. 1, *Nature, Addresses and Lectures*, edited by James Elliot Cabot, 150–80. New York: Houghton Mifflin, 1887.

[Emerson, Ralph Waldo, William Henry Channing, and James Freeman Clarke?]. *Memoirs of Margaret Fuller Ossoli.* Boston: Phillips, Sampson and Co., 1852.

Faber, Frederick W. *All for Jesus; or, the Easy Ways of Divine Love.* 23rd American ed. Baltimore: John Murphy, 1854.

———. *Devotion to the Pope.* Baltimore: John Murphy, 1860.

———. *Growth in Holiness; or, The Progress of the Spiritual Life.* Baltimore: John Murphy, n.d.

———. *The Foot of the Cross; or, The Sorrows of Mary.* Baltimore: John Murphy, n.d.

———. *The Precious Blood; or The Price of Our Salvation.* 10th U.S. ed. Baltimore: John Murphy, n.d.

Farina, John. *An American Experience of God: The Spirituality of Isaac Hecker*. New York: Paulist Press, 1981.

Ferraro, Thomas J., ed. *Catholic Lives / Contemporary America*. Durham, NC: Duke University Press, 1997.

Fiedler, Leslie. "An Almost Imaginary Interview: Hemingway in Ketchum." 1962. Reprinted in *A New Fiedler Reader*, 153–64. Amherst, NY: Prometheus Books, 1999.

———. *Love and Death in the American Novel*. New York: Criterion, 1960.

Finke, Roger, and Rodney Stark. *The Churching of America, 1776–1990: Winners and Losers in Our Religious Economy*. New Brunswick, NJ: Rutgers University Press, 1992.

Fisher, James T. "Clearing the Streets of the Catholic Lost Generation." In *Catholic Lives / Contemporary America*, edited by Thomas J. Ferraro. Special Issue. *South Atlantic Quarterly* 93 (Summer 1994): 603–30.

Fisher, Philip. *Hard Facts: Setting and Form in the American Novel*. New York: Oxford University Press, 1987.

Franchot, Jenny. *Roads to Rome: The Antebellum Protestant Encounter with Catholicism*. Berkeley: University of California Press, 1994.

Frederic, Harold. *The Damnation of Theron Ware*. 1896. Reprint, New York: Penguin, 1986.

Frink, Sandra. "Women, the Family, and the Fate of the Nation in American Anti-Catholic Narratives, 1830–1860." *Journal of the History of Sexuality* 18 (2009): 237–64.

Fuller, Margaret. *Woman in the Nineteenth Century*. 1845. Reprinted in *The Essential Margaret Fuller*, edited by Jeffrey Steele, 243–378. New Brunswick, NJ: Rutgers University Press, 1992.

Garaventa, Louis Theodore. "Bishop James Gibbons and the Growth of the Roman Catholic Church in North Carolina, 1868–1872." Master's thesis, University of North Carolina, 1973.

Gatta, John. *American Madonna: Images of the Divine Woman in Literary Culture*. New York: Oxford University Press, 1997.

Gauchet, Marcel. *The Disenchantment of the World: A Political History of Religion*. 1985. Translated by Oscar Burge. Reprint, Princeton, NJ: Princeton University Press, 1997.

Gibbons, James Cardinal. *The Faith of Our Fathers: Being a Plain Exposition of the Church Founded by Our Lord Jesus Christ*. 83rd rev. ed. Baltimore: John Murphy, 1917.

———. "The Relative Condition of Woman under Pagan and Christian Civilization." *American Catholic Quarterly Review* 11 (1886): 651–65.

———. "Restless Woman." *Ladies Home Journal*, Jan. 1902, 6.

———. *A Retrospective of Fifty Years*. Vol. 1. Baltimore: John Murphy, 1916.

Giemza, Bryan A. "Joel Chandler Harris, Catholic." *Logos: A Journal of Catholic Thought and Culture* 14, no. 3 (Summer 2011): 86–103.

Gilbert, Sandra. "Introduction: The Second Coming of Aphrodite." In *The Awakening and Selected Stories*, by Kate Chopin, 7–33, edited by Sandra M. Gilbert. New York: Penguin Classics, 1984.

Giles, Paul. *American Catholic Arts and Fictions: Culture, Ideology, Aesthetics*. Cambridge: Cambridge University Press, 1992.

Gilhooley, Leonard. *Contradiction and Dilemma: Orestes Brownson and the American Idea*. New York: Fordham University Press, 1972.

Gilmore, William J. *Reading Becomes a Necessity of Life: Material and Cultural Life in Rural New England, 1780–1835*. Knoxville: University of Tennessee Press, 1989.

Gleason, Philip. *The Conservative Reformers: German-American Catholics and the Social Order*. Notre Dame, IN: University of Notre Dame Press, 1968.

Griffin, Susan M. *Anti-Catholicism and Nineteenth-Century American Fiction*. New York: Cambridge University Press, 2004.

Grimké, Sarah M. Selections from *Letters on the Equality of the Sexes, and the Condition of Woman* (1838). In *The American Intellectual Tradition: A Sourcebook*, 3rd ed., vol. 1, *1630–1865*, edited by David A. Hollinger and Charles Capper, 220–37. New York: Oxford University Press, 1997.

Guiney, Louise Imogen. "On Catholic Writers and their Handicaps." *Catholic World* 90 (1909): 203–15.

Gura, Philip F. *The Wisdom of Words: Language, Theology, and Literature in the New England Renaissance*. Middletown, CT: Wesleyan University Press, 1981.

Gustafson, Sandra. *Eloquence Is Power: Oratory and Performance in Early America*. Chapel Hill: University of North Carolina Press, 2000.

Gutjahr, Paul C. "Diversification in American Religious Publishing." In *A History of the Book in America*, vol. 3, edited by Scott C. Caspar et al., 194–202. Chapel Hill: American Antiquarian Society/UNC Press, 2007.

Hall, David D. *Cultures of Print: Essays in the History of the Book*. Amherst: University of Massachusetts Press, 1996.

Halttunen, Karen. *Confidence Men and Painted Women: A Study of Middle-Class Culture in America, 1830–1870*. New Haven, CT: Yale University Press, 1982.

Hassard, John. "Catholic Literature and the Catholic Public." *Catholic World* 12 (1870): 399–410.

Hawthorne, Nathaniel. *The Blithedale Romance*. 1852. Centenary ed., vol. 3. Columbus: Ohio State University Press, 1985.

Hecker, Isaac Thomas. *Aspirations of Nature*. New York: James B. Kirker, 1857.

———. "The Catholic Church in the United States." *Catholic World* 29 (1879): 431–56.

———. "The Catholic Publication Society." *Catholic World* 3 (1867): 278–83.

———. *The Diary*. Edited by John Farina. New York: Paulist Press, 1988.
———. *Questions of the Soul*. Reprint of the 1855 edition published by D. Appleton. Introduction by Joseph F. Gower. New York: Arno Press, 1978.
———. "The Transcendental Movement in New England." *Catholic World* 23 (1876): 528–37.
Hecker, Isaac Thomas, and Orestes Brownson. *The Brownson–Hecker Correspondence*. Edited and introduced by Joseph F. Gower and Richard M. Leliaert. Notre Dame, IN: University of Notre Dame Press, 1979.
Higham, John. *Strangers in the Land: Patterns of American Nativism, 1860–1925*. Westport, CT: Greenwood Press, 1980.
Hofstadter, Richard. "The Paranoid Style in American Politics." 1964. Reprinted in *The Paranoid Style in American Politics and Other Essays*, 3–40. New York: Alfred A. Knopf, 1966.
Hollis, Charles Carroll. "The Literary Criticism of Orestes Brownson." PhD diss., University of Michigan, 1954.
Holmes, Oliver Wendell. *The Complete Poetical Works of Oliver Wendell Holmes*. Boston: Houghton Mifflin, 1899.
———. *Elsie Venner: A Romance of Destiny*. [1861, serialized in *Atlantic Monthly*, starting Dec. 1859]. New York: A. L. Burt Company, 1883.
Howard, June. "Unraveling Regions, Unsettling Periods: Sara Orne Jewett and American Literary History." *American Literature* 68, no. 2 (June 1996): 365–84.
———. "What Is Sentimentality?" *American Literary History* 11 (Spring 1999): 62–81.
Howe, Daniel Walker. *The Unitarian Conscience: Harvard Moral Philosophy, 1805–1861*. Cambridge, MA: Harvard University Press, 1970.
———. *What Hath God Wrought: The Transformation of America, 1815–1848*. New York: Oxford University Press, 2007.
Howlett, W. J. *Life of the Right Reverend Joseph P. Machebeuf, D.D.* Pueblo, CO: Franklin Press, 1908.
Huntington, Jedediah Vincent. *Alban: A Tale of the New World*. New York: George P. Putnam, 1851.
———. *The Forest*. Clinton Hall, NY: Redfield, 1852.
———. *Lady Alice; or the New Una: A Novel*. New York: D. Appleton, 1849.
———. Letter to Orestes A. Brownson, Aug. 19, 1855. Online: www.archives.nd.edu (accessed Apr. 15, 2011).
———. *Rosemary, or, Life and Death: A Tale of Our Own Time*. New York: D. J. Sadlier, 1860.
Johnson, Glenn. "Ralph Waldo Emerson on Isaac Hecker: A Manuscript with Commentary." *Catholic Historical Review* 79 (1993): 54–64.
Kane, Paula M. *Separatism and Subculture: Boston Catholicism, 1900–1920*. Chapel Hill: University of North Carolina Press, 1994.

Kazin, Alfred. *On Native Grounds: An Interpretation of Modern American Prose Literature.* Garden City, NY: Doubleday, 1942.

Kehoe, Lawrence. Letter to Father Daniel E. Hudson, C.S.C., May 18, 1882. University of Notre Dame archives. Online: archives.nd.edu/calendar/c188205.htm (accessed June 6, 2011).

Kelley, Mary. *Private Woman, Public Stage: Literary Domesticity in Nineteenth-Century America.* New York: Oxford University Press, 1984.

Kelly, Blanche Mary. "John Rose Green Hassard." *Historical Records and Studies* (U. S. Catholic Historical Society) 15 (Mar. 1921): 19–34.

Kelly, Ruth M. "Journey to Faith: Isaac Hecker and Nineteenth-Century American Reform." In *Mapping the Catholic Cultural Landscape*, edited by Sister Paula Jean Miller and Richard Fossey, 199–210. Lanham, MD: Rowman & Littlefield, 2004.

Kelso, Isaac. *Danger in the Dark: A Tale of Intrigue and Priestcraft.* Cincinnati: H. M. Rulison, Queen City Publishing House, 1855.

Kohlmann, Anthony. *A True Exposition of the Doctrine of the Catholic Church, touching the Sacrament of Penance, with the Grounds on Which This Doctrine is Founded.* 1813. Reprinted in William Sampson, *The Catholic Question in America.* New York: E. Gillespy, 1813.

———. *Unitarianism Philosophically and Theologically Examined: A Complete Refutation of the Leading Principles of the Unitarian System.* 3rd ed. 2 vols. Washington City: H. Guegan, 1821.

Labrie, Ross. *The Catholic Imagination in American Literature.* Columbia: University of Missouri Press, 1999.

Lacomb, Michele. "Frying-Pans and Deadlier Weapons: The Immigrant Novels of Mary Anne Sadlier." *Essays on Canadian Writing* 29 (1984): 96.

Lathrop, George Parsons. "Orestes Brownson." *Atlantic Monthly* 127 (1896): 770–80.

Lears, T. J. Jackson. *No Place of Grace: Antimodernism and the Transformation of American Culture, 1880–1920.* New York: Pantheon Books, 1981.

Lee, Hermione. *Willa Cather: Double Lives.* New York: Pantheon Books, 1989.

Lefkowitz Horowitz, Helen. *Rereading Sex: Battles over Sexual Knowledge and Suppression in Nineteenth-Century America.* New York: Vintage, 2002.

Lewis, R. W. B. *The American Adam: Innocence, Tragedy, and Tradition in the Nineteenth Century.* Chicago: University of Chicago Press, 1955.

Lindemann, Marilee. *Willa Cather: Queering America.* New York: Columbia University Press, 1999.

Lippy, Charles H. *Being Religious, American Style: A History of Popular Religiosity in the United States.* Contributions to the Study of Religion 37. Westport, CT: Greenwood Press, 1994.

Liptak, Dolores. *Immigrants and Their Church.* New York: Macmillan, 1989.

Longfellow, Henry Wadsworth. *The Poems of Henry Wadsworth Longfellow*. Edited by Louis Untermeyer. New York: Heritage Press, 1943.

Loughran, Trish. *The Republic in Print: Print Culture in the Age of U.S. Nation Building*. New York: Columbia University Press, 2007.

March, John. *A Reader's Companion to the Fiction of Willa Cather*. Edited by Marilyn Arnold, with Debra Lynn Thornton. Westport, CT: Greenwood Press, 1993.

Marcus, Steven. *The Other Victorians: A Study of Sexuality and Pornography in Mid-Nineteenth Century England*. New York: Basic Books, 1966.

McCole, Camille. "New Books: *Shadows on the Rock*." *Catholic World* 133 (1931): 752–53.

McDannell, Colleen. "Catholic Women Fiction Writers, 1840–1920." *Women's Studies* 19 (1991): 385–405.

———. *The Christian Home in Victorian America, 1840–1900*. Bloomington: Indiana University Press, 1986.

———. *Material Christianity: Religion and Popular Culture in America*. New Haven, CT: Yale University Press, 1995.

McGee, J. G. "On Catholic Literature." *Catholic World* 14 (1872): 707–15.

McGill, Meredith. *American Literature and the Culture of Reprinting, 1834–1853*. Philadelphia: University of Pennsylvania Press, 2002.

McInerny, Ralph. "Willa Cather." Notre Dame Center for Ethics and Culture. 2005. Online: http://ethicscenter.nd.edu/about/inspires/Willa_Cather.pdf (accessed July 16, 2010).

McSorley, Joseph. *Isaac Hecker and His Friends*. 1952. Rev. ed. New York: Paulist Press, 1972.

Meehan, Thomas F. "Catholic Literary New York, 1800–1840." *Catholic Historical Review* 4, no. 4 (1919): 399–414.

Melville, Herman. *Pierre; or, the Ambiguities*. 1852. The Writings of Herman Melville 7. Edited by Harrison Hayford, Hershel Parker, and G. Thomas Tanselle. Reprint, Evanston, IL: Northwestern-Newberry Library, 1971.

———. "Hawthorne and His Mosses." In *The Piazza Tales: And Other Prose Pieces, 1839–1860*, The Writings of Herman Melville 9, edited by Harrison Hayford et al., 239–53. Evanston: Northwestern-Newberry Library, 1987.

Messbarger, Paul R. *Fiction with a Parochial Purpose: Social Use of American Catholic Literature, 1884–1900*. Brookline, MA: Boston University Press, 1971.

Michaelidis, Chris. "The Tree of the Choctaws: Live Oaks in the Sacred Poetry of Father Adrien Emmanuel Rouquette." In *Mapping the Catholic Cultural Landscape*, edited by Sister Paula Jean Miller and Richard Fossey, 43–54. Lanham, MD: Rowman & Littlefield, 2004.

Mielke, Laura L. *Moving Encounters: Sympathy and the Indian Question in Antebellum Literature*. Amherst: University of Massachusetts, 2008.

Miller, Perry. *The Raven and the Whale: The War of Words and Wits in the Era of Poe and Melville.* New York: Harcourt, Brace, 1956.

Monk, Maria. *Awful Disclosures of Maria Monk, or, the Hidden Secrets of a Nun's Life in a Convent Exposed!* Philadelphia: T.B. Peterson, 1836.

Murray, John O'Kane. *A Popular History of the Catholic Church in the United States.* 5th ed. New York: D. and J. Sadlier, 1877.

Nevils, Coleman. *Miniatures of Georgetown, 1634 to 1934: Tercentennial Causeries.* Washington, DC: Georgetown University Press, 1935.

Nicolson, Murray W. "Bishop Charbonnel: The Beggar Bishop and the Origins of Catholic Social Action." *CCHA Historical Studies* 52 (1985): 51–66.

Nord, David Paul. *The Evangelical Origins of Mass Media in America, 1815–1835.* Columbia, SC: Association for Education in Journalism and Mass Communication, 1984.

North American Review 70 (Jan. 1850): 225–37. Review of *Lady Alice; or the New Una. A Novel,* by J. Huntington.

O'Brien, David J. *Isaac Hecker: An American Catholic.* Mahwah, NJ: Paulist Press, 1992.

———. *Public Catholicism.* New York: Macmillan, 1989.

O'Brien, Sharon. *Willa Cather: The Emerging Voice.* New York: Oxford University Press, 1987.

O'Connell, Rev. Dr. J. J., O.S.B. *Catholicity in the Carolinas and Georgia: Leaves of its History.* New York: D. and J. Sadlier, 1879.

O'Connor, Flannery. "The Catholic Novelist in America." 1963. Reprinted in *Collected Works,* edited by Sally Fitzgerald, 853–64. New York: The Library of America, 1988.

Orsi, Robert A. *The Madonna of 115th Street: Faith and Community in Italian Harlem, 1880–1950.* New Haven, CT: Yale University Press, 1985.

Parkman, Francis. *The Jesuits in North America in the Seventeenth Century.* 1867. Introduction by Conrad E. Heidenreich and Jose Brandao. Reprint, Lincoln: University of Nebraska Press, 1997.

Parrington, Vernon Louis. *Main Currents in American Thought.* 3 vols. New York: Harcourt, Brace and Company, 1927–30.

Pilkington, John Jr. *Francis Marion Crawford.* Twayne United States Authors Series 67. New York: Twayne Publishers, 1964.

Poe, Edgar Allan. *Collected Tales and Poetry of Edgar Allan Poe.* New York: Viking, 1975.

Porter, David H. *On the Divide: The Many Lives of Willa Cather.* Lincoln: University of Nebraska Press, 2008.

Portier, William L. "Isaac Hecker and the First Vatican Council." *Catholic Historical Review* 71, no. 2 (1985): 206–27.

Reid, Christian [Frances Fisher Tiernan]. "In the Sierra Madre." *Catholic World* 90 (1908): 156–71, 309–22.

———. *Morton House*. New York: D. Appleton, 1871.

———. *Nina's Atonement*. New York: D. Appleton, 1873.

———. *Valerie Aylmer*. New York: D. Appleton, 1870.

Reiff, Philip. *The Triumph of the Therapeutic: Uses of Faith after Freud*. New York: Harper and Row, 1966.

Repplier, Agnes. "Catholicism and Authorship." *Catholic World* 90 (Nov. 1909): 167–74.

Reynolds, David S. *Beneath the American Renaissance: The Subversive Imagination in the Age of Emerson and Melville*. Cambridge, MA: Harvard University Press, 1988.

———. *Faith in Fiction: The Emergence of Religious Literature in America*. Cambridge, MA: Harvard University Press, 1981.

Rooney, James A. "Reminiscences of Early Days." Jubilee issue. *Catholic World* 101 (1915): 89–98.

Rosowski, Susan J. *The Voyage Perilous: Willa Cather's Romanticism*. Lincoln: University of Nebraska, 2001.

Roy, Jody M. "Nineteenth-Century American Catholicism and the Catholic Response." PhD diss., University of Indiana, 1997.

Ryan, Mary P. *The Cradle of the Middle Class: The Family in Oneida Country, New York, 1790–1865*. Cambridge: Cambridge University Press, 1981.

Ryan, Thomas A. *Orestes Brownson: A Definitive Biography*. Huntington, IN: Our Sunday Visitor, 1976.

Sadlier, Mary Anne. *Bessy Conway; or, the Irish Girl in America*. New York: Sadlier, 1861.

———. *The Blakes and the Flanagans: A Tale Illustrative of Irish Life in the United States*. 1850. Reprint, New York: Sadlier, 1858.

Samuels, Shirley. Introduction to *The Culture of Sentiment: Race, Gender, and Sentimentality in Nineteenth-Century America*, 3–8. New York: Oxford University Press, 1992.

Sánchez-Eppler, Karen. "Bodily Bonds: The Intersecting Rhetorics of Feminism and Abolition." *Representations* 24 (1988): 28–59.

Schaff, Philip. *America: A Sketch of the Political, Social, and Religious Character of the United States of America, in Two Lectures*. New York: C. Scribner, 1855.

Schlesinger, Arthur M., Jr. *Orestes Brownson: A Pilgrim's Progress*. Boston: Little, Brown, 1939.

Seyersted, Per. *Kate Chopin: A Critical Biography*. Baton Rouge: Louisiana State University Press, 1969.

Shea, John Gilmary. *Memorial of the First Centenary of Georgetown College, D.C., Comprising a History of Georgetown University and an Account of the Centennial Celebration*. New York: P.F. Collier, 1891.

Shuster, George N. *The Catholic Spirit in Modern English Literature*. New York: Macmillan, 1922.

Sklar, Kathryn Kish. *Catharine Beecher: A Study in American Domesticity*. New Haven, CT: Yale University Press, 1973.

Smith, Albert E., and Vincent de P. Fitzpatrick. *Cardinal Gibbons, Churchman and Citizen*. Baltimore: O'Donovan Brothers, 1921.

Smith, Anthony Burke. *The Look of Catholics: Portrayals in Popular Culture from the Great Depression to the Cold War*. Lawrence: University of Kansas Press, 2010.

Smith, Bonnie G. *Changing Lives: Women in European History Since 1700*. Lexington, MA: D. C. Heath, 1989.

———. *Ladies of the Leisure Class: The Bourgeoises of Northern France in the Nineteenth Century*. Princeton, NJ: Princeton University Press, 1981.

Smith, Henry Nash. *Virgin Land: The American West as Symbol and Myth*. Cambridge, MA: Harvard University Press, 1950.

Smith, John Talbot. *The Catholic Church in New York: A History of the New York Diocese from Its Establishment in 1808 to the Present Times*. 1905. 2 vols. Reprint, New York: Cosimo, 2008.

Smith, Samuel B. *Rosamond: or, a Narrative or the Captivity and Sufferings of an American Female Under the Popish Priests, in the Island of Cuba . . . Written By Herself.* Pittsburgh: John Shapp, 1848.

Southern Literary Messenger 34–35 (1851): 702. Review of *Alban. A Tale of the New World* by J. Huntington.

Stearns, Edward J. *The American Catholic Quarterly Review and "Faith of Our Forefathers": The Case As It Stands*. New York: Thomas Whittaker, 1880. [Duke Divinity School microfiche collection: ATLA 1986–2068.]

Stoddard, Charles Warren. *The Lepers of Molokai*. Notre Dame, IN: Ave Maria, 1908.

Stowe, Harriet Beecher. *Uncle Tom's Cabin; Or, Life Among the Lowly*. 1852. Reprint, New York: Penguin, 1986.

Szabo, Liz. "'My Heart Bleeds to Tell It': Women, Domesticity and the American Ideal in Mary Anne Sadlier's 'Romance of Irish Immigration.'" 1996. Online: http://xroads.virginia.edu/~hyper/SADLIER/Intro.htm (accessed May 15, 2010).

Taves, Ann. *The Household of Faith: Roman Catholic Devotions in Mid-Nineteenth-Century America*. Notre Dame, IN: University of Notre Dame Press, 1986.

[Tenney, Sarah Nicolena Brownson]. *At Anchor: A Story of Our Civil War*. New York: D. Appleton, 1865.

———. *Marian Elwood; or, How Girls Live*. New York: E. Dunigan and Brother (James B. Kirker), 1859.

Thorp, Willard. *Catholic Novelists in Defense of their Faith, 1829–1865*. 1968. Proceedings of the American Antiquarian Society 78. Reprint, New York: Arno Press, 1978.

Tompkins, Jane. *Sensational Designs: The Cultural Work of American Fiction, 1790–1860*. New York: Oxford University Press, 1985.

Toth, Emily. *Unveiling Kate Chopin.* Jackson: University Press of Mississippi, 1999.

Turner, James. *Without God, Without Creed: The Origins of Unbelief in America.* Baltimore: Johns Hopkins University Press, 1985.

Tweed, Thomas A. *Crossing and Dwelling: A Theory of Religion.* Cambridge, MA: Harvard University Press, 2006.

———. *Our Lady of the Exile: Diasporic Religion at a Cuban Catholic Shrine in Miami.* New York: Oxford University Press, 1997.

———, ed. *Retelling U.S. Religious History.* Berkeley: University of California Press, 1997.

Valenti, Patricia Dunlavy. *To Myself a Stranger: A Biography of Rose Hawthorne Lathrop.* Baton Rouge: Louisiana State University Press, 1991.

Waldstreicher, David. *In the Midst of Perpetual Fetes: The Making of American Nationalism, 1776–1820.* Williamsburg, VA: Omohundro Institute/UNC Press, 1997.

Walsh, James J. "Doctor Jedediah Vincent Huntington and the Oxford Movement in America." *Records of the American Catholic Historical Society of Philadelphia* 16 (1905): pt. 1, 241–67; pt. 2, 416–42.

Warner, Susan. *The Wide, Wide World.* 1850. Reprint, New York: Feminist Press, 1987.

Welter, Barbara. "The Cult of True Womanhood: 1820–1860." *American Quarterly* 18 (1966): 151–74.

———. "From Maria Monk to Paul Blanshard: A Century of Protestant Anti-Catholicism." In *Uncivil Religion: Interreligious Hostility in America,* edited by Robert N. Bellah and Frederick E. Greenspahn, 43–71. New York: Crossroad, 1987.

Wheeler, Kathleen. *Bloom's Modern Critical Views: Kate Chopin–Updated Edition.* New York: Infobase, 2007.

White, James A. *The Era of Good Intentions: A Survey of American Catholics' Writing Between the Years 1880–1915.* 1958. New York: Arno Press, 1978.

Widmer, Edward. *Young America: The Flowering of Democracy in New York City.* New York: Oxford University Press, 1998.

Will, Allen Sinclair. *Life of Cardinal Gibbons, Archibishop of Baltimore.* 2 vols. New York: Dutton, 1922.

Williams, Michael. Review of *Death Comes for the Archbishop,* by Willa Cather. *Commonweal* 6 (Sep. 1927): 490–92.

Woodress, James. *Willa Cather: A Literary Life.* Lincoln: University of Nebraska Press, 1987.

Zboray, Ronald J. *A Fictive People: Antebellum Economic Development and the American Reading Public.* New York: Oxford University Press, 1993.

Index

Academy of the Sacred Heart (St. Louis), 148–50, 159
Acocella, Joan, 172
Aeschylus, 75
Ahlstrom, Sidney, 19
Alcott, A. Bronson, 46
Alcott, Louisa May, 79
America (periodical), 173
American Antiquarian Society, 8
American Catholic Quarterly Review, 125, 214n33
Americanism controversy, 52, 196n3
American Renaissance, 33, 82
American Revolution, 7, 72, 113
American Tract Society, 18, 23, 60, 74, 199n23
Anglicanism, 86, 88
anti-Catholicism, 6, 8, 31, 38, 43, 51, 60, 62, 76, 83, 85, 93, 110, 112, 138, 167, 177, 182, 189n6, 193n26
anti-Catholic literature, 6, 51, 83
Atlantic Monthly, 59, 200n48, 213n29, 220n6
Austria, 4, 105
Ave Maria, 104, 140, 199n26

Baker, Carlos, 146
Baltimore, 10, 17, 48, 81, 86, 103, 105–6, 119–22, 127, 139–40
Balzac, Honoré de, 30
Bancroft, George, 63
Baym, Nina, 121, 124, 202n2
Beecher, Henry Ward, 27
Belgium, 47, 72, 73
Bercovitch, Sacvan, 19
Bible, 6, 74, 81; Bible commentaries, 6
Billington, Ray Allen, 38
Boston Pilot, 60, 104
Boston Quarterly Review, 13, 24, 197n7
Brook Farm, 15, 46–47, 62, 66, 70
Brown, Charles Brockden, 33
Brown, William Hill, 79
Brownson, Orestes A., 12–16, 21–44, 46–48, 50–55, 58, 61, 63, 65, 71, 77–78, 83–84, 86, 89–94, 99–103, 112–15, 118, 120, 137, 162, 165, 168, 178–79, 183–84, 186; *Charles Elwood*, 78; *The Mediatorial Life of Jesus*, 40; *The Spirit-Rapper*, 78
Brownson's Quarterly Review, 13, 23, 25, 89, 186
Brown University, 36
Bryant, William Cullen, 64, 205
Bulwer-Lytton, Edward, 30
Buntline, Ned (Edward Zane Carroll Judson), 83
Bunyan, John, 137; *Pilgrim's Progress*, 137
Butler, Alban, 137; *Lives of the Saints*, 137
Byron, George Gordon (Lord Byron), 30

Cable, George Washington, 153
Cadegan, Una M., 57, 198n17
California, 4, 223n29
Callon, David Jerome, 105–6
Calvinism, 73, 85, 97–98, 121, 202
Canada, 4, 106–7, 141, 172
Cannon, Charles James, 16
Carey, Mathew, 8, 10–11

Carlyle, Thomas, 64
catechisms, 6, 9, 10, 17–19, 80, 103, 116, 117–44, 184–85, 211n15, 213n29, 214n33
Cather, Willa, 12, 18, 19, 57, 109, 150, 164, 181, 185–86; *Death Comes for the Archbishop*, 169, 171–73, 176–81; *A Lost Lady*, 168; *My Mortal Enemy*, 169–71; *One of Ours*, 168, 173; *O Pioneers!*, 172; *The Professor's House*, 169; *Shadows on the Rock*, 172
Catholic Encyclopedia, 82, 166, 198n17, 204n13
Catholic Publication Society, 51, 56–57
Catholic World, 15–16, 51, 53, 56–62, 76, 101, 104, 120, 140, 165, 173, 198n16, 198n18, 199n26, 200n35
Cavanaugh, Mary Stephana, 8
Channing, William Ellery, 33, 35–36, 40, 64; "Remarks on National Literature," 35
Charbonnel, Armand-Francois-Marie de, 84, 107–8, 208n62
Child, Lydia Maria, 78
children's literature, 51, 54, 68
Choctaws, 54
Chopin, Kate, 12, 18–19, 145–81, 185–86; *The Awakening*, 145–46, 150–51, 157–63, 222n20; *Bayou Folk*, 153; *At Fault*, 154; "Lilacs," 159–60, 163; "Love and Easter," 153; "Love on the Bon-Dieu," 153; "Madame Celestine's Divorce," 154–56; "A Sentimental Soul," 156; "Two Portraits (The Nun and the Wanton)," 158–59; *Two Tales*, 153; *A Vocation and a Voice*, 161
Chopin, Oscar, 150
Civil War (American), 7, 15, 16, 23–24, 29, 56–57, 104, 107, 109, 137–40, 144, 147, 163, 223n29
Columbus, Christopher, 133
Columbus Press, 52
Commonweal, 172–73, 186
Concord, Massachusetts, 62
Congregation of Missionary Priests of Saint Paul the Apostle. *See* Paulist Fathers
convent exposés, 6, 31, 43, 51, 83, 93, 139, 193n26, 219n98
convents, 110, 149, 158, 159–60, 169, 179, 212n25
Cooper, James Fenimore, 27, 33, 78, 107, 177
Crane, Stephen, 156
Crawford, Francis Marion, 166–68, 222n6; *The Novel: What It Is*, 166–68
Cummins, Maria, 78–79

Dante, 64, 141
D. Appleton & Company, 82, 204n13
Dartmouth College, 37
Darwin, Charles, 156
devotionalism, 114, 117–44, 189n5, 195n50, 201n48
devotional literature, 6, 10, 17, 57, 82, 100, 103, 105, 107, 117–44, 199n20, 211n15; and Irish American publishers, 6
Dickens, Charles, 30, 78, 109; *A Christmas Carol*, 78; *Little Dorrit*, 78
Dickinson, Emily, 4, 33, 183
didacticism, 9, 17, 23, 81, 83, 89, 92–93, 101, 105, 108, 124, 140, 142–44, 162–66, 175, 186, 194n30, 196n56, 203n7, 211n10
Dolan, Jay, 82, 104, 114, 127
domesticity, 17, 80, 112–13, 118, 121–42, 147, 152, 159, 179, 192n9, 215n53
Donahoe, Patrick, 81, 104
Dornin, Bernard, 81
Dorsey, Anna Hanson McKenney, 12, 16, 18, 77, 84, 103–15, 147, 162, 168, 177, 179–80, 183, 208n57, 208n59; *Coaina*, 84, 106–12, 179–80; *Nora Brady's Vow*, 106; *The Oriental Pearl*, 104–5
Dorsey, Ella Lorraine, 104, 207n49
Dorsey, Lorenzo, 104
Douglas, Ann, 121, 135, 192n15
Douglass, Frederick, 4, 9, 183

Dreiser, Theodore, 156, 160, 186; *Sister Carrie*, 160
Durkheim, Emile, 5

Elliott, Walter, 45, 58–59, 72, 74, 196n2
Emerson, Ralph Waldo, 9, 13, 23, 33–36, 46, 48, 62, 64, 67, 69, 76, 194, 200; "The American Scholar," 34–36, 62; "Literary Ethics," 34; "The Poet," 69
Episcopalians, 86–87, 96, 129, 167–68, 172–73, 177
Erdrich, Louise, 186

Faber, Frederick W., 125–26, 212n23
Farina, John, 47, 57–58
Farrell, James T., 186
Faulkner, William, 153
feminism, 40, 61, 66–67, 78, 80, 146, 148, 151–52, 155–56, 172, 176, 178–79; and fiction, 6, 147, 152, 157–59, 163, 203n5
Ferraro, Thomas J., 115
Fiedler, Leslie, 78, 121, 202n3, 210n10
Finke, Roger, 50
Finney, Charles Grandison, 48, 197n5
First Things, 186
Fisher, Philip, 131, 202n2
Fitzgerald, F. Scott, 186
Florida, 4, 50
Fordham College, 60
Foster, Hannah, 79
Fourier, Charles, 46
Foxe, John, 137–38, 217n77; *Book of Martyrs*, 137–38
France, 34, 72
Freemasons, 129
French Catholics, 39, 50, 73, 84, 110, 148, 150; literary depictions, 171, 176, 177
French literature, 65–66, 91
French Revolution, 126
Fruitlands, 46–47, 62, 70
Fuller, Margaret, 40, 66–67, 195n37, 201n52; *Memoirs*, 67; *Woman in the Nineteenth Century*, 40

Gairdner, James, 138
Garesché, Katherine Milligan ("Kitty"), 148–49
Gauchet, Marcel, 18, 152, 163
Georgetown College, 12
Germans, 39, 46, 48, 51, 63, 65, 72–73, 75, 104, 105, 107, 125, 169, 190
Germany, 4, 72, 190, 218n89
Gibbons, James, 10, 12, 14, 17–19, 48, 179, 184; *Faith of Our Fathers*, 17, 105–44, 184–85, 184n33
Gilbert, Sandra, 146
Giles, Paul, 126
Goethe, 57, 64–66
Greeley, Andrew, 12
Greeley, Horace, 60–61

Halttunen, Karen, 14, 175
Hansen, Ron, 186
Harvard College, 7
Hassard, John, 55, 59–62, 99, 114, 120, 137, 200n35; "Catholic Literature and the Catholic Public," 59
Hawthorne, Nathaniel, 4, 19, 37, 85, 111, 208n69, 208n70, 213n29; *The Blithedale Romance*, 37; *The Scarlet Letter*, 24, 85, 111
Hawthorne, Rose, 19, 190n16, 213n29
Hecker, George, 56
Hecker, Isaac, 10, 12, 15, 16, 23, 45–77, 83, 86, 89, 93, 99, 101, 114–15, 137, 165, 168, 178–79, 183–84, 186, 196–97; *Aspirations of Nature*, 70–75, 201n65; *Questions of the Soul*, 48, 55, 62–75
Hemingway, Ernest, 177, 186
Herbert, George, 64
Hollis, Charles C., 36
Holmes, Oliver Wendell, 133–35, 215n58
Howe, Daniel Walker, 3, 82
Hudson, Daniel, 77, 104–6, 207n51, 221n2
Hughes, John, 47
Hugo, Victor, 30
humanism, 40, 48, 65, 67
Hungary, 4

Huntington, Benjamin, 86
Huntington, Daniel, 86, 205n19
Huntington, Jedediah Vincent, 12, 16, 49, 77, 84–116, 162, 165, 177, 183; *Alban*, 95–99; *The Forest*, 91, 104, 108–9; *Lady Alice*, 84–99; *Rosemary*, 99–102
Huxley, Thomas H., 156

idolatry, 29, 36–41, 43, 66–67, 76, 110, 194n46, 195n50
immigrants, 6, 19, 38–39, 46, 49, 51, 53–54, 57, 72, 84–85, 94, 104, 115, 121, 127, 165, 167, 204n14; German, 218n89; Irish, 49–50, 57, 85, 88–90, 94, 95, 103, 107, 148, 152, 208n62, 215n53; and religious literature, 6, 14, 105
immigration, 4–5, 9, 10, 13, 38, 39, 49, 50, 74, 85, 89, 90, 96, 167, 186, 210n4
Industrial Revolution, 113, 126, 174
Iowa, 50
Ireland, 4, 13, 49, 50, 72, 85, 205n26, 206n27, 218n89; and Catholic Emancipation, 13; potato famine, 10, 49
Ireland, John, 50
Irving, Washington, 33
Italy, 4, 53, 61, 72, 87, 166, 198

Jacksonian politics, 30, 35–36, 193n27
James, Henry, 161; *Portrait of a Lady*, 161
Jesuits (Society of Jesus), 12, 51, 57, 83, 107, 110, 169
Jesus, 40, 112, 117–18, 125, 130, 132, 134, 138
Jewett, Sarah Orne, 153, 220n6, 221n24

Kant, Immanuel, 24, 75
Kazin, Alfred, 174, 176
Kehoe, Lawrence, 56, 200n27
Kelly, Ruth M., 48, 52
Kelso, Isaac, 51
Kempis, Thomas à, 137
Kenedy, John, 81, 209n79
Kennedy, William, 186
Kerouac, Jack, 186
Knights of Labor, 126
Know-Nothing Party, 38–39, 121, 218n89
Kock, Paul de, 30
Kohlmann, Anthony, 12, 76, 185, 190n11

Lalleman, Louis, 57
Lane, Charles, 46
Lathrop, George Parsons, 19, 190n16, 213n29
Lathrop, Rose Hawthorne, 19, 190n16, 213n29
Leader (periodical), 86
Lears, T. J. Jackson, 175
Lee, Hermione, 172
Leo XIII, 105
Ligouri, Alphonsus, 125
Lindemann, Marilee, 178
Lingard, John, 138
Literary World, 63
liturgy, 124, 154
local color fiction, 18, 92, 95, 98, 108–12, 145–48, 152–53, 155, 161, 164, 166, 173, 176–78, 180, 220n6, 221n24
London, Jack, 156
Longfellow, Henry Wadsworth, 7, 18, 26, 135, 150, 216n65; *Evangeline: A Tale of Acadie*, 7, 26–27; *Golden Legend*, 134–35; *The Song of Hiawatha*, 75
Loughran, Trish, 7, 189n3, 190n9
Louisiana, 4, 50, 54, 199n22; and Kate Chopin's fiction, 19, 145, 147, 150, 152, 153, 157, 162, 173, 180
Lowell, James Russell, 28, 35, 64; *The Vision of Sir Launfal*, 28
Lowell, Robert, 186, 205n18
Lyceum, 22, 49, 51–52

Macaulay, Thomas Babington, 149
manifest destiny, 13, 22, 28–29, 70, 72, 177, 201n61
Mariolatry, 14, 134. *See also* Virgin Mary
Maryland, 119
masculinity, 41, 195n51
McDannell, Colleen, 152, 189n5, 215n53

McInerney, Ralph, 164
medievalism, 37, 126
Meehan, Thomas J., 13
Melville, Herman, 4, 22, 23, 33, 63, 85, 86, 107, 183, 191n1, 218n80; "Hawthorne and His Mosses," 63; *Moby-Dick*, 85; *Pierre*, 22
Methodism, 129, 169, 199n23
Methodist Book Concern, 199n23
Metropolitan Magazine, 86
Mexico, 4
Miles, George Henry, 16
Miller, Perry, 19
Millerites, 131
Milton, John, 64, 66
Minnesota, 50
Monk, Maria, 31, 51, 83, 138, 193n26, 217n80
Moody, Dwight L., 127
Mormons, 131, 136–37, 194n48
Murphy, John, 81, 209n79, 212n23
Murray, John O'Kane, 53
mysticism, 47–48, 57–58, 64, 69–70, 76, 151, 157–58, 175

Native American religion, 75, 107–9
nativism, 38–39, 90, 194n48
Nebraska, 50, 168
Newman, John Henry, 64–65, 86
New Mexico, 176–81; 223n29
newspapers, 13, 34, 53–54, 57, 60, 82, 86, 104, 184, 198n17
New York Tablet, 90, 203n12
New York Tribune, 60–61
North American Review, 87, 92, 94
North Carolina, 17, 119–22, 129, 137, 139–41
nuns, 14, 31, 112, 139, 148–49, 151, 158–61, 169, 172, 179–80

O'Brien, Sharon, 172
O'Connor, Flannery, 145, 186
Olsen, Charles, 186
O'Meara, Mary, 148–49
O'Neill, Eugene, 186
O'Shea, Patrick, 81
"Ouida," 61
Oxford Movement, 86, 98

papal states, 52–53
parishes, 8; and Catholic revivalism, 127, 199n20, 201n48, 204n14; development, 8, 19, 51
Parkman, Francis, 107; *The Jesuits in North America*, 107
Parrington, Vernon Louis, 19
Parton, James, 59
Paulist Fathers, 15, 46, 51–54, 58–59, 74, 197n12, 198n14, 198n16, 200n35
Paulist Press, 52
Paulist Productions, 52
Plato, 75
Poe, Edgar Allan, 135; "The Fall of the House of Usher," 135
polygamy, 135–36
popular culture, 13, 26, 32, 112, 134, 138, 184
pornography, 42–43, 91, 93, 98–99, 206n43, 217n80
Porter, David H., 174
Protestantism, 9, 13, 17, 25, 39–40, 44, 67–68, 73, 76, 112, 121, 130, 133, 140, 153–54; and religious publishing, 10, 18, 29, 143, 199n23
Puritanism, 85, 95, 98, 111
Putnam, George B., 98

Ramé, Marie Louise ("Ouida"), 61
Reconstruction, 119, 122
Redemptorists, 46–48, 50–51
Reed, Rebecca, 83
Reid, Christian (Frances Fisher Tiernan), 105, 140, 147, 218n92, 221n2; *Morton House*, 140; *Nina's Atonement*, 140; *Valerie Aylmer*, 140
Repplier, Agnes, 56, 198n18, 200n35
Republicanism, 24
revivalism (Catholic), 48, 50, 52, 54, 127, 185
Reynolds, David S., 10, 80–81, 142–43
Rice, Anne, 186
Richardson, Samuel, 78

Richmond, Virginia, 87, 122
Rodriquez, Alphonsus, 137
Romanticism, 15, 54–57, 63–67, 70, 75
Rosowski, Susan J., 171
Rouquette, Adrienne-Emmanuel
Rousseau, Jean-Jacques, 65
Rowson, Susanna, 78
Russia, 4, 177, 190
Ryan, Patrick John, 91

Sadlier, Denis, 81
Sadlier, James, 81, 205n26
Sadlier, Mary Anne, 16, 39, 89–90, 95, 99, 104–5, 147, 204n12, 205n19, 205n26; *Bessy Conway*, 89; *The Blakes and the Flanagans*, 39, 89
St. Catherine of Genoa, 57
St. Francis de Sales, 137
St. John of the Cross, 57
St. Patrick's Cathedral (New York City) 12
saints, 14–15, 68, 105, 108, 125, 132, 136–37, 159, 170, 195n50
Samuels, Shirley, 79
Sánchez-Eppler, Karen, 79, 203n5
Sand, George, 30, 65, 98–99
Schaff, Philip, 49–50
Schiller, Johann Christoph Friedrich von, 21, 57, 64
schools (Catholic), 51, 147, 190
Scott, Walter, 102–3
secularism, 18, 30, 133, 176
sentimentality, 14–15, 17, 25, 35, 37–43, 78–81, 89–94, 105–6, 108, 111, 113, 117–44, 147, 165, 184, 191n6, 202n2, 203n3, 203n5, 210n10, 215n53, 215n56
sermons, 9, 12, 59, 102, 121–23, 128, 163, 185; published, 199n23
Sexton, Anne, 186
sexuality, 91–93, 206n30; and women, 40–41, 93, 112, 146, 151, 156, 161–62, 176, 178, 195n51, 204n17, 206n30
Seymour, M. Hobart, 138; *Evenings among Romanists* ("Nights among Romanists"), 138
Shakespeare, William, 64, 216n59
Shelley, Percy Bysshe, 30
Shuster, George N., 48, 78
Sinclair, Upton, 156
Smith, Anthony Burke, 222–23n23
Smith, Bonnie G., 126, 212n25
Smith, John Talbot, 164–65
Society of Jesus. *See* Jesuits
Southern Literary Messenger, 87–88, 98–99
Spain, 72, 199n21
Spalding, Martin John, 48, 120, 200n35
Spencer, Herbert, 156
Spenser, Edmund, 64
Spirit of the XIX Century, 38
Stark, Rodney, 50
Stoddard, Charles Warren, 165; *The Lepers of Molokai*, 165, 221n2
Stowe, Harriet Beecher, 4, 9, 27, 54, 78, 85, 110, 123, 150, 183, 192n15, 203n8, 215n56, 217n56; *Defence of Lady Byron*, 27; *The Minister's Wooing*, 27; *Uncle Tom's Cabin*, 85, 110, 123, 217n80
Sue, Eugène, 30
Swift, Jonathan, 42; *Tale of a Tub*, 42

Taves, Ann, 118, 125
Taylor, Bayard, 64
Tennyson, Alfred Lord, 64
Texas, 50
Third Plenary Council, 57
Thomas, Isaiah, 8
Thoreau, Henry David, 23, 33, 46,
Thorp, Willard, 16, 87, 102, 143
Tiernan, Frances Fisher. *See* Christian Reid
Tompkins, Jane, 80, 209n72, 211n10
transcendentalism, 13, 15, 23–24, 33, 36, 46, 48, 62, 64–65, 67, 96, 183, 196n1, 210n8
transportation: effect on commercial publishing, 5–6, 12, 51, 189n3
Turner, James, 162, 168
Twain, Mark, 107
Tweed, Thomas A., 5

Unitarianism, 13, 26, 33, 35, 63, 73, 96, 190n11
University of Notre Dame, 105

Vatican Council (1869–70), 48, 59, 125, 196n3, 198n14
Virgin Mary, 14, 17, 41, 106, 107, 110, 125, 132–35, 154, 158, 176, 179, 215n56, 215n58

Walsh, James, 91
Ward, Anna Barker, 62, 200n37
Warner, Susan, 78, 79, 124
Welter, Barbara, 41
Wharton, Edith, 161; *The House of Mirth*, 161
Whitman, Walt, 4, 33, 218n80
Williams, Michael, 164, 172
Wilmington, North Carolina, 119, 122–23, 210n5
Wiseman, Nicholas (cardinal), 105
woman's suffrage, 25
Woodress, James, 172
Wordsworth, William, 64, 75, 132–35

Young America, 13, 21–44, 191n1, 201n61
Young Catholic, 51

Zboray, Ronald J., 11, 190n9

STUDIES IN AMERICAN THOUGHT AND CULTURE

The American Jeremiad
Sacvan Bercovitch

Back to the Land: The Enduring Dream of Self-Sufficiency in Modern America
Dona Brown

Margaret Fuller: Transatlantic Crossings in a Revolutionary Age
Edited by Charles Capper and Cristina Giorcelli

Channeling the Past: Politicizing History in Postwar America
Erik Christiansen

Ernest Hemingway: Thought in Action
Mark Cirino

Creating the College Man: American Mass Magazines and Middle-Class Manhood, 1890–1915
Daniel A. Clark

Robert Koehler's "The Strike": The Improbable Story of an Iconic 1886 Painting of Labor Protest
James M. Dennis

Emerson's Liberalism
Neal Dolan

Observing America: The Commentary of British Visitors to the United States, 1890–1950
Robert P. Frankel

The University and the People: Envisioning American Higher Education in an Era of Populist Protest
Scott M. Gelber

Picturing Indians: Photographic Encounters and Tourist Fantasies in H. H. Bennett's Wisconsin Dells
Steven D. Hoelscher

Cosmopolitanism and Solidarity: Studies in Ethnoracial, Religious, and Professional Affiliation in the United States
David A. Hollinger

Thoreau's Democratic Withdrawal: Alienation, Participation, and Modernity
Shannon L. Mariotti

Seaway to the Future: American Social Visions and the Construction of the Panama Canal
Alexander Missal

Faithful Passages: American Catholicism in Literary Culture, 1844–1931
James Emmett Ryan

Imaginary Friends: Representing Quakers in American Culture, 1650–1950
James Emmett Ryan

Countercultural Conservatives: American Evangelism from the Postwar Revival to the New Christian Right
Axel R. Schäfer

The Trashing of Margaret Mead: Anatomy of an Anthropological Controversy
Paul Shankman

The Presidents We Imagine: Two Centuries of White House Fictions on the Page, on the Stage, Onscreen, and Online
Jeff Smith

Unsafe for Democracy: World War I and the U.S. Justice Department's Covert Campaign to Suppress Dissent
William H. Thomas Jr.